TAKE
CHARGE
OF YOUR LIFE

BEFORE IT TAKES CHARGE OF YOU

Rich Blessings in Jesus!

Mark Gay

"Ephesians 1:3"

Books by Dr. Richard Ganz

THOU SHALT NOT KILL: The Christian Case Against Abortion
FREE INDEED
SOLD-OUT (with Dr. William Edgar)
PSYCHOBABBLE
THE SECRET OF SELF-CONTROL
TWENTY CONTROVERSIES THAT ALMOST KILLED A CHURCH
TAKE CHARGE OF YOUR LIFE
TODAY IS YOUR LIFE (soon to be published)

TAKE CHARGE

OF YOUR LIFE

BEFORE IT TAKES CHARGE OF YOU

DR. RICHARD GANZ

LANDMARK
PROJECT &
PRESS

Remove not the ancient landmark...

All Scripture references are author's paraphrase unless otherwise indicated.

Editor: Amy Cameron
Cover Photo: Al Goyette

First Printing - June 2008
Second Printing - August 2008

Published by Landmark Project Press

13524 - 38 Street
Edmonton, Canada
T5A 2W7
press.landmarkproject.net
press@landmarkproject.net

Printed in the United States of America

Library and Archives Canada Cataloguing in Publication

Ganz, Richard L
    Take charge of your life : before it takes charge of you / written by Richard Ganz.
    Includes bibliographical references.
    ISBN 978-0-9780987-4-2 (pbk.)
    1. Self-actualization (Psychology)--Religious aspects--Christianity.
    I. Title.
BV4598.2.G35 2008   248.4   C2008-903417-1

To my wife, Nancy -
it's still love at first sight

Contents

Thanks...

Thanks to my wife of thirty-five years, Nancy. My first thought in the instant that I saw you standing alongside a bridge in San Marco's Plaza in Venice was, *This is the most beautiful girl I have ever seen. I'm going to marry you.* Boy, was I thankful I was lost, when I saw this vision of beauty standing in front of me holding an open map! Thank you for marrying me and for giving us our four beautiful daughters. Thank you as well for helping me to learn the skills of self-mastery that are so necessary to succeed in anything, but that are especially necessary in the writing of books.

Thanks to Jordan Dohms of Landmark Project Press for his skill in taking my manuscript and using his techno-wizardry to transform it into the book you now hold in your hands.

Thanks to Amy Cameron. In Amy, I have discovered a special way to utilize the brilliance of a soon-to-be Ph.D. in Mathematics. Just as I have been dazzled by her logic and masterful ability to prove to me that $2 + 2$ does not always equal 4, I have been equally dazzled by her ability to take my words, phrases, and thoughts, and find exactly the right word or thought that I have never even considered. She has helped to turn this project into what is an extremely valuable and helpful book. Amy, your work has been appreciated more than you can imagine.

Special thanks to God for giving me the ability, strength, and grace to help His people achieve a Take-Charge life.

GREETINGS!

Take Charge of Your Life is what I had hoped a previous book, *The Secret of Self-Control*, could have been, but wasn't. My new book will show you a revolutionary way of life. You are about to enter the world of power-charged, super-charged, God-charged, Take-Charge living.

In *Take Charge of Your Life*, you will see how to live the life God intends for you. You will see God's power unleashed in your mortal body. I present a way of living, which I call a Take-Charge Life. It is nothing other than bringing into daily reality the fully abundant life (John 10:10) God intends for you.

I grew up on the streets of the South Bronx. My mother was a crippled widow with a twelve year old and ten year old son. I worked from the time I was twelve to help my mother make ends meet in our home. Coming from a home filled with many difficulties, I grew into a disillusioned and isolated teen. As I got older, disillusionment and isolation developed into anger and rebellion. Then God broke in and changed my life. God's amazing grace notwithstanding, I have often wondered how I could grow up and become one of the world's leading authorities on life transformation.

In *Take-Charge of Your Life*, you will learn how God brought about the transformation of my life, and how this transformation can take place in your life as well. I am convinced that each one of you who knows Jesus can become far more than you have ever thought or even imagined (Ephesians 3:20).

This book is about the *real* power that is involved in an abundant life. You are going to see that real power is not what you exercise over *others*. Real power is what you exercise over *yourself*.

Here's the plan. We are going to use the Bible as our foundation. What a foundation! It provides us with "everything necessary for life and right living" (2 Peter 1:3). My job is to get you to move from sloppy, careless, indifferent, improper, out of control living, to a Take-Charge life. I will help you attain the often seemingly impossible dream of a power-charged, super-charged, God-charged, Take-Charge life. I guarantee you, it *is* attainable.

We all want a full and abundant life. Sadly, most of us simply seem to be alive. God does not just call us to live. He calls us to live *fully!* He calls us to a "full and abundant life" (John 10:10). As you use this book, I will be coaching you towards the achievement of a full and abundant Take-Charge life.

As we used to say at every Bar-Mitzvah and wedding I either attended or worked at as a waiter while growing up in the Bronx, *"L'Chaim!"*, *"To Life! Abundant life!"* Here's to a Take-Charge life!

PART ONE

The

Start

of a Take-Charge Life

1

HOW NOT TO LIVE A TAKE-CHARGE LIFE

You can live a Take-Charge life, even if you come from the least likely background. Neither your failure nor your success determines whether you can have a Take-Charge life.

I went to an all male high school. How that happened, I still cannot completely figure out. How I managed to live in the Bronx and go to an all male high school near the tip of Brooklyn, to this day defies my imagination. I have always felt that my "debt to society" was paid in my "imprisonment" at Brooklyn Technical High School. Graduation was like parole after four miserable years of incarceration.

Here's how life at Brooklyn Tech worked out for me. At the end of the first semester, my grades were straight A. At the end of four years, I graduated 1300th out of 1400. It seemed as if I were powerless against the forces running roughshod over me. My life had Taken-Charge of me, and it did not stop there.

How Not to Choose

When it came time to choose universities, I had only one requirement—girls! I did not care about anything else. It did not even matter if my professors spoke languages I did not understand.

I took advantage of every moment of my first two years in university. I joined the fraternity that was known for one thing alone: Partying. My life became one huge party. I was so out of touch with academic reality, that I would go to the fraternity house to study for my exams. What could be more ridiculous than studying for a final exam with some of your most imbecilic fraternity brothers, and a group of tag-along girls? Within five minutes of studying, the night would invariably deteriorate into a party.

I still remember a huge sociology final exam for which I was preparing. I do not remember it because of the content of the exam, but because of the intensity of the watermelon fight that lasted until dawn. I also remember the incredulous look of my professor as I walked into her exam room covered from head to toe in watermelon juice.

At the end of my first two years of university, I was the proud possessor of a 2.004 grade point average. Considering that one needed a 2.00 average to remain in university, I saw my academic career as a complete success. I was still free to party my way through my last two years of university.

For some bizarre reason (i.e. my Jewish mother's wishes), I was planning a career as a tax lawyer. By the end of the introductory year-long course in accounting and tax law, I was doing miserably, but had struck up a friendship with the professor. We had a few things in common. We were both Jewish. We both had strong Jewish mothers. We were both dating the same girl!

I met with the professor. He explained to me that I needed to pass the final exam of his course in order to pass the entire year of study. The night before the final exam, he handed me several pieces of paper and said, "If you look really carefully at these pages, you may find yourself doing very well on the exam." As I was to find out later, this *was* the exam, only without the title "Final Exam" on it.

The following morning, I quickly looked through all the pages. All I could see were numbers. I did not have the energy or the interest to do anything with the questions. When I received my final exam grade, I learned that I had set the curve in the class—my 29% was the lowest grade the professor had yet seen in his short professorial career. The professor met with me, and did something that was incredibly gracious (if not possibly a bit illegal). He told me that if I promised to never, ever take another accounting course, he would give me a C for the year (that was one more 2.00 for Rich!).

I didn't know what I was going to do next. I had no real interest in anything. Surfing struck my fancy, but I had never done it. It just seemed like a great way to spend my life. I had not worked at academics since my first semester in high school six years earlier.

A Take-Charge Seed

One day, a friend handed me a book that he had found interesting. It was *The Interpretation of Dreams* by Sigmund Freud. I read the first chapter, and was hooked. I signed up the next year for every psychology course I could take. I told my fraternity brothers that I was about to become a *real* student. One of them laughed so hard, that he sprayed his mouth full of coffee all over me in his amusement.

Something happened shortly afterwards that changed the course of my life. I overheard a conversation between a couple of my fraternity brothers. They were taking bets against *me*. The going odds were 5 to 1 against me being able to have the B average I said I would have at the end of the coming academic year.

It was at that very moment that the seed of a Take-Charge life sprouted within me. I would not have called it that at the time, but that is what it was. I made several decisions right on the spot. First, I was going to leave the fraternity. Second, I was going to make new friends with the top students I could find at the university. Third, I set my sights even higher. I was going to have a straight A average.

I dropped out of the fraternity, and had nothing to do with it ever again. I became friends with students who encouraged me to read classical literature, who studied five or six hours every day, and who had really intelligent things to say. The only goal that I did not entirely attain was to have a straight A average. Over my next two years of university, in which I took approximately twenty courses, I received one B. All the rest were A's.

I applied for graduate studies in Clinical Psychology. I knew that my chances were slim for acceptance into an APA approved Ph.D. program. These programs had thousands of applicants, most of whom were straight A students for four years.

I was astounded the day I opened a letter from the one graduate school that accepted me into their Ph.D. program. For an entire day, I carried that letter around, showing it to one person after another. Late in the day, someone said to me, "Congratulations on your scholarship." I asked, "What scholarship?" He replied, "This one," pointing at the letter.

In my excitement, I had overlooked the second paragraph, which revealed to me that I had received a U.S. Public Health Fellowship. This scholarship covered all of my tuition and living expenses. It was such a good scholarship that at the end of each of the first two years of graduate studies, I had enough money left over to take a trip to Europe. In fact, during the second summer, I met my future wife, Nancy, in Venice, Italy, while hitchhiking through Europe.

I have never sat down and analyzed what was taking place in my life back then. Looking at it now, I can see that at the particular crisis moment, I began to make real and serious decisions. I decided to do what was good and what was right, even if it was hard. I was also very successful in my internship and postdoctoral work.

I was now ready to begin my career as a Clinical Psychologist. I was already teaching at a university. Now I would also be on the faculty of a major medical center. By all standards, I had arrived. I was a totally different person than the kid who stood before his professor drenched in watermelon juice on the day of his final exam.

On the human level, I was now a success. Is such human success what I mean when I speak of a Take-Charge life? The answer is *No*, and we will see why in a moment.

TAKE-CHARGE ACTION INITIATIVES

1. *What does a Take-Charge life NOT look like?*

    _____

    _____

    _____

2. *If you wanted to have your life Take-Charge of you, what would you do?*

    _____

    _____

    _____

    _____

3. *What commitments do you have to break, and what commitments do you have to make, for you to achieve a Take-Charge life?*

    _____

    _____

    _____

    _____

2

BREAKING INTO A
TAKE-CHARGE LIFE

How long will it take you to come to a Take-Charge life?
It may take you a great deal of time. It may happen to you
in the twinkling of an eye. For me, it happened between
the time my eyes glanced from a name on a page, to the
face of a person in front of me. You will know when you
get there.

If a Take-Charge life is not success, wealth, strength, or power, what is it? Did my new job at the medical center achieve it? Let's see.

Another turning point in my life was about to happen. I was not long into my work at the medical center. I was sitting in a case-conference and watching the leading psychoanalytic psychotherapist in the city conduct a psychotherapy session in front of the entire psychiatric and psychological community. Dr. Chernoff also happened to be my therapist, and watching him, I appreciated even more just how good he was at what he did. Then, as if out of nowhere, a strange thought entered my head: *This is useless nonsense. Clever, but meaningless.* This thought terrified me. It seemed as if I were saying goodbye to what seemed to be a lifetime of preparation for this kind of work. Once again, my life seemed to be out of control and Taking-Charge of me.

I could not help asking myself how this could be happening to me *now* when I had finally achieved everything. One day, I was traveling from the medical center to my psychiatrist's office for my psychotherapy session. I decided to tell Al Saunders, my colleague at the medical center who was also traveling to his psychiatrist's office (what a messed up world we were living in!), just what I was going through. I said, "Al, psychotherapy is useless and meaningless. We aren't *really* helping anyone to have a great life. Al, we don't even have that great life ourselves."

With both hands, Al grabbed my shirt and tie, and hurled me into the window of the bus. He said, "Rich, take a look. What do you see?" I answered, "I see men covered with dirt and sweat digging ditches in the road." Al replied, "That's right Rich, and that will be you really soon if you keep talking like that."

Al brought me back to my senses—at least for a while. I tried to not think about these things. I tried to tell myself that things like meaning and truth did not matter, especially since there was no meaning and there was no truth. I thought I had resolved the issue by telling myself that in a meaningless, senseless world, at least I would be able to have everything that I wanted.

COMING HOME

Before I knew it, Nancy and I were off for a month-long trip to Europe. We were traveling just the way we traveled when we met two years earlier in Venice—hitchhiking. One evening, we found ourselves knocking on the door of a home belonging to people we did not know. They opened the door, smiled at us, and said, "Welcome, you've arrived." This is an interesting greeting, considering that they did not know us or know that we were coming! We were ushered into a living room filled with people sitting on the floor, chairs, and couches. We were about to listen to a lecture from a professor of theoretical physics from Massachusetts Institute of Technology on quantum mechanics and its relationship to God.

That was the first moment of my life in which I realized that a person does not have to be stupid to believe in God. After the lecture, someone came up to Nancy and me and asked me how we had come to L'Abri. I asked him what L'Abri was. He said, "This is L'Abri." He was quite amazed that we had come to this place without knowing what it was. We had no idea that we were standing in the living room of a Christian community whose purpose was to reach young people who were struggling with questions about the meaning of life. My questions were not stupid questions to the people at L'Abri. As far as they were concerned, my questions were what life is all about.

At a certain point, someone came over to me and asked if he could read something to me from the Bible. When I said, "Go ahead," he read to me words about a man who was beaten and bloodied. He read to me about a man who had nothing attractive about him. He read to me about a man who was despised and rejected. He read to me about a man who was filled with sorrow and grief. He read to me about a man who was wounded and crushed for our sins. He read to me about a lamb that was led to the slaughter. He read to me about a man whose life was an offering for sin. He read to me about a man who bore the sins of many.

My response was rage. It was a rage that deepened with every verse that was read. I thought, *How dare he read to me, a Jew, about his New Testament Gentile deity?* I told him, in no uncertain terms, what I thought. He never said a word to me. He simply handed me the Bible from which he had just read.

The instant I saw the name at the top of the page, was the instant that my life was changed forever. The name was *Isaiah*, the great Old Testament prophet. Looking at his name, I felt as if I had died. I knew that Isaiah had lived over seven hundred years before Jesus. In the time it takes to scream, I realized this prophet was speaking of Jesus. I felt as if someone had stabbed me through and through. I knew in that instant that everything I had been wondering about, everything regarding life and death, meaning and purpose, was about to be answered by this Galilean carpenter. His name had been my favorite curse. Now it was to become to me that Name which is above every name.[1] I had been captured by Christ.

I was now at the place where I could see. I could see that life was not in partying. I could also see that life was not in academic accomplishment and a successful psychotherapy career. Life was to be found in this Galilean whose voice spanned the ages and reached, two thousand years later, into my heart. If I had known these words concerning Jesus much earlier, I certainly would have pondered them: He is to be "appointed for the rise and fall of many in Israel."[2] I did not know if I was rising, or falling, or just spinning madly out of control. What I knew was this: Jesus has the answer about life, and if I want to know it, I must surrender my life completely to Him.

That is what I did in the time between reading the name *Isaiah*, and lifting my eyes from that page. I was now in contact with the God of Israel; the God of Abraham, Isaac, Jacob, and Richard. This wandering Jew had come home.

Take-Charge Action Initiatives

1. *What place does God have in your life?*

   _____

   _____

   _____

2. *Is there anything that you think is stupid about believing in God?*

   _____

   _____

   _____

3. *Are there any aspects about Christianity that bring you to rage?*

_____

_____

_____

4. *Have you ever committed your life to Jesus? If not, why not, and what can you do about it?*

_____

_____

_____

3

WHAT IN THE WORLD IS A TAKE-CHARGE LIFE?

A Take-Charge life is a full time life action plan. You live out God's saving work through you, for the sake of others.

We live at a time when true leadership is rarely found. True leadership is never the exertion of our power over others. True leadership is the exertion of our power over ourselves.

This is what a Take-Charge life involves. It is nothing more, and nothing less, than being "energetic to submit ourselves to God's saving power working through us."[1]

Such a lifetime is not a pastime. It is full time. It is from our hearts. We live a Take-Charge life knowing that we are enabled by God to have "both the desire and the power to do what pleases Him."[2] A Take-Charge life then, is a submitted, energetic, God-directed, God-pleasing life.

THIS IS THE TIME

It is time for us to Take-Charge of our life. I have absolutely no question about that. *This is the time.* The time is NOW. A decisive commitment is necessary. We are capable of making just such a decisive commitment. I made life-changing commitments when the only impetus was to prove that my fraternity brothers were wrong. I made life-changing commitments when I realized that psychoanalysis is wrong. We are capable of such commitments.

The only life-changing commitment that matters forever is our commitment to Jesus. From the moment that He Takes-Charge of our life, He will enable us to live a Take-Charge life.

As we progress through this book, we will learn more and more about how to live a Take-Charge life. We must never forget that we already possess everything we need to live a life pleasing to God. What seems impossible now, will soon be second nature. We *will* Take-Charge of our lives. No longer will our lives Take-Charge of us.

TAKE-CHARGE ACTION INITIATIVES

1. *Is there any decisive commitment you need to make right now?*

   To be a good stewart of the body God gave me. To let go of anger and a desire to control others.

2. *In what ways is your life (A) energetic, (B) God-directed, (C) God-pleasing?*

   _____

   _____

   _____

   _____

3. *From what you have read so far, what is a Take-Charge life?*

   _____

   _____

   _____

4. *What Take-Charge areas are you hoping will be covered in this book?*

Self-control in general. Trusting
that the LORD will provide.

5. *Have you made the life-changing Take-Charge commitment mentioned at the end of this chapter? If not, why not?*

Well, that's why I'm reading this
book, I don't know how to.

PART TWO

The

Heart

of a Take-Charge Life

4

The Basic
Principle Of A
Take-Charge Life

*Living out of rules or living by issues will never achieve for
you a Take-Charge life. The heart of a Take-Charge life
is God's grace directing your life. You are not directed by
rules.*

I will not deny a single word that I said as we ended the last chapter. We really do possess everything necessary for a Take-Charge life.
At the same time, when we are honest about it, we know how easily
our lives can still Take-Charge of us. At these times, we assume that
if we just make some minor alteration, or if we just correct "this" or
change "that," then we are well on our way to a *real* Take-Charge life.
We NEED to know deep within, that we can only *really* Take-Charge
of our lives when our lives have first been Taken-Charge of, by God.

We often live, as I did in my years of academic commitment, in our
own strength. The results, as they were for me, seem to be excellent.
We create rules of all kinds to help us live a "successful" life. What we
need though, is to live out of God-inspired principles, not simply to
live out of a system that *seems* to work. It is all too easy to get comfortable in a seemingly well-working system. What keeps us strong, what
keeps us on the course to a Take-Charge life, is not primarily our own
efforts. When we live out of the grace of God, all of our efforts flow
out of such grace-filled principles.

WHEN RULES OVERPOWER GRACE

Let me show you how this works itself out in our lives. Several years ago, I debated a Chasidic Jew who was a professor at a Lubavitch Chasidic Yeshiva. Lubavitch Chasidism is the most religious, the most rules and regulations oriented branch of Judaism in the world.

Following the debate, we continued to write to each other for about a year. One of the aspects I noticed in our continuing dialogue was that the professor would not write the name *God* in his letters to me. Instead, he would write *G_D*. This practice of not writing out all the letters of God's name is not unique to him alone. In fact, every observant Jew does the same. Not only that, but they will not even speak the name, *God.*

The history of this practice goes back to Israel's captivity in Babylon. They believed that the reason for their exile from Israel was because they had misused the name of God. In order to protect against that *ever* happening again, they erected numerous safeguards against such a danger. They did not speak the name of God, nor did they even write it.

The Israelites' main concern was to protect themselves against the dangers connected with the misuse of God's name. In the process, the added rules they invented to safeguard the use of the Name, lost them the blessing of that Name. In fact, they were so fastidious in their avoidance of the use of God's name, that God's written name became unused and, soon after, unknown. They forgot how God's name should be written, and is meant to be written!

The result is amazing. To this day, there is no certainty, even amongst Evangelical Christians, about the *exact* pointing of the vowels in the spelling of God's covenant name *Yahweh*. This is the most sacred name of God in the Bible. Losing this name has produced very tragic results. Today no one—not one single person in the world—can, with absolute certainty, state how God's name is even pronounced. The Jewish people, in protecting themselves against abusing the name of God, *lost* the name of God. Their efforts centered on rules they invented. Their misuse of God's name could never be safeguarded against by removing a series of letters on a page, or by saying "HaShem," "The Name," instead of saying "God."

When we live out of the grace of God, we see that such "self-effort" as the Lubavitch extend, such a life of rules and regulations, is useless in pleasing God, or in developing strong, moral character. Theirs can only be a "Self-Charged," but never a "Take-Charge" life. The basis of a Take-Charge life is the grace of God in our hearts, not the rules we set up.

One of my deepest concerns is just how easy it is to be satisfied with a life that just follows rules. It is so easy to turn the grace of God into a list of rules and regulations. When we do this, it becomes as impossible for us to live a Take-Charge life as it is for a Chasidic Jew today, or a Pharisee in the days of Jesus. Without realizing it, our lives slowly come to Take-Charge of us. Like the Chasid, or the Pharisee, we become enmeshed in rules. Like the Chasid, or the Pharisee, the grace and blessing of God disappear. Since the rules seem good, we enshrine them. Over time, we come to live by rules and miss the grace.

Remember, it was a Jewish nation *deeply concerned* for the higher life that lost the very name of the God *of* that higher life. This type of life can never be a Take-Charge life, either personally, or for the church.

I remember as I sat and stared at the page of that Bible, how my heart was opened to Jesus. Then, at some point fairly early on, a series of issues became central. The wonder of this new life became lost. When issues become central, Jesus becomes peripheral.

TAKE-CHARGE WITH GRACE

A Take-Charge life is not a rules oriented life, nor is it an issues oriented life. We so easily slip into a rules and issues oriented life whenever grace is lost as the dynamic of our lives. When we do this, we are insubstantially different than my Lubavitch Chasidic professor friend who diligently refused to mention the name *God*. He really believed a rule such as that would give him a blessed life. Sadly, it kept him from greater blessing.

Let us not be confused. A graceless life is a disempowered life. A Take-Charge life is a grace-charged life.

TAKE-CHARGE ACTION INITIATIVES

1. *How do you let God Take-Charge of your life?*

   I have no idea.

2. *What is the problem with a rules oriented life, especially if the rules are good ones?*

   You protect yourself from God really pushing God away and taking His place.

3. *What does it mean to live out of the grace of God?*

   I don't know.

4. *Comment on this statement: Rule keeping is unnecessary and only leads to legalism.*

   ?
   _____

   _____

   _____

5. *What are some of the consequences when we live by rule keeping?*

   We try to be in command of everything in our lives instead of
   ourselves.

5

THE GRACE OF A TAKE-CHARGE LIFE

God's grace is so magnificent, that the more you see and experience it, the more you realize how limitless it actually is. As you Take-Charge of your life, you realize that there is nothing in your experience that compares with God's grace.

It is easy to be a rule keeper. It is easy to be proud about the issues we believe are important. It is easy to look down upon others who see these issues from a different perspective than we see them. The problem is that we let our devotion to certain issues and principles define us. The problem is that our adherence to these issues and principles can easily become rigid rules and regulations keeping. In the process, the beauty and simplicity of Jesus is lost.

I want us to understand that grace has to be a living reality, not simply a doctrine to which we give assent. The grace of God is so magnificent that the more we see and experience it, the more we realize that we can never say, "I have fully grasped it," any more than we can ever say, "I have grasped a sunrise or a sunset." It is a huge underestimation to think we can grasp grace by quoting a theological definition: "God's grace is undeserved favor." This can *never* explain grace. It would be like thinking we understand love when we say, "Love is when two people get married."

New Life is Really New

When Jesus came, He brought a NEW Covenant. It was really new. It was so new, that it was just about impossible for His earliest disciples to understand. In fact, what He did is *unimaginable*. What He did is irrational to every category of thought that we possess. That is why His disciples could not get it. What He was doing in His love for them, what He was doing in His grace for them, was contrary to every idea they had about the nature of true religion.

We look back at the disciples, and we wonder, "What in the world was wrong with them? How could they not get it?" The reality is quite the opposite. We should ask instead, "How *could* they get it?" It is impossible. It is beyond comprehension. The Old Covenant sacrifices, as powerful a pointer as they were, had a limited purpose. Their purpose was simply to show us how even the most rational and beautiful picture of grace—a blood sacrifice for sin—falls flat in front of what Jesus *actually* did.

Jesus trained men who, because of their background, should have been ready for the great blood sacrifice of Jesus on the cross. They weren't. They were still *utterly incapable* of "getting it" just from the facts. This is understandable. The ultimate fact is that it is absolutely impossible to come to an understanding of God's grace just from an assessment of all the facts.

There is nothing in human experience *alone* that can awaken a person to the *full* reality of God's grace. What Jesus did for us, the grace that His life and death is for us, is eternally impossible to *fully* comprehend. The fact that people like us will live with God FOREVER is purely His gracious gift to us. Sadly, even though we know so much about grace, we continue to make obeying rules the high watermark of our lives, rather than grace.

An Early Experience of Grace

I remember the first experience of what I would now call grace in my life. It happened over half a century ago. I was a little kid, and I had just been given a gift that I had wanted for a long time. It was a cowboy suit. It had everything. It had the pants, the vest, the cowboy hat, the boots, and spurs on the boots. It had a holster and two guns.

"Gunsmoke" was my favorite television show. The bad guys would often get their heads hit with the butt of Marshall Dillon's gun. To me, my brother was the "bad guy." I remember taking out my toy gun and doing what Marshall Dillon always did. It was just a quick crack on my brother's head. I was stunned when my mom was furious, but I shouldn't have been. She told my dad to give me a spanking. I was terrified. I was also distraught, because she said she was taking away my cowboy suit.

My dad took me into my bedroom, where I was to be spanked. I was five or six years old, and I waited in pure fear as he took off his belt and told me to bend over the bed. Then he did something I still weep about even as I write these words. He proceeded to hit the *bed* instead of me. I was flooded by a sense that because of what he did, I had escaped a terrible punishment. It had a powerful impact on me, and remains for me my first experience of grace. In the encounter with my father, the punishment I deserved was received by my bed instead of me.

God, though, looks upon us all; every one of us who would ever belong to Him. He sees the punishment we justly deserve, but He does not punish us. He also does not take it out on the cross. He punishes *His Son* instead, and He does it with an anger that could have justly been poured out upon us. In my situation, I understood something about grace as a son who had just escaped punishment. With God, His justice and His holiness demand that the punishment be paid in full. There are only two payment options: Either we pay it, or He pays it for us.

The Fullness of Grace

God's grace-filled love involves, as the Bible says, a height and depth and length and breadth that is beyond *comprehending*.[1] He therefore chose to punish His Son instead of punishing us. He chose to hurl His white hot, legitimate fury upon His Son, so that we would go free, even though we deserve every stroke that fell upon His own Son, who deserved only love.

When we come to Him, we come believing that He is truly God our Savior. We know that He is a good and loving God. We see, perhaps slowly, His unconditional forgiveness. With that forgiveness, we see that we are to live, but not by rules. We live instead out of the new heart that we are given.

We are meant to live a brand new life. This is a glorious life; not a life of rules and regulations, but a life of love. This is why He says, "In this is love . . ." In what? In THIS: ". . . NOT that we loved God." This is the starting point of a Take-Charge life. We had no love—none for the people around us, but even less for God. We were loveless, and lost in our selfishness.

God came after us. God came for us. God came and found us. *Not that we loved God.* He wants us to know that. It is the first principle of a truly TAKE-CHARGE life. We had nothing of love in us. "BUT..." Here is where our lives really begin to change. It is like the criminal who is standing before a judge. He is told he is guilty. Yet if the judge says, "But...," the prisoner knows immediately that mercy is coming. If judgment is coming, the judge will say, "You are guilty, AND I'm throwing the book at you." If there is to be mercy, the judge will say, "You are guilty, BUT I'm going to give you a break."

Here is the place where the break comes for us. God has just declared us guilty—guilty of pridefulness, guilty of selfishness, guilty of lovelessness. He has made it clear: "The wages of sin is death."[2] That means ALL sin, even the sins we think are insignificant and foolish. These, before God, are all capital offenses worthy of death. "You are woefully, sinfully, selfishly prideful and loveless, BUT I love you nonetheless."*Not that we love God, but that He loves us.*

"So what?" you say, "Talk is cheap; love is cheap." How many women reading this book, have heard "I love you," and all it meant was "I want you"? "So He loves us," you say, "So what?" Well here's what: "In *this* is love, not that we loved God, but that He loves us AND GAVE HIS SON TO DIE ON THE CROSS IN ORDER TO MAKE THE JUST PAYMENT FOR OUR SINS."[3] This is love. The One who loves, dies for His beloved. We are His beloved. He loves us. We hated Him, but He loves us anyway. Humanly speaking, it makes no sense to die for people who hate you, but that is what He did. When we come to love Him, we should see our ability to love Him as a miracle.

This is grace, pure and simple. "In this is love, not that we loved God, but that He loves us and gave His Son to die on the cross in order to make the just payment for our sins."*It does not stop here.* Grace is freely given, but it can only be grace for us as we see how powerfully it *transforms* us, and enables us to live a truly Take-Charge life.

Take-Charge Possibilities

When we ask, "Is it really possible for us to live this Take-Charge life?" the answer is *Yes!* "In this is love, not that we loved God, but that He loves us, and gave His Son to die on the cross in order to make the just payment for our sins. BELOVED IF GOD SO LOVED US, SO ALSO OUGHT WE TO LOVE ONE ANOTHER."[4]

This is what a Take-Charge life is all about. It is a life of love. It is not a self-empowered excuse for selfishness. It is a God-breathed vision in which we see ourselves as an offering poured out on the altar of His grace. We see ourselves extending His love across the earth. Amazingly, we are the means, the hands and feet so to speak, by which God accomplishes His glorious purpose. This purpose is to extend His invitation to lost and broken people. Through us, they receive the message of love, healing, and restoration that comes from heaven.

How have we so messed it up? How have we so missed the mark? God calls us to simply "be like Jesus." Let us give ourselves to that life. Let us determine in our hearts to take hold of the Take-Charge power that is waiting to be ignited in us. This power is, remarkably, all of God's grace. It leads us so that as we live our lives, we come to see that all that we are, and all that we have, is to be used for Him. God delights in us living just such lives, lives of love. Lives that really know grace, *will* become gracious lives. Lives that are *truly* touched by God's love, *will* truly love as well.

We do not have to be afraid of grace. We must not let *anyone* set up a barricade between us and grace, not even a barricade of good things. Grace, pure, free, unmerited grace, is to be the heart of everything. As we let the grace of God Take-Charge of our lives, it will kindle a fire of love and devotion that will reveal through us the Savior who graciously "loves us and gave Himself for us."

With this in view, you are ready, dear reader, to TAKE-CHARGE OF YOUR LIFE, knowing that if you do so by His power, then your life will *never* Take-Charge of you!

TAKE-CHARGE ACTION INITIATIVES

1. *In what concrete ways would your life be different if you lived by grace rather than by rules?*

_____

_____

_____

2. *What kept the early followers of Jesus from grasping His message of grace?*

_____

_____

_____

3. *If grace is the heart of our lives, what place do biblical rules have?*

_____

_____

_____

4. *What is the place of grace in a Take-Charge life?*

_____

_____

_____

5. *What is a Take-Charge life all about?*

_____

_____

_____

PART THREE

The

Action

of a Take-Charge Life

6

LIVING A TAKE-CHARGE LIFE

When you determine to live your life with passion, integrity, and intensity, you are on your way to a Take-Charge life. God desires your heart. When you live your life following Him, He will change you into an extraordinary man or woman.

At the time, I did not realize the significant consequences of the simple question I asked myself in 1979: *If I had a year to live, how would I spend it?*

My wife and I had two beautiful children. We lived in a lovely country cottage in the heart of a rural area of the United States. I was teaching in a counseling program that cooperated with a leading seminary's theological training program. Life was going great!

A problem arose when I realized that I would not continue to do the work I was doing if I had only a year to live. Then a deeper question arose. *Why,* I wondered, *should I keep doing something I obviously don't view as what I should do with my life—even if I have sixty more years in which to live?*

A new personal journey then began! Our family ended up living above a barn in the mountains of Switzerland, where I had accepted a request to write a film script. We also experienced fifteen months of traveling and living out of the trunk of our car while I worked as an itinerant teacher/preacher. While it was an exciting time for us, it was also a gruelling time for my wife. Through it, we gained a sharpened focus of how God was going to use us, even though once again it was not what either one of us had ever imagined.

I began to see how easy it is for me to deceive myself about my hopes, dreams, and aspirations. I began to understand how incredibly easy it is to justify our self desires as the call of God. If I had not realized this, I could have gone through my entire life and never known that although my hopes, dreams, and aspirations are important, the call of God is of ultimate importance.

These personal experiences compelled me to look at people in new ways, and what I saw startled me. I saw a lack of conviction and integrity in our society. Many people have given up living according to principles higher than self-indulgence and self-absorption. I came to believe that people have done this because they have given up on the only foundation from which absolute, transcendent principles for living can be derived: The Bible. Consequently, they have come to disregard principle. Men and women who possess character and principle simply do not fit into their world.

Do you remember when a man's word was his bond? He "struck hands," and, no matter what happened, his word could be counted on—even if it cost him in some way. Today, in contrast, a person armed with a team of attorneys can sign a contract and have it mean nothing because integrity is lacking. We have all met people who do not want to *be* honest; they just want to *appear* honest. They want to parade their honesty, but when the crunch comes they are not prepared to be radically honest.

This crisis of integrity affects all of us in various ways. For example, burglars robbed the home of a friend of mine and stole many valuable possessions while he and his family were vacationing. When he returned home, the police advised him to immediately call his insurance company. The insurance representative, in turn, told him to figure out the exact cost of the stolen items.

Later, the insurance adjuster came by, went over the figures my friend and his wife presented, and said, "These seem fine. We'll be sending you 75 percent of this total."

"What do you mean?" my friend asked, surprised.

"It's a known fact that everyone inflates the prices of their stolen property," the adjuster replied, "and the insurance company always gives 75 percent in order to adjust for these inflated estimates. Everyone accepts it."

"We will never accept 75 percent," my friend answered. "Before almighty God we arrived at these figures. We have put down our loss as carefully as we can, to the penny."

Confused, the adjuster explained that people were always slightly less than honest with adjusters.

My friend, in turn, explained that his family had to "stand before a far greater 'adjuster' than they would ever meet on this earth" and thus they would never do what the adjuster had said was always done. A short time later, the family received notice that they would be granted the entire amount of their claim even though the insurance company had never done that before.

This situation was a minor event in the lives of individuals who will never be known publicly and will probably never accomplish great things according to the world's standards. In fact, my friends would be surprised that I found their situation noteworthy. They are committed to doing what is right "even when it hurts" in an age that generally lacks such commitment. People may talk about honesty or integrity, but rarely does it go beyond just plain talk.

A well-known Christian who was hosting a Christian radio show introduced a commercial break by saying something like this: "You know, Thrifty Sam sells the best tires on the road. I wouldn't drive my car without them, and I hope you won't either." After the commercial break, he launched into his testimony by saying, "You know how sincere I am about Thrifty Sam's tires. Well, I am just as sincere about the Gospel." He saw no problem in comparing his sincerity about the tires he was promoting to his sincerity for Jesus Christ.

This illustrates a real problem. Quite often Jesus is not viewed as the eternal Lord and King who shatters evil and presumption. Instead, He is viewed as just another commodity, like car tires or car batteries. Some of us find it all too easy to speak in the fashion of that Christian celebrity who owns great tires and has a great Savior. We do not care to acknowledge that Jesus desires to rule every inch of our hearts. When we live our lives in submission to His rule, He is able to change us into extraordinary men and women.

Notice that I did not write that God necessarily wants us to *do* extraordinary things (although He may), but that by His power we *are* extraordinary. According to *Webster's New World Dictionary*, the word *extraordinary* means "more or better than what is normal." God does not want us to be this way so that we can boast about how great we are. He wants us to be this way because Jesus is extraordinary, and we are to be like Him. As we become more and more like Him, a Take-Charge life is not a pipe dream. It is a reality. It is the standard.

It is an absolute contradiction to belong to Jesus and yet live like the world and possess its values, drives, goals, and character. Sad to say, this is just how many of us live.

Extraordinary Living

Throughout the history of the Christian church, individuals such as the Apostle Paul, the Apostle Peter, Saint Augustine, Martin

Luther, John Calvin, George Whitefield, John Wesley, Charles Spurgeon, Billy Graham, and Francis and Edith Schaeffer have stood out prominently among God's people.

As we read through these names, we might be tempted to think that the Apostles Paul and Peter were unique because they received God's direct revelation. Did they sit around waiting for revelation? I do not believe that Paul, for example, thought, *Life's a breeze. God speaks directly to me.* We need only to read the following passage from the Apostle Paul to learn that he faced trials that are more substantial than what just about anyone else has faced: "I have worked much harder, been in prison more often, been beaten more severely, and been exposed to death over and over again. Five times I received from the Jews thirty-nine lashes. Three times I was beaten with rods. Once I was stoned. Three times I was shipwrecked. I spent a night and a day in the open sea."[1]

None of the people in the list above were lazy people who sat around waiting for God to do something. What empowered these ordinary men and women to live extraordinary Take-Charge lives was their shared faith, which was deeply and pervasively rooted in Jesus, their Savior and Lord. They believed that God would truly move mountains as they exercised their faith.[2] They possessed what each of us is supposed to possess—a *living* faith. Such a living faith dominated their lives. Everything else took second place.

These heroes of the faith found themselves facing dramatically new situations. What separated them from the rest of their generation was this: They carefully determined how to accomplish what they believed God had called them to do in their lives. They were no longer *career-oriented*, they were *called*. Their purpose in life was to accomplish their calling. Seeking to implement their vision, they worked, prayed, and planned as they believed the Bible directed them. They are examples of Take-Charge men and women.

Amazingly, the world was changed through them. They lived out a simple Take-Charge faith in Jesus, and it changed them—and the world! Without God, they were fear-ridden and prone to live simply to save themselves. With Him, they turned the world of their day upside down—after they had first been changed from the inside out. They were not elitist believers. They simply acted on the faith that had shaken their whole being.

Consider another dramatic example of Take-Charge living faith, which was demonstrated by Elijah when he confronted the 450 false prophets of Baal. As the story unfolds, Elijah meets King Ahab and asks him to summon people from throughout Israel and have them meet him on Mount Carmel. There he will assemble the 450 prophets of Baal. At the outset, Elijah challenges the Israelites to either follow God or Baal. "But the people say nothing."[3]

Elijah sets up a test. The 450 prophets of Baal are to choose a bull to sacrifice, and Elijah will do the same. Each bull is to be cut into pieces and placed on a separate wooden altar. "Then you call on the name of your god," Elijah shouts, "and I will call on the Name of the Lord. He is the One who answers by fire, for He is God."[4]

The Israelites and the prophets agree to this test, and all morning the prophets of Baal call on their god and dance around their altar. Baal does not answer. Elijah taunts them. "Shout louder!" he calls out, "Perhaps he is deep in thought, or busy, or traveling. Maybe he is sleeping and must be awakened."[5]

The prophets of Baal shout louder and continue to prophesy frantically. Still nothing happens.

In the evening, Elijah calls the Israelites to his side and repairs the ruined altar of the Lord, using twelve stones to represent the twelve tribes of Israel. He then arranges the wood, cuts up the bull, and lays it on the altar. At this point, three times the people pour four large jars of water onto the bull and the altar until water runs everywhere.

Elijah then calls upon God to answer him so that the people will know that He is God. Immediately, God's fire burns up the sacrifice, the wood, the twelve stones, the water, and even the nearby soil. Elijah next has the 450 false prophets executed.

Do you know what I find particularly exciting about this example of faith? We read that "Elijah was a man just like us."[6]

LETTING LIFE PASS

When we consider how God has used Elijah and other men and women of God throughout the ages, it is tragic how we let life pass us by.

We can be rid of the hindrances and live the Take-Charge life that God intends for us. A life of unimaginable joy and fulfillment awaits us as we allow God to have His way with us.

This is more than just fulfilling our dreams. It is about being a people of life-energizing vision. The Bible makes this clear, when it says: "Without a vision, the people perish."[7] At a time when the pressures of secularism, materialism, and selfism loom so large in our society, the character of Jesus is being seen in fewer and fewer people.

The challenge is for us to live a Take-Charge life. In order to accomplish this, we need to know who we are and who we are meant to be.

Nothing need keep us from principle-centered Take-Charge lives of power, meaning, and vibrancy. When we live such Take-Charge principle-centered lives, we move from selfhood into servanthood, from self-absorption to concern for others. Nothing need keep us, once we have made this determination, from the freedom, the passion, and the joy of a Take-Charge life.

Remember: Real leadership is not the exertion of our power over others. Real leadership is the exertion of our power over *ourselves*. When we understand this, we are well on the way to a Take-Charge life.

TAKE-CHARGE ACTION INITIATIVES

1. *If you had one year to live, would you live differently? If so, how would you live? If not, why not?*

   _____

   _____

   _____

2. *Have your hopes, dreams, and aspirations been an important part of your life? If so, why? If not, why not?*

   _____

   _____

   _____

3. *Write down a few words that define your faith in God right now. Be honest.*

   _____

   _____

   _____

4. *As you look at that description on paper, how would you like your faith in God to be different?*

   _____

   _____

   _____

7

TAKE-CHARGE TODAY

Today you have the opportunity to Take-Charge of your life. You can stop living your life with denials, rationalizations, and justifications. Instead, live with honesty, integrity, and fidelity.

Many of us assume that we are powerless to change anything about ourselves. We feel as if we have little or no control over ourselves. We feel as if our best efforts at improving and reforming ourselves are thwarted by who and what we are and by our circumstances. When we disempower ourselves, we fail to be what we want to be. Instead, we become what we despise.

We try to make our way through a performance-filled life comprised of countless "to-do's" either imposed upon us by others, or imposed upon us by ourselves. Our expectations are often so high that failure is inevitable; or our expectations are so low that, likewise, failure is inevitable.

We feel powerless. Millions of people respond to such a sense of powerlessness by becoming extremely depressed. According to some estimates, about 25 percent of the population of Canada and the United States is at least mildly depressed at any given moment.[1] That's about 75 million people!

Contrary to what we might think, people who were born before World War II experience far less depression than the Baby Boomers. Why? The answer is really quite simple. As the 20th century progressed, life became more and more performance-oriented. As a result, people began running at a faster pace just to keep up with all the expectations on them. As the standard of living increased, the standard of ethical living rooted in the Bible decreased. People obtained more material things, but lacked a foundation for how to live.

As people struggled for a resolution, a state of depression emerged over society as a whole. Dr. Gerald Klerman, a former director of the U.S. Alcohol, Drug Abuse, and Mental Health Agency, coined this "The Age of Melancholy."

In addition to the millions who suffer from depression, millions of others live with deep anxiety or fear. Still millions more attempt to use sex, food, toys, or work to ease their pain and fill the void in their lives. The media is filled daily with stories of people who turn to violence hoping to regain a sense of personal power.

Should it be surprising, then, that so many people become violent, commit suicide, become dependent upon psychiatric medication, or remain in therapy seemingly forever? It is easier now than ever to become despairing. With all the medical and technological advances, it is also harder than ever to break free from the problems of modern life.

It is Time to Take-Charge

Many of us have a very difficult time battling against anger, depression, worry, or fear. Many of us no longer have a clue as to who we really are. We must not give up. We must not think that by doing wrong or hurtful behavior, we will ever Take-Charge of our lives. Memorizing clichés also will not help us. Spending years going to a psychologist is also not the answer. We live in a drug culture. Psychiatric drugs are rarely the answer for the struggles in living that we face.

There is another way! It is a call for you to Take-Charge of the only person you can Take-Charge of—yourself! TODAY, you can Take-Charge of your life. You can be all you are meant to be.

You may be thinking, *I don't know who I am supposed to be. I don't know how to Take-Charge. I don't know how to stop being a victim and face my problems.* If that is what you are thinking right now, that's okay. You have to start somewhere. Let's start from where you are.

WHERE ARE YOU?

I would like us to consider carefully the following four principles:

1. We have to want to change our life. The motivation has to come from us.

2. We are extraordinary. Each of us is unique. We can have a powerful impact on others.

3. God will empower us as we seek to Take-Charge of our life. He even goes so far as to change us into new people.[2]

4. Living this extraordinary life requires commitment, effort, and practice. Only then will we achieve our goals. As we read the Bible, God's goals for us will become our goals.

WHERE DO YOU WANT TO GO?

Many of us want to become more "spiritual." We want to know the Bible better, enjoy a deeper walk with God, and see God work daily in our lives. At the same time, many of us want an easy solution. We are not willing to expend any effort to accomplish these goals. Like world-class athletes who must spend years training for just one Olympic race, those of us who truly want to take a stand for God must spend our lives in daily spiritual training. There are no shortcuts.

Unfortunately, more and more people are disagreeing with that reality, as is evidenced in the following two examples. In the 1994

winter Olympics, Tonya Harding was placed in competition with
Nancy Kerrigan, who was a better figure skater. Harding arranged
for someone to ruin Kerrigan's career, by smacking her leg with a
lead pipe when she was leaving the ice after a figure skating work-
out. There is also the case regarding the mother who tried to get a
cheerleader killed, so that her own daughter could be in the lime-
light. While these incidents are not typical, they reflect a growing
tendency of people to attempt to receive benefits without working for,
or deserving them.

Changing is the Hardest Change to Make

If we desire a Take-Charge life and are prepared to work towards
it, it will be ours. I am convinced that each of us can attest to that
fact. Change is possible! There is nothing about our lives that is
insurmountable. We need to face our beliefs, thoughts, and actions
honestly.

When we face an impasse, it is often nothing more than our ineffective behavior multiplied by countless trials and errors that leaves
us feeling helpless and hopeless. Based on our past failures, we come
to believe that we have done all we can do. This elicits another "failure
response." We stop trying to Take-Charge of our lives. We also stop
believing that we can ever face our difficulties and regain control of
our lives.

This is wrong thinking and wrong action! We are capable of
replacing a failure response with one that will lead us to victory, hope,
joy, and positive change. As we do so, we come to Take-Charge of
the responses that got us into trouble in the past. We learn how to
choose new responses to the life-destroying difficulties of the past
that continue to give us trouble in the present.

Here is a simple illustration. Let's say that an executive is often
asked to give oral presentations during important meetings. Every

time the executive gets up to speak, he gets wet, clammy skin, and shaky, wobbly knees. This nervousness obviously makes the presentation less effective. This same ineffective scenario occurs over and over again.

The executive is accomplished in achieving emotional and physical responses that demonstrate the expectation of an ineffective ability to communicate, and failure. When the executive fails, he is not disappointed. What though, if he learns to respond more appropriately? Think about how much better he will feel about getting up in front of the team, and how much better the presentation will probably be!

When my oldest daughter was a college student, she struggled about whether or not to switch majors. She was a straight "A" student, and on the way to receiving full scholarships to various graduate schools in that area of study. She had never taken a single course in the new area of study she was considering, and had no guarantee of success if she pursued it.

When we talked about what she should do, she said, "I don't feel that I'll ever use what I have studied to be of any real help to people. I know that I'll always sail through a program in the area I am in. I recognize that I may not do well in this other area of study."

As we talked further, she realized that fear of failure was keeping her from trying something she felt called to pursue. She chose not to live dominated by a fear-of-failure response, and changed her area of study. She did not allow herself to continue to live in fear. She knew that she might not do as well with this new challenge. She was willing to try nonetheless. She had chosen to live by faith. The years have passed, and today she is a professor at a major university.

A Better Way

I often mention in my seminars that we have the power to choose our responses to difficult situations. I encourage people to know that they do not have to be gripped by destructive patterns that have ruled their lives. The people in my seminars suggest to me that what I am talking about seems like it will leave them as less of the person they know themselves to be, and more like choice-making robots. As they succeed in choosing healthy life-empowering responses, however, they realize that such fear is groundless and in fact counterproductive. They come to realize that the new behavior they are learning leaves them more fully human than they ever were when they were trapped by life-dominating fears.

How could any of us want, for any reason, to stay trapped and crippled by fear, anxiety, or panic? How could we want to wander through life terrified of all the situations we *may* face? There is a better way!

That better way is to Take-Charge of our life. We need to choose to Take-Charge of who we are instead of having everything we say, hate, or fear Take-Charge of us. Why let these things control us? Even the benefits fear and anxiety bring, are disempowering benefits. They are hurtful to us. We must not hang onto them, no matter how hard it is for us to let go.

If we really want to be free of the snares and stressors that choke our lives, we can be *free indeed!*[3] We are all creatures of habit. At different times, all of us have seen our best intentions and efforts turn out badly. Why habituate them? We know that when we learn bad habits, they seem impossible to break. Take heart! When we learn good habits, they are also hard to break.

We need to put off habitual, destructive patterns of response, and replace them with what is good, right, beautiful, and excellent. Let us look at several basic patterns of response that we all use to one degree or another. These self-destructive patterns have one thing in common: They keep us from being all that we are meant to be.

Although we will use a college student as an example, the truths of these patterns apply to all of us.

THE MINIMIZING PATTERN

After receiving a bad grade on a final examination, the minimizing student says, "Oh well, who cares? Grades don't matter anyway."

THE PERMANENTIZING PATTERN

In the same situation, the permanentizing student says, "My situation in that class is horrible, my life is horrible, everything is horrible. It's always going to be horrible. I will never get a good grade again."

THE DESTROYING PATTERN

This student refuses to face the situation honestly, and instead destroys anyone connected with it. He says, "I am a stupid, incompetent, useless kid," or, "My professor is a useless ignoramus." Whatever the case, everyone is treated destructively.

THE RETALIATING PATTERN

The retaliating student does not minimize, permanentize, or destroy. All he cares about is getting even, and that with a vengeance. The whole problem is based on the perception he has about what the professor did. The student views it as a personal attack, and works on a response to get even.

A P.A.T. A.N.S.W.E.R.

Many of us hope for magical solutions that will automatically make everything okay in our lives. We hope for guaranteed success.

It is not that simple. There are no magic answers that do not challenge us to act on all that we believe, think, and do. Within this context, there is though, a rather simple response that breaks the patterns of response above. We can call this response a *maximizer*. We can remember it as a "P.A.T. A.N.S.W.E.R."[4] The first aspect contains three parts.

"P"—Problem: Understanding the Problem

During a snowstorm I moved our car down our quarter-mile country lane to make sure that I would be able to get out about an hour later in order to travel to a conference. I did not want to come out in knee-deep snow and discover that the car was stuck. When I gingerly pushed on the gas pedal to return to the house, the car did not move. I had a *problem!*

"A"—Attitude: Choosing Your Attitude

I sat in the car wondering, *How could this happen to me when I am so busy? I have handled this entire situation correctly. I planned ahead to make sure I would not get stuck. This can't happen.* I tried again, and heard that sickening sound of tires spinning on what had become ice.

As I exhausted myself running through a snowy field to get home, my next response was anger—at myself, at my car, and at the snow which was greatly inconveniencing me. I even became angry at the lane for causing me so much difficulty.

When I stormed through the door and saw my wife happily working, I became impatient, frantic, and self-centered in the way I communicated the situation.

"T"—Technique: Getting it Done

Nancy kindly agreed to stop what she was doing and help me, and we went outside. Despite our best efforts, the tires continued to spin.

"Where are those orange things you bought years ago with the claws that dig into the ice so that the tires can move?" Nancy asked.

I had not been able to find them for years, but she had given me a new idea. *What can I use?* I thought. So I tried another technique. I pulled out carpeting from the trunk and placed it under the tires. Soon the tires flung the carpet onto the snow, and the car still did not move.

My next attempt to find the right technique was to jam a tree limb under the tires. That did not work either.

As I stood there angry, frustrated, depressed, and sweaty, a car stopped, and someone asked if he could lend us a hand. Within seconds the car was free. Until that moment, I felt as if my day was ruined. Worse yet, I could have ruined Nancy's day as well. If my kids had been home, I could have ruined their day also.

Here's the point. It was not necessary to allow a stuck car to ruin my day. We need to understand this point. One horrible experience did not have to make the entire day horrible.

My attitude toward getting stuck prompted me to think in a disempowering way: *How can this be happening? I'll never get out of this. Everything else has to stop because all that matters is my problem.* Instead, what if I had shut off the engine as soon as my tires began to spin, prayed for wisdom, and said aloud, "This is no big deal. I'll just flag down the next few people who drive by. We will push the car over and through the ice, and I'll be out in no time"?

EVALUATE YOUR PATTERNS

We all face problems. Life is filled with them. Some of us think through our problems and create a plan for solving them. Others of us react to them without much thought. When we respond in reactive ways again and again, we set up a reactive rather than a thoughtful pattern of response.

Reactors create far more stress than thinkers, because reactors' solutions to their problems are far less effective. This means that more trouble will be created, which will lead to more problems, which will cause reacting people to fly around and react to one thing after another and accomplish virtually nothing.

The Bible teaches that we can be of good cheer even when we face serious problems.[5] God uses those problems as building blocks for our character development. "Suffering produces endurance, which in turn leads to our character being proven."[6]

In my case, when I spoke with Nancy about the pattern of response I had exhibited when faced with the car stuck in the ice and snow, she said, "You respond that way so often."

Although she was right, I did not want to hear that. I had let myself become trapped in a wrong pattern of response. I began to see that I could break that pattern. I realized the importance of evaluating a problem situation, recognizing my attitudes towards it, and devising a better technique to deal with it.

I had a choice whether or not to learn and apply new attitudes towards my difficulties. I also had a choice to develop my character or damage my character. Each of us faces the same choice. What we determine is crucial. Will we determine right now to use the problems in our life to grow? Will we commit ourselves to Take-Charge of our life, even when our life seems to be charging out of control?

TAKE-CHARGE ACTION INITIATIVES

1. *List three problems you have faced recently, and the attitudes
   with which you faced each of them. Now list the techniques you
   used to try to handle each problem. List honestly what happened
   and how you really responded.*

   _____

   _____

   _____

   _____

   _____

   *Do you see any patterns of response emerging? If so, what are
   they?*

   _____

   _____

   _____

2. *Consider each of the following situations. For each one, list the
   Problem, and then write down the Attitude(s) you would typically
   have toward each situation, and the Technique(s) you would typically try to apply in order to solve the problem:*

   *The principal calls to say that your child just got into another
   fight at school.*

   _____

   _____

   _____

   *A person with a cart full of groceries cuts in front of you in the
   supermarket line.*

   _____

   _____

   _____

You are overlooked for a significant promotion at work. Everyone agrees that the person who received the new position has much less ability than you.

_____

_____

_____

You and your wife have a battle over finances.

_____

_____

_____

3. *For each of the above situations, what Attitude(s) and Technique(s) could you have implemented instead?*

_____

_____

_____

_____

_____

_____

8

A Take-Charge Way Of Life

The world lives by a way that seems right, but leads to death. The Bible teaches a way that IS right, and leads to life. The Take-Charge way brings abundant life.

We all face problems. Sometimes our problems leave us feeling as if we are hurtling out of control. In the last chapter, we looked at the Problem, the Attitude, and the Technique—P.A.T. Now we are going to look at the A.N.S.W.E.R. This is significant in living a Take-Charge life. The principles identified by each of these six letters will help us Take-Charge of our life.

"A"—Appeal: Appeal to God

If trusting God is important, why do so few of us consult Him? We consult doctors, attorneys, teachers, and accountants, but rarely do we consult God.

God loves to help us through our difficulties. "Cast all your cares on Him, because He cares for you."[1] "God is a shield for all who seek to be sheltered by Him."[2] "Call to Me and I will always answer you and tell you great and wonderful things you need to know."[3] "Do not worry or be anxious about anything, but throughout your life just pray to God, ask God, and thank God, as you come before God."[4]

It makes great sense for us to appeal to the God who loves us! He will always be alongside of us. He will always help us. He will always work on our behalf. Are we appealing to Him when we face difficulties?

"N"—Nonnegotiable: The Nonnegotiables

All of us have a system of belief. For each of us, some of these beliefs function with greater certainty than others. When we know that our belief is true, that it is an absolute, then we need to put it into practice.

Consider these true illustrations:

- Harold knew it was time to change jobs. He was offered a great job that required him to work at least two Sundays a month. Some people might think that this would be a small price to pay for a superior job, but he refused to consider the offer because he held the conviction that it was wrong for him to work on Sundays.

- Robert, a young salesman, received pressure from his manager to sell customers audiovisual materials they didn't need, and to do virtually anything to close a sale. Valuing integrity, he continued to keep his customers' best interests in mind and eventually chose a different career.

- Karen spoke to me about her relationship with Michael. "He is exactly what I have always dreamed of," she said. "He is considerate, sensitive, and a good listener. He is handsome and about to be promoted to a higher management level. But he does not share my faith." Many people never think about this issue, but for Karen this point became central.

- A teenager caught off guard by a school principal who demanded to know the truth about a situation, answered, "I don't know." He did know. Later, he became upset because he had overstepped a nonnegotiable belief—always to tell the truth.

Many years ago, the Davy Crockett television show was popular. Davy tried to conduct his actions based on this slogan: "Be sure you are right, then go ahead." When you know what is right, act on it.

Our beliefs are the substance out of which everything else flows. Our beliefs motivate and dominate all that we are and all that we do. If we believe that we are a failure, everything we do will substantiate that belief and cause it to come true. On the other hand, we may over-compensate by spending our lives trying to prove to everyone that we are not a failure.

What we believe is powerful. Here is an example. Hypnotized individuals do many unusual things through posthypnotic sugges-tion. In an article in *Science Digest*, Dr. Theodore Barber wrote, "The hypnotized subject behaves differently because he *thinks and believes* differently. . . . When a subject *believes* that he is deaf, he behaves as if he is deaf. . . . When he *believes* that he is insensitive to pain, . . . he can undergo surgery without anesthesia."

Later, we will explore the power of belief in more detail. For now, we will look at one further illustration. It goes back to the time when I was a staff psychologist in a psychiatric hospital. Nearly all the patients had one thing in common—they believed they were crazy. This belief caused them to live accordingly. One of the most empow-ering things I did for them was to communicate that I truly believed they were not crazy. When they came to believe that, it often changed their lives.

I asked one patient, Tom, what his problem was. He answered, "I'm mentally ill." When I asked how he had arrived at this assess-ment, he described how he had removed all his clothes, burned his college books in the campus square, and danced around the fire until the police took him to the psychiatric hospital. As we talked further, he saw that his behaviour was wrong, but not psychotic. Sin, not illness, had overtaken him. His belief changed. His eventual release from the psychiatric hospital occurred.

"S"—STRATEGIZE: BE STRATEGIC

What is a strategy? It is a method used to obtain an advantage—during wartime, in business, in politics, and in many other situations. Many companies, for instance, create business strategies—ways to create new markets, increase profitability, improve customer service, etc.

We are not talking about the word *strategy* in the context of gaining advantage over another person. We are talking about obtaining an advantage over ourselves so that we can, with God's help, Take-Charge of our life and be prepared for the myriad battles we all face.

The Bible teaches an important lesson on strategy when it says, "Though we live in the world, we do fight a war as the world does. The weapons we fight with are different than the weapons of the world. Amazingly, our weapons have God's power connected to them and are able to smash strongholds."[5] We need to recognize that human weapons are useless in the immense battles we face in our lives. We need to know how to use weapons that can smash spiritual strongholds that are able destroy our lives. We need to know and pursue God's strategies in our battles. Such strategies may rarely seem reasonable to us.

For example, does it make sense for the Israelite army to walk around the walled city of Jericho for seven days and then to blow trumpets to make the walls fall down?[6] Does it make sense to ask Gideon to take 300 selected men and rout more than 100,000 Midianites?[7] Does it make sense for a lowly shepherd boy to use a slingshot against Goliath, a giant warrior who was nine feet, nine inches tall and whose armor weighed about 125 pounds?[8]

Goliath was insulted by David's strategy and said, "Am I a dog, that you come at me with sticks?" David replied that he came "in the name of the Lord Almighty."

When we have appealed to God and identified our nonnegotiable beliefs, our strategies become vital. As we Take-Charge of our lives, we will be able to face the "giants" that are in front of us.

Unfortunately, many of us go through life without having a strategy. We just try to get through each day. Is that all there is to life? The slogan says: "Life is hard, and then you die." Is there nothing more?

In my book *Free Indeed*, I describe a logger in the wilderness of northern Canada. He became lost one bitterly cold evening. Seeing lights in the distance, he rushed toward them, only to stop in terror when he had to cross a river. It seemed frozen, but as he walked on it, he began to think he could hear the ice cracking. He walked more carefully and slowly.

Eventually, the logger began crawling inch by inch toward the other side. Sweat poured down his face. Then he heard the distant sound of bells. The sound grew louder, and soon a horse-drawn wagon filled with logs and singing loggers crossed the ice. As if in a dream, the logger stood up, shook himself as if to come out of his stupor, and ran the rest of the way to the other side of the river.

Both the wagon's occupants and the terrified logger made it from point A to point B. The only difference is *how they got there!*

The same truth applies in our lives. Will we get from point A to point B consumed by fear, panic, and depression? Or will we go through life singing and with sleigh bells ringing?

"W"—Wisdom: Discovering the Way of Wisdom

We read that "there is a way which seems right to us, but in the end it leads to destruction."[9] What a contrast between this, and what follows: "Now choose life, so that you and your children may live."[10] The Bible contrasts the way that only *seems* right with the way that *is* right. It also goes on to detail that the right way is to "love the Lord our God by listening to Him and by hanging onto Him."[11]

Consider another contrast: "The fear of the Lord is the beginning of wisdom,"[12] and, "fools despise wisdom and discipline."[13]

In Proverbs, which could also be called "The Book of Catchy Sayings," we learn that people who are wise will find protection from those who are evil[14] as well as from those who are immoral.[15] The wise will share the road with those who are good.[16] They will live long and prosperous lives.[17] They will stay healthy even when they are old.[18] They will live at peace.[19] They will not be afraid, and they will have a good night's sleep.[20] Because they are confident in God, they will avoid getting their lives caught up in bad things and with bad people.[21] This list could go on and on!

This "way-of-wisdom" theme runs through the Bible, and is summarized most beautifully by the man whom God called the wisest man on earth—Solomon—who wrote, "Wisdom is supreme. Make sure to get it."[22]

When our life seems to be out of control and Taking-Charge of us, the answer will not be found in some mysterious, ethereal, mystical revelation of a deep, unconscious, archetypal experience. The answer is found in true wisdom—the wisdom of God.

"E"—Empower: Empowered by God

We have appealed to God. We have discovered our nonnegotiable beliefs. We have planned our strategy. We have committed ourselves to implementing our strategy with wisdom. We are ready to see how such a process can lead to complete empowerment in our lives.

The Bible calls us to be full of power. It teaches that although "we have this treasure in bodies that are breaking apart," it is this way in order "to show that the explosive power we possess is from God and not from us."[23] We see this idea again when we read that "My grace is all you need, because My power is made perfect in weakness."[24]

God delights in empowering us. He delights as well to use us for His service. Service is the channel for such empowerment. It is the means by which our lives can be refocused.

We are not powers unto ourselves. Instead, when the pressures get "far beyond our ability to endure,"[25] we rejoice because we have been allowed to face these pressures, so that we learn to trust God and not rely on ourselves. We come to see that God's empowering grace should fill each of our lives.

When Jesus and the disciples face tremendous pressure before He returns to heaven, He says to them, "You will be empowered when the Holy Spirit comes on you. You will tell everyone about Me, starting in Jerusalem, going out to Judea and Samaria, and finally reaching the ends of the earth."[26]

Soon afterward, Jesus' disciples experience this promise. Peter and John heal a crippled beggar.[27] The authorities who investigate this "seditious" activity, ask only one question: "By what power or by what name did you do this?"[28]

The answer leaps off the lips of Peter and John when they say that "it is by haShem Yeshua haMashiach of Nazareth, whom you put to death on the cross but whom God raised from the dead, that this man stands before you healed."[29]

The empowerment we receive from God is not something we can sustain by ourselves. It does not come from us or from our efforts. It comes from the work of Jesus Christ and the Holy Spirit in our lives. He gives us "great power to continue to testify to the resurrection of the Lord Jesus."[30] We are empowered in this way so that many people may come to life in Jesus.

Sometimes empowerment leads to death. Stephen was a man "full of grace and power."[31] In his witness, he spoke of life in Jesus. His "reward" was being stoned to death.[32]

We are empowered to live. We are empowered, like Stephen, to die. We are empowered to help people who are hurting. We are empowered to reach out to those around us and bring them hope. This is why Paul prayed that "the God of hope would fill you all with joy and peace as you trust Him, so that you may overflow with hope through the power of the Holy Spirit."[33]

Empowerment from God is not something that demands a waiting period. As His people, we are already empowered. We have passed from spiritual darkness into His light. If we are spiritually weak, it is perhaps because we are unfocused. We do not look where we should look. We look intensely at the difficulties, instead of lifting our eyes to God.[34]

Here is an example of the importance of having a correct focus. My daughter won a free winter hazard driving lesson from a company that offers a driver training program. Since she could not attend, I took her place. The teacher showed us a video involving a skid. He pointed out that the main reason the car continued in the skid was because the driver focused on the skid. In order to get out of the skid, he should have focused on the direction he desired the car to go, not the direction of the skid. The right maneuver requires tremendous effort and concentrated focus. It is worth it, because it can save our lives.

Many of us go through life in the skids. We focus on our skids. We put great effort into our skids. We hope fervently that our skids will be reduced and redirected, yet we live as if we have no control over the direction of our lives. Living that way, it is no surprise that our lives consist of one skid after another. Even the name of the place where society's down-and-outers wind up is called Skid Row.

How can we get out of our skids? *We need to focus on the direction in which we want to go.* We read: "Let us fix our eyes on Jesus."[35] These words were written just after the mention of numerous heroes of the faith.[36] These heroes were flogged, chained, stoned, imprisoned, and put to death. Our empowerment is not designed to keep us from difficulty. Our empowerment does, however, enable us to go through our difficulties hopefully.

After encouraging us to focus on Jesus, the Bible challenges us to resist behaviors that will tempt us and lead us into trouble, to take self-mastery seriously, remain encouraged, endure hardship, strengthen themselves, live in peace, be holy, and worship God "with fear and awe."[37]

It is easy to believe that only "supermen" and "superwomen" can achieve these goals; that ordinary people will be left far back in the pack because the struggle to change will be too hard. The Scriptures teach that we can accomplish incredible things because "God does not give us a spirit of timidity, but a spirit of power, of love and a sound mind."[38]

God calls us to be Take-Charge men and women of courage, character, power, love, and self-mastery. Without a doubt, that is what God's empowerment is all about. Many of us want to be empowered for the wrong reasons. What we mistakenly desire, is power for power's sake, rather than empowerment for the sake of others.

True empowerment completes our character. When God empowers us, He completes our character. Remember: "Suffering enables us to endure even more suffering, which in turn brings about a change, a developing, a maturing, and a proving of our character."[39] The concern is our character, even beyond our behavior.

"R"—Respond: Choose Your Response

When my counselees have trouble in implementing change, it is often because they are locked into a very damaging "either/or" approach to solving their troubles. They see things as either *do everything right* or *do nothing at all* to promote personal change. They do not seem to grasp that doing nothing will simply perpetuate their troubles, and that doing everything right is unattainable. They doom themselves for failure.

For example, a depressed woman I will call Helen came with her husband for counseling. When I asked her to describe her depression, she answered, "My home is a complete wreck. I have six children, the youngest of whom is a toddler. If I don't get things under control, I'll remain depressed forever." As it turns out, she had tried to organize the entire house, and, after an hour's effort, had sat down defeated, exhausted, and more depressed.

Certainly, various things were happening in her life on biological, hormonal, emotional, and spiritual levels. However, it was easy for me to see how her all-or-nothing mentality had thrown her deeper into despair as she faced the inevitable defeat of trying to organize in sixty minutes an entirely disorganised and dishevelled house.

I discovered what Helen believed to be her easiest, more difficult, and most difficult household responsibilities. We then worked together to create a program that helped her and her husband cope with the mountain of responsibilities. She started with the easiest one first. All she did day one was dust. The next day she washed laundry. Day three she vacuumed the upstairs. She was also excited because her husband had been included in helping her with the housework.

Within weeks, Helen was transformed. She had achieved real success. She had realized that she could accomplish meaningful tasks, and such accomplishment encouraged her to try even harder. "I have accomplished more in just one week," she exclaimed happily, "than I have during the past two years!"

I can summarize why that simple approach worked so well for Helen by telling a story about professional basketball coach Pat Riley. His teams have won the most professional basketball games in history.

When Pat was coaching the Los Angeles Lakers in 1985, they had a great year but did not win the NBA championship. The next season did not seem to offer great prospects. The team members began thinking, *We've given it everything, and there's nothing more we can give. If we didn't win last season, how can we win now?*

Pat devised a plan. He challenged each of the ten team members to improve by just the smallest margin: 1 percent. When this was done in five skill areas, this would produce a team that was 50 percent better! The team was convinced that they could improve just 1 percent in each area.

What happened? The 1986-87 Lakers team is considered by many to have been one of the greatest basketball teams ever. How did Pat do it? The same way Helen did—by negotiating a workable, manageable portion that almost certainly guaranteed success.

How to Improve

I spent one summer teaching in Japan, where I marveled that a nation nearly annihilated more than sixty years ago is a wealthy, leading industrial power today. Many people have given in-depth reasons for Japan's rise to power. One easily overlooked factor in particular merits consideration. The Japanese are convinced that producing high-quality goods is ultimately less expensive. They are also committed to constant quality improvement. They call this *kaizen*. This concept of *kaizen* is foreign to many of us who live in the West. We rarely think about quality, let alone how to constantly improve it.

One day our family visited the town of Omiya, where Japan's bonsai masters live. These masters tend tiny little trees and shrubs that are often as much as 600 years old. They have handed down their skills from family member to family member throughout the generations.

I watched one man work in the presence of his grandfather, a bonsai master, and make minuscule adjustments to tiny trees worth thousands of dollars each. He knew that the tiniest refinements eventually make an enormous difference.

Just as refocusing on quality improvement is important in keeping nations competitive in world economic markets and in pruning tiny trees, it is vital to us if we are going to advance on a personal level.

To help us gain this competitive edge, I have created a little response device to help us. I have also given it a Japanese-sounding name to stimulate us in our quest for personal spiritual development. I call it GISI-DICI, and this is what it stands for:

> Gradual Improvement, Steady Improvement
> Daily Improvement, Constant Improvement

What most people lack is not intelligence, but a workable approach that will help them put into practice what they already possess. GISI-DICI provides us with the basis for reasonable change that we can expect to make. Our improvement will be gradual, steady, daily, and constant.[40]

Let's suppose we have just met someone who is discouraged, who has given up finding a job, and who no longer cares about looking attractive. We could say, "Get your life into shape," and walk away.

If we did that, the person might have reason to be discouraged and think, *What does he mean? How am I to accomplish that?*

Instead, we need to be concrete in our help. For example, we can say to people who have come to us for help, "Let me tell you how to have greater success in finding a job. You need to dress better. Your pants and your shirts should be ironed. Your clothing should match. You need to comb your hair. You need to brush your teeth. You need to have someone help you create a one-page carefully worked-out résumé. You need to learn how to use the internet to find a list of every potential employer." Doing this, we have helped the person begin having a Take-Charge life. We have helped them take responsible, concrete steps and actions. These actions will be completed successfully because people *can* accomplish manageable amounts.

As we respond differently and excitedly to the challenges that God brings into our lives, our entire life experience will change. Not only will our lives no longer Take-Charge of us, we will Take-Charge of our lives. Others around us, our family and friends, will get to see what a Take-Charge life looks like. We will encourage other people as we help them to think of living and enjoying a powerful Take-Charge life day by day and step by step.

God will bless us as we step out in faith. God will bless us when we are not content to just exist but desire instead to Take-Charge of our lives. God will bless us so that, empowered by Him, our lives will never again charge out of control. Dear reader, you already have *everything* you need for an abundant Take-Charge life. Use it!

TAKE-CHARGE ACTION INITIATIVES

1. *Reread each of the A.N.S.W.E.R. steps. List personal difficulties to which you can apply these TODAY.*

   _____

   _____

   _____

   _____

2. *Do you believe that trust is an important part of your relationship with God? Why or why not? Give an illustration from your life.*

   _____

   _____

   _____

3. *In a difficult situation, do you find yourself going to other people before you go to God? Why or why not?*

   _____

   _____

   _____

4. *List six nonnegotiable beliefs to which you will cling.*

   _____

   _____

   _____

   _____

   _____

   _____

5. *In which area(s) do you tend to blame other people or circumstances when you face difficulties?*

_____

_____

_____

   What are you going to do about that?

_____

_____

_____

6. *List three areas in your life in which you can apply GISI-DICI.*

_____

_____

_____

7. *What do you hope to accomplish in each of these areas?*

_____

_____

_____

9

TAKE-CHARGE ACTION

Even seemingly insignificant actions lead to significant outcomes. Deliberately choose not to wait for someone or something to change you or your circumstances. Act now. Take-Charge of your life. Begin TODAY.

As a young child, I found that my most difficult moments each day occurred just after I opened my eyes in the morning. I would lie in my warm bed knowing that I had to get up, and dreading it. I would put it off, experiencing moment after moment of dread until my mother or father forced me to get up and get dressed.

I am sure that many of us can resonate with this simple childhood dilemma. In fact, the military wake-up song *Reveille* contains these words: "You can't get 'em up. / You can't get 'em up. / You can't get 'em up in the morning. / You can't get 'em up. / You can't get 'em up. / You can't get 'em up today." Unfortunately, I lived out those words for many years, getting up only after torturously debating with myself about the merits of doing so.

Looking back, I realize that if I had gotten up quickly, I would have experienced little, if any, dread, and accomplished more with less pressure. The solution was so simple. I just needed to *Take-Charge*. As a human being, I had been created to act, not to be a passive blob. Obviously I had to get up in the morning and get on with my responsibilities, no matter how miserable that option seemed.

When we start to Take-Charge of our life, we come to see how a seemingly insignificant but responsible action can lead to a significant outcome. Most of us would not, for example, imagine that hopping out of bed right away in the morning rather than waiting desperately for a reason to want to do so is really a big deal. It is. Such seemingly insignificant decisions and resultant actions affect many aspects of our lives, from the way we get out of bed, to our perspectives on the activities of a given day, to the way in which we live out the 86,400 seconds of each day.

We live in an age of entitlement. Millions of people in the United States believe that it is the responsibility of the government to take care of them. These people refuse to accept the fact that they are responsible both for TODAY and for their lives.

This entitlement mentality, this unwillingness to accept personal responsibility, is even more prevalent, and a greater problem, in Eastern Europe. This is especially true after the fall of communism in 1991. The media highlighted the numerous opportunities that were opening up over there. At the same time, however, a new problem surfaced. Millions of Eastern Europeans did not have a clue about personal initiative. For so many years, they were given jobs, apartments, and other benefits and services. Several years after the opening of Eastern Europe, many people still sat around waiting to be told what to do.

When I worked with a mission group in Moscow, one mission worker had completed all the required forms for the past several weeks. The paperwork revealed that he had visited everyone, followed up all his visits, and kept detailed records. The director of the mission became suspicious, telephoned people who supposedly had been contacted, and discovered that none of them had been visited.

Challenged to explain the false claims he had made, the worker readily confessed them without remorse. "You gave me the forms," he said, "and I filled them all out just as you wanted. Everything is in place. What more is necessary?" Having lived and worked under communism, he had learned that the actual work did not matter as long as all the forms were in order. He had no concept of what even beginning to Take-Charge of his life was really all about.

Many others, in contrast, would love to Take-Charge of their lives, but nonetheless experience no meaning or purpose. Instead, they drift along trying various things. They remain unfocused, hungering for a reason to live, and longing for responsibilities that will make a difference to something or someone, including themselves.

Recently, I spoke with a young woman who grew up on a Native Canadian reservation. Kim described how virtually every young person on the reservation was involved in a drug-filled, alcohol-filled, sex-filled lifestyle. She then added, "But they aren't having fun." Their lifestyle seemed to them to be all they had and all they would ever have until they died. As a consequence, many of them did not care if they lived or died. They had no sense that their lives mattered. They could not imagine projecting themselves into a vantage point from which they could see any meaning or purpose in their lives. Consequently, many of them committed suicide. They never experienced the hope of a Take-Charge life.

When Kim became a believer in Jesus, her entire life changed dramatically. She realized that her life matters. She understood that what she thinks and does matters. She now knew that decisions she makes have enduring significance, both for herself and for others in her life. Kim began to Take-Charge of her life. Gradually, the initial difficulties of Taking-Charge of her life passed. She became more confident as she experienced the blessing that comes from accepting the personal responsibility that is a consequence of a life of faith in Jesus.

What is disturbing, if not as readily apparent, is that many people in North America are now responding like the young people in Kim's community. They eat and breathe, but cannot see that their lives have any meaning. They wait for something significant and positive to happen. It rarely does. They wander aimlessly, or deliberately, into death, without any sense of meaning or purpose. They never experience the joy of living a Take-Charge life.

It is no secret that scholastic performance in many North American schools has deteriorated considerably. Many students no longer believe that they have to work hard and make something of themselves. *Why do all that?* they reason. *We'll get by, or the government will take care of us if we can't make it on our own.* Such a view of life is catastrophic.

Likewise, many adults have no clue about the meaning of their life. They do not know why their life is worth living. They experience as well a deep spiritual void. Unlike previous generations, they no longer think about, or even recognize, truth or absolutes. If the subject of truth enters into a discussion, they receive it with the intolerance they once felt that an absolutes-dominated society demonstrated toward them. Since our culture has moved away from Bible-based absolutes and towards changing cultural norms, there is now no cultural rest or safety. Unborn babies are slaughtered, damaged people are truly endangered, and violent criminals are given all the benefits and protection that law-abiding citizens deserve.

In a society such as ours that so easily discards the deepest held values, it is hard for people growing up in such an environment to think about commitment and life, and take it seriously.

Think of the cultural forces that subtly, or even blatantly, pressure us to live commitmentless lives. Think of the rationalizations that we allow to encourage us to blame others for our predicaments. In order to become the Take-Charge men and women we are meant to be, we must instead become committed to honestly appraising ourselves and all that we do. The P.A.T. and A.N.S.W.E.R. tools are designed to help us do that.

The hugely successful movie *Sleepless in Seattle* portrayed characters who had no control over their lives. They waited for something "magical" to happen. The movie became popular because many people are miserable, just like the main characters in the movie. They want something magical to happen, but have little interest in working to make it happen.

There is obvious unwillingness to work at what is important. This is one reason why divorce has become so prevalent. People do not even want to work on their marriage. Mostly women, but even men, fantasize about instant, easy, and magical romance. This is why *Sleepless in Seattle* so powerfully resonated with movie-goers. It played right into their fantasies without ever helping them in real life.

Most couples are deeply in love when they consider marriage. At the same time, they never bother to learn the principles that make a relationship succeed after the "magic" has worn off. These principles require initiative, knowledge, effort, and work. Before entering marriage, instead of committing to these principles, most people are committing to marriage contracts. These contracts are designed only to help them get out of those marriages rather than work through those marriages.

Consider as well, that most people today will go after the best paying jobs, not the work which would help them accomplish their calling in life. One of my daughters reported to me with dismay a speech the career counselor gave to the students in her high school. Speaking about the future, he said, "I wanted a good-paying job because I wanted all the toys." He did not go on to say that this was youthful ignorance. Rather, he was commending this way of life. All too often, what we do is done superficially or frivolously. It is no wonder that our work is unfulfilling and our marriages are disinte-grating. "Without a vision, the people perish."[1]

In contrast, look at the lives of people who live in ways that make a difference. These are people who risk. These are people who fulfill the calling on their lives. These are people who Take-Charge. Notice what is involved in a Take-Charge life:

- ▸ They do not wait until the right job opens up. They make things happen.

- ▸ They do not wait for people to affirm their significance so that they can start to feel good about themselves. They recognize their significance and identity, and press ahead. They make things happen.

- ▸ They do not sit around wishing things were different. They use their God-given abilities and talents to live. They make things happen.

This is all so simple. We do not wait around for things to happen. We make things happen. We do not sit around wishing things were different. We make things different. We stand up and make things happen. Think about it. As soon as we stand up, things are different. If we wonder, *How are things different?* the answer is simple. We are no longer sitting down. We have made a change. We have acted. We are making things happen.

God's Action Call

When I was on the staff of a psychiatric department in a univer-sity medical center, one of the most common problems we faced was a ward full of people who would not get up in the morning. I certainly understood this dilemma, and realized that I would not exactly call it a psychiatric problem! Did this mean that they *could not* get up? Of course not! They simply chose to sleep away each day. No amount of psychotherapy, investigation, or insight was able to get them out of bed; that is, until a staff member discovered their aversion to icy water being poured on them.

It is amazing how quickly this simple act changed their attitude about getting up. They were capable of what we can call in the simplest sense a Take-Charge Action. They were able to do this because of a simple truth: They hated cold water far more than they hated getting up and facing the day. I do not recall a single patient staying in bed after being drenched, or a single patient who had to be drenched twice.

Life involves action, not just contemplation. Those people in the psychiatric hospital often comforted themselves because they *wanted* to get out of bed. Wanting and doing are two different things. God calls us to action. Our lives are never meant to simply think about the good things we are to do.

Remember: God tells us that we are to think about the good, beautiful, and true things, but God does not stop there. He says that "these are the things that we are to put into action."[2] The word for *action* means to "exercise, practice, undertake, accomplish." We are to exercise and accomplish all that God has for our lives. It is then, the passage continues, that "the God of peace is with us."[3]

God desires us to be men and women of action, to know the right thing, and to do it. If psychiatric patients can be motivated enough to get up every morning whether they like it or not, we can do the right thing that is pleasing God, whether we like it or not as well.

Start Today

The action of starting is fundamental. None of us can ever do anything with our lives if we do not take that first step. As the Bible puts it, "I energetically push myself toward the goal, so that I will win the prize that God has for me, as I get closer and closer to heaven through my life in Jesus."[4]

God has given each of us the ability to "push forward" from wherever we are in life. This means that we do not have to be "pushed back." The difference between the two is the difference between someone who is free and someone who sees himself as enslaved. Each of us can always choose to Take-Charge, even in the most trying circumstances. We become imprisoned, however, when we believe that other people have the power to Take-Charge of us. This belief can occur at any time, even when we seem to be the most free.

When we live as if others have Taken-Charge of our lives, it is easy to move to the next step and simply blame them for the way we are today. Each of us is influenced by many factors, including relationships with people who do not always treat us the way we think we should be treated. We must not allow ourselves to continue to be shaped by what others think of us. We must take the lessons from the past, and push ourselves forward. By our actions, we must repudiate our false beliefs.

Some of us believe that a higher level of economic prosperity will set us free. Sadly, this kind of thinking enslaves us to the false notion that freedom is found in the abundance of things. True freedom is not dependent upon prosperity. We will never be joyfully free simply because we have all kinds of things. Thus we read: "It is for freedom that you have been set free. Stand strong and do not let yourself ever be enslaved again."[5] In relationship to our freedom, "We need to be happy if we have great wealth. We need to be equally happy if we are as poor as a church mouse. We are happy when we learn the secret and know that we can do everything we have to do. We can bear everything we have to bear. We can endure everything we have to endure. We can do it all! We can do it all because Jesus loves us, cares for us, hears us, provides for us, and has given us everything we need."[6]

Many of us live at the mercy of the market or the whims of our employers. We do not have to live this way. We are not puppets. We are free.

The psychologist B. F. Skinner hoped that modern men and women would see themselves as nothing other than animals that can be easily conditioned by stimulus-response techniques. He is wrong! We have the power to choose, and are responsible before God for what we have been given. Our genetics do not cause our behavior. We are free to change any and every pattern of response. This includes our most negative patterns of behavior that have persisted for decades.

My brother clearly illustrates this freeing truth. About thirty years ago, he became a follower of Jesus after leading a dissolute life. Shortly after experiencing God's healing forgiveness and gaining new purpose and direction, he knew that he needed to get serious about finding employment. He had never done that before. He realized that he needed Take-Charge Action. He needed to take simple, basic steps that would get him moving in the right direction. So he filled out job applications and agreed to take a job with an agency in New York that transported disabled people. He agreed to do the work even though it only paid minimum wage.

Before he started his new job, he was offered another job selling potato chips for a significantly higher wage. Although he was torn between the two choices, he chose to drive the disabled people because he believed that it could be a ministry and that it was important for him to honor the commitment he had made to accept that job.

Before long, his employer asked my brother to line up contracts with hospitals and nursing homes. Since he would no longer be a driver and was being asked to consider a new position, my brother realized that he should consider career options. He saw that he could do this new sales job on his own. Although it involved risk, there was a huge market for what he could offer, and he was ready to try it.

Within a few years, my brother owned about forty vans, had sixty employees, and had the opportunity to really be of help to many other people. Several years later, while he was in the process of selling his business, he asked me for advice about his options. He had two serious offers. The first person was willing to pay hundreds of thousands of dollars more than the second, yet my brother sold his business to the second person. Why? The first buyer wanted to consolidate his business with another one in the city and thus remove most of my brother's employees from the payroll. The second buyer wanted to keep all of the employees.

"I'm responsible for the financial well-being of sixty people and their families," my brother said to me. "I can't just take the higher price if it means that they will lose their jobs."

As my brother discovered, our first step in starting to Take-Charge of our life TODAY is not the exertion of our power to make an impact on the world. Our first step is the exertion of our power to make an impact on ourselves, one step at a time.

With this in mind, we can remember that most of the so-called "big" changes just *seem* big. In reality, these seemingly big changes are really nothing other than the results of many small, simple, successive changes.

Each of us has the power and freedom to live with action, even TODAY. Dear reader, Take-Charge of your life one step at a time. Remember: Do not let your life Take-Charge of YOU.

Take-Charge Action Initiatives

1. *Describe a time in your life when you took a series of small, purposeful steps in order to accomplish a goal. What happened?*

   _____

   _____

   _____

2. *What gives you a sense of real meaning and purpose in your life? Be honest!*

_____

_____

_____

3. *How can you use the Bible as a solid foundation for your life TODAY?*

_____

_____

_____

_____

4. *Have you ever blamed other people or circumstances when something in your life did not go well? If so, when?*

_____

_____

_____

5. *Do you think it is easier to blame other people and circumstances, rather than accepting personal responsibility and making the necessary changes? If so, why? If not, why not?*

_____

_____

_____

6. *Why is it often hard to take the first step in a positive direction? What reason(s) do you give for not Taking-Charge of your life?*

_____

_____

_____

10

THE BENEFITS OF A TAKE-CHARGE LIFE

You must Take-Charge of your life. This includes your thoughts, attitudes, and intentions. If you do not Take-Charge of your life, then you are allowing circumstances, influences, and people to Take-Charge of you. Choose the better way. Choose the Take-Charge way.

I speak with people all over the world, and most of them would give almost anything to have a Take-Charge life. It is not that they are doing all sorts of rotten things. It is just that they cannot seem to put on the brakes and find out which way to go in order to make necessary changes and Take-Charge of their lives. Pulled in different directions, they move in just about every direction except the direction they really want to go, that is, the one God encourages them to pursue. Some of these wonderful people ask me, "Is it right for us to Take-Charge of our lives? Isn't God supposed to be Taking-Charge of our lives instead?" Do they realize that what they are asking is to make God completely responsible for everything they think and everything they do? Do they realize that in thinking this way, they are trying to absolve themselves of any personal accountability?

In contrast, millions of people seek to be in charge of their own lives and their own destinies. From the days of Adam onward, people have been trying to be like God. The powerful poem "Invictus" by William Ernest Henley, makes this proud boast: "I am the master of my fate, the captain of my soul." This must not be confused with a

Take-Charge life. We are not striving for autonomy. We are not seeking to create our own laws and standards. We must go beyond "doing what is right in our own eyes."[1] Sadly, countless people reject the standards of the Bible and attempt to replace them by running their own lives, by creating their own standards.

At the same time, we are to live Take-Charge lives. When we do not, our lives begin to Take-Charge of us. Sarah is an example of this point.

Sarah came to me for help in as medicated a condition as anyone I had ever met. She had lost her job, received disability benefits, and was in danger of losing her children. She wanted drugs and doctors to take care of her. It was difficult for her to accept my conclusion that she was not mentally incapable, and that she needed to Take-Charge of her life or she would lose everything. "I know," she said quietly, "but I'm tired and lonely and scared."

How often we allow fatigue, loneliness, fear, anger, and other emotional and physical factors to dictate and control our lives. We hope that someone or something will turn everything around for us without our having to do anything. As in Sarah's case, when we live this way, who we are and what we have slips away from us.

We must Take-Charge of our lives. This includes our thoughts, attitudes, and intentions. If we do not, then we are allowing circumstances, influences, and people to Take-Charge of us. Instead, we must allow God to empower us to Take-Charge of our lives right now, TODAY!

We may be facing seemingly impossible situations. No matter how bad things seem, the Bible teaches us that we already have everything we need to live a Take-Charge life. In fact, a Take-Charge life is our mandate. Listen to the Bible's encouragement in this respect: "God's divine power has given us *everything* we need for life and upright living."[2]

DESTRUCTIVE EXCUSES

Over the years, many people have told me, in one way or another, that they cannot imagine ever living a Take-Charge life. What they are really saying is, "I can't do anything until I'm zapped. I want something outside of me to change me." All of us at one time or another use similar excuses when what we have to do seems a little beyond what we are ready and willing to do.

Solomon was the wisest man who ever lived. He understood what a Take-Charge life is all about. He said, "Like a city whose walls are broken down is a man who does not Take-Charge of his life."[3] What Solomon is saying is that if we refuse to Take-Charge of our lives, we will wind up broken down like a ghost town. We are to rule over ourselves. We are to exercise mastery over ourselves. We are to Take-Charge of our lives.

When we meet people who say, "My problem is anger," they are really saying, "I am telling you that I am the kind of person who does not Take-Charge of his life. Please don't expect me to Take-Charge of my life while I am with you, because I don't do it with anyone. I get away with doing this because I tell people that I am not accountable. I do not exercise mastery over myself. I do not Take-Charge of my life."

Of course, they do not consider that this is what they are saying. They would not like it if we responded to them, "You mean that you are like a city with walls that are completely broken down? You are nothing more than a ghost town?" We are meant to live a Take-Charge life of mastery and rule over ourselves.

We need to use all that we are and all that we have to begin this Take-Charge process. Consider the Bible's encouragement for us in this:

> Do you not know that in a race all the runners run, but only one gets the prize? Run in such a way as to get the prize. Everyone who competes in

the Olympic Games goes into strict training. They do it to get a crown that will not last, but we do it to get a crown that will last forever. Therefore, I do not run like a man running aimlessly; I do not fight like a man beating the air. No. I beat my body and make it my slave so that after I have preached this to others, I will not fail to walk the talk. I do not want to be disqualified from getting the prize.[4]

Paul wrote these words for the same purpose they are intended for us. They are meant to bring encouragement and a clear focus. Paul wrote this so that he too would not lose his focus. He determined to Take-Charge of his life in every way. He kept the goal in sight. His pursuit of the crown was determined and energetic. Disqualification was not an option.

Paul's desire to Take-Charge of his life was all-consuming. He dedicated himself to Taking-Charge of every area of his life. He did not want his life to be aimless. He did not want his efforts to be wasted. He wanted his efforts to find their mark, so that he would not be veered from the God-inspired direction of his life. He did not want to run aimlessly through his life.

Similarly, when I have run in a race I have needed to keep my focus on the course. If I had ever run backwards, or in circles, or in a completely different direction from the other runners, what would have happened? Clearly I would not win the race. Instead, I would wind up wasting time and my energy running in the wrong direction.

Do you want to live a purposeful, Take-Charge life? It is yours for the taking.

A Fruitful Take-Charge Life

Our life is to evidence abundance. It is to be fruitful. "The fruit of the Spirit is love, joy, peace, patience, kindness, goodness, faithfulness, gentleness and self-control."[5] Interestingly, self-control is in this list. Actually, self-control, or, as it *could* be translated, *self-*

mastery, is involved in every aspect of this fruit. It is just another way of talking about a Take-Charge life. When we Take-Charge of our lives, we are able to face all our difficult challenges while reflecting the goodness, patience, joy, and kindness of the Spirit. After all, how can we be patient, joyful, etc., if we have not developed a Spirit-directed self-mastery? Living a fruitful, Take-Charge life reflects a life of Spirit-inspired self-mastery in every way.

This fruit we are speaking about may not grow all at once. As we live a Take-Charge life day by day, TODAY, we will see a blossoming in our lives.

WE CAN DO IT

Many of us think, *I can't Take-Charge of my life. That's only for others, not me.* In fact, all of us struggle day by day to live a Take-Charge life.

The Bible tells us that *"those of us who belong to Christ Jesus no longer live by the old ways with the old passions and desires. Rather, we live by the Spirit, so we need to keep in step with the Spirit."*[6]

We can Take-Charge of our lives because our old ways no longer control us. Our lives no longer have to be filled with careless, irresponsible living. Jesus died to free us from the bondage to such self-serving, love-denying lives. Each day, we can choose to use the fruit of our new lives. God is always available to help us Take-Charge of every area of our lives.

This being the case, why do so few of us experience this freedom? Why are not more of us living Take-Charge lives? Why do so many of us still seem enslaved by old passions and desires? Why don't we give up these desires and Take-Charge of our lives?

Many of us have never even realized that God calls us to action, that He calls us to Take-Charge. We do not consider that we are not meant to wait passively for something to happen to us. We must Take-Charge! We have the power to do it.

Take-Charge Action Initiatives

1. *In which area(s) of your life do you especially need to Take-Charge right now?*

   _____

   _____

   _____

2. *Which excuses have you found yourself using to avoid Taking-Charge in each of those areas?*

   _____

   _____

   _____

   _____

3. *Do you allow circumstances, influences, and people to direct your life rather than Taking-Charge of your life by God's power? If so, how might you begin to Take-Charge TODAY?*

   _____

   _____

   _____

4. *What is keeping you from getting rid of the improper and immoral passions and desires in your life that need to be changed, and running the best race and fighting the best fight you can?*

   _____

   _____

   _____

5. *How can you, as Paul expressed, "Run in such a way as to get the prize"?*

_____

_____

_____

6. *To which "prize" do you think Paul was referring?*

_____

_____

_____

11

SELF-MASTERY OF A TAKE-CHARGE LIFE

Self-mastery is integral in a Take-Charge life, and produces many lasting benefits. The process of self-mastery involves effort. Your new goals in a Take-Charge life demand that you break through the barriers that kept you mired in failure and defeat. As you achieve self-mastery, you may wonder if the results are worth the effort. Yes, if you consider a Take-Charge life a worthy goal!

Emil Zatopek won three Olympic gold medals during the 1952 Olympic Games—in the 5,000-meter race, in the 10,000-meter race, and in the marathon. His rival in the marathon, Les Perry of Australia, narrated the highlights of that race in a television documentary. He described how Zatopek finally reached him at the twenty-mile mark known as "the wall," the place where greatness and presumed greatness are easily separated.

Zatopek, with his thick Czechoslovakian accent, asked, "Perry, zee pace . . . too fast?"

Knowing that Zatopek had only competitively raced in a few marathons, Perry decided to thoroughly discourage him. He imitated Zatopek's accent: "Zatopek . . . zee pace . . . too slow!"

"Zank you, Perry," Zatopek answered, innocently looking him in the eye. Zatopek then surged ahead, never looking back.

During a post-race interview, Zatopek was asked, "Have you trained a full four years for these Olympic games?"

He looked at the interviewer incredulously and responded, "A full four years? I have trained a full fourteen years."

Zatopek had learned that in order to become an Olympic gold medalist, disciplined training was absolutely necessary. No matter how much effort it took, he had determined to stick with it until he achieved his goal. His gold medals were merely the result of countless small steps along the way.

Why did he put in fourteen years of ceaseless effort? He was determined to win his race. He was determined to achieve his goal!

Pursue Your Goals

Self-mastery is an integral part of a Take-Charge life. The Bible reinforces this when it says that we are to "discipline ourselves [exercise self-mastery] for the purpose of godliness."[1] The Bible goes on to say that we must "make every effort" in this endeavor.[2] We must devote our efforts to reaching this goal of a holy and God-pleasing Take-Charge life.

If we really want to accomplish something with our lives, it takes effort. It takes effort that is expended over time as we work toward a specific goal.

What are our goals? What is required to reach them? For us to achieve our goals, we will have to live the moments of our lives consistently moving in that direction. If we start moving in another direction, we will not attain our goals. We will attain something else. Then we will have many excuses as to why we never got to where we wanted to be, or accomplished what we wanted to accomplish. In other words, we have to stay focused.

A person who spends time and energy on everything that crosses his path—even things that he does not want to do—is not disciplined. Such a person is simply involved in ceaseless activity. The Bible calls this "running aimlessly."[3]

The "Pareto Principle," named after its founder Vilfredo Pareto, shows us the dangers of running aimlessly. The principle teaches that 20 percent of our activities will account for 80 percent of our results. This means we really have to be careful about what we do. Here is a helpful suggestion in that regard: Keep a list each day of the ten most important things that you need to do, listed in order of importance. Start with the first one, the most important item. Remember: The top two items will be worth more to you than all the rest put together.

Brian Tracy, in his book *Eat That Frog*, says, "Each of the ten tasks may take the same amount of time to accomplish. But one or two of those tasks will contribute five or ten times the value of any of the others... This task is invariably the frog that you should eat first."[4] For Tracy, eating that frog means "to start on the most important task that is before you. You force yourself to eat that frog, whatever it is. As a result, you accomplish vastly more than the average person."

Whatever our goals may be, we have to apply effort and training in order to reach them. We need to think with the mindset of a skilled athlete. The athlete chooses a desired result and practices over and over again. This repetition is often thousands of times. The athlete does this until the execution of the task necessary to obtain the desired result becomes second nature, and can practically be done in his sleep.

LASTING PURSUIT

As an adult, my daughter Natanyah is still an avid basketball player. When she was a young teenager, I watched her sink more than a dozen foul shots in one game. How did she achieve this level of mastery? Part of the answer lies in hours and hours of practice. Also, every night when she got into bed, she would take her basketball and lay there for ten to fifteen minutes, visualizing shot after shot going through the hoop. Everything—including hand and finger movements—necessary to accomplish the desired result was done by her with each shot. When she closed her eyes, she would watch the ball arc perfectly into the basket every time. This was the determination she had to accomplish her goals even while she was still in junior high.

This determination has continued on into Natanyah's adulthood. I do not even want to begin to tell you the level of effort that was necessary for her to work and achieve an A+ *average* for university. You might wonder why she worked so hard. Ask her that question this May, when she graduates from Georgetown University Law School, having gone through it with a full scholarship.

Let me give you another basketball illustration, this time of a person who highly motivated Natanyah. It is Larry Bird, the Hall of Fame star of the Boston Celtics. Someone asked Larry to shoot a basket and miss. The problem was, Larry had trained and disciplined himself so masterfully that he had to shoot many, many times before he could actually miss. This is a reflection of the kind of discipline that makes us ready to achieve success or mastery in any area of our lives.

RECEIVE YOUR REWARD

We have much more to strive for than just the perishable rewards that athletes receive. The Bible says that athletes "enter into strict training to get a reward that will not last. We exert *this* effort to get a crown that will last forever."[6]

We are reminded in this passage that as we exercise self-mastery, we move closer and closer to a reward that is infinitely greater than any reward a vigorous Olympic athletic attains. We should demonstrate more effort in these important areas in our lives than even the athlete. Remember: The eternal crown we will receive will endure forever.

Self-mastery has interesting results that affect every area of our lives. What we learn as we deepen in self-mastery, is that no problem is too difficult for us to conquer. Once we master the skill of working through a problem to its conclusion or a task to its completion, we have learned how to focus, master, and solve the problems that are part of *every* difficult challenge in our lives.

If we are not achieving our goals, we need to take a look at the time we have spent moving towards them or away from them. Whatever our goals—becoming a great shortstop, playing the piano for huge audiences, graduating from medical school, serving in an inner-city clinic, rearing godly children—we will need to spend time pursuing what we want to achieve. The first reward is in the doing. The eternal reward comes later.

Directed Energy

It is a truism: Old habits die hard. Consider our lives. We have grown our habits. We have watered them. We have nurtured and pruned them. We have helped them blossom. What if our flowering habits turn into weeds? What do we do then?

Most of us do not like weeds. A garden full of weeds is an eyesore. Weeds, though, can be very difficult to eradicate. They can be as difficult to get rid of as our old, engrained, unprofitable habits. If we wind up leaving them around, they take over everything. We would all like our weeds and our problems to be eradicated in an instant, without having to really work at it. This is one reason why drugs are so popular. They offer people an instant surge, an instant change in their feelings, an instant blast of confidence. The problem is, this blast of confidence does not resolve their problems. When the high is over, the problems still exist.

When I think of the discipline and work required to produce a lasting change, I think of the old willow tree that recently blew over on our farm. We had to get rid of it, and we could only do so much with a chain saw. Then we had to hire a backhoe operator to remove the stump. He was amazed by the depth and strength of the root system, and had a very difficult time removing roots that had been embedded for so many years.

Likewise, bad habits we have built in the past (and still may love) are often difficult and painful to eliminate from our lives. That is one reason why diets are so hard to maintain. It is not that dieting people do not want to lose weight. It is that they love the food that causes them to gain weight in the first place, and they love the food more than they love being trim.

Here is another simple truth to consider: *We will become more and more like the things to which we devote our time.* If we are couch potatoes, we should not assume that watching Arnold Schwarzenegger movies will magically transform us into Arnold Schwarzenegger look-alikes. Such a transformation requires weight training, a proper diet, interval training, and other lifestyle changes. Similarly, we will never achieve biblical scholarship by reading newspapers and magazines two hours a day, while only spending five minutes a day reading the Bible.

If we are committed to a particular goal, we have to spend time achieving it. We will have to drop other activities from our schedule. We will always experience some pain and loss as we apply discipline to our lives and choose to do new things. These losses are inconsequential when they are weighed against the gains we will achieve. This is all part of developing deepening self-mastery.

Many of us think, "I have no self-mastery." This is not accurate. When we think this way, we are giving ourselves false information. What we have communicated to ourselves is that we do not possess the self-mastery necessary to strive toward and achieve our goals. The truth is, we have the self-mastery to pursue whatever we want to pursue.

Strange as it may seem, a person exercises discipline even to live a bad life. We need to Take-Charge of our discipline as much as we need to Take-Charge of everything else in our lives. A couch potato who does not exercise is not undisciplined; he has just learned to discipline himself to sit on the couch and watch television for extended periods of time, rather than being physically active and productive. He does not use the term "discipline," but that is what he is doing.

RESPONDING TO PAIN

We are reminded in the Bible that "no training is pleasant while we are going through it."[7] The process of training to become more and more upright is indeed difficult. It goes against our natural tendencies. While training from God does not seem pleasant, "later on, however, it produces a harvest of uprightness and peace," but only "for those who have been trained by it."[8]

Most of us do not like pain, because pain is not pleasant. Let's not focus on the pain. When we "stick to the race [life] marked out for us,"[9] we have two choices. We can focus on the pain that we feel in the training of our life, become discouraged, and possibly stop running altogether. Alternatively, we can focus joyfully on the fact that we have started running. We know where we are going. We are committed to getting there. We can see how far we have come. We know we can make it in God's strength if we just stick to it.

A common mantra of coaches is: "Focus on the gain, not the pain." Often this is shortened to: "No pain, no gain." In spite of the fact that physical pain can signal potential trouble in our bodies, this phrase remains popular.

Real success and mastery in athletics or any other area requires us to go beyond past limitations. It requires us to extend ourselves further than we ever have before. Such success demands that we concentrate and focus on the goal. Without such a mindset, we will not break the barriers that have slowed us down or have stopped us.

We are all in a race whether we like it or not. As we train ourselves to pursue our goals with God's help, we will make progress. The process involves effort, but it is effort that is well worth it. It is an effort that will never hurt you, but always strengthen you. It will help you to live the way you are meant to live.

Have you ever spoken to someone who did something wrong and then chose to make things right? I have experienced this many times when I have been counseling people. As I hear what has taken place, I will state that I am glad things have worked out. I will then ask, "How do you feel about it?" Often the response is, "I'm glad I did make things right, but it really . . . hurts."

We do not like to really make diligent efforts in our lives. We prefer things to be easy. We do not realize that the effort is not the real issue, but how we respond to the difficulties associated with such effort. We must not let the expenditure of effort keep us from Taking-Charge of our lives. We must not focus on the effort and decide that the change we deemed necessary is not worth such effort. The tension, conflict, or struggle is just part of life. We must not let it stop us.

It is easy for us to look at others and say, "You've got it made. You have such an easy time with struggles that are so difficult for me. Why do I have to have such a difficult time with these things?" We do not recognize that others may have had to go through the same struggles we are facing. Maybe they have battled with an area of temptation, or sin, or catastrophic illness. Maybe they have had to change careers in mid-life. Perhaps they have struggled deeply with a terribly unhappy marriage.

As we begin to Take-Charge of our life, we will overcome barriers. We will go to heights we have never before experienced. It is not enough to simply want new and positive changes in our life. These changes demand work and effort. Such training, in the deepest sense, involves molding and perfecting our thoughts and our actions. It will lead to blessing in both the inner and outer aspects of our life.

Life is filled with struggle. This is a positive thing. The Bible teaches us to "endure such struggle as training for life."[10] When we stick to it through the training, we learn how to stick to it when we face hardship and difficulty. Life is inevitably filled with hardship, but through the hardship God is gracious, and brings deliverance. We must not forget that in times of difficulty and hardship we can learn a great deal and find that our hearts have been comforted. As the Bible says, "Do not make light of the Lord's discipline. Do not lose heart when He corrects you. Remember that the Lord trains all those whom He loves, and He corrects all His children."[11]

The Vital Link

When we speak of correction, most of us consider it as something negative. We equate it with punishment. This view of correction is a misunderstanding of what correction really is. When something that is wrong is corrected, this is very positive. If a teacher only marks a child's answers to a math quiz with an "X" for "wrong," that is not correction. Correction involves something very positive. It is the communication of what is right. The person being corrected is given the opportunity to learn something that will help him in his life.

When a mother really understands correction, she will not say to her child, "Don't do that." Instead she will say, "This is what you can do," or, "Here is why doing this would be better than what you are doing." Likewise, when God corrects us, He always teaches us what is right.

Even people whom God loves will face difficulties. The love of God is a key belief for believers, and the Bible links God's love with training. We are to treat the struggles and difficulties that come into our lives as our *resource for training*. The reason is simple. "God trains us for our good, so that we may share in His holiness."[12]

God corrects us because He loves us. He wants us to use everything He brings our way to help us become more and more like Him. He wants our training to be fruitful.

We can choose whether or not to receive and accept God's correction. The Bible tells us about a person who hates training and correction. This person says, "I hate training! My heart loathes correction."[13] Listen to the result: "My life is utterly ruined."[14] When we hate God's training and correction and reject it, the result is a completely ruined life. It is a life filled with trouble, sorrow, and regret.

The results of a person rejecting God's training and correction do not end at a ruined life. The Bible tells us that the ruined life happens "in the presence of all his friends, colleagues, and family."[15] If we hate correction, we will end up being publically humiliated and disgraced.

There is another, more encouraging, side: "When we pay attention to training, we walk on the path of life."[16] When we ignore correction, we not only live a corrupt life, but we will also "lead others astray."[17] The depth of consequences to our behavior is amazing. How few of us have considered that our good behavior encourages others to follow suit. So too our bad behaviour impacts others negatively.

Here is an example. A parent who smokes two packs of cigarettes a day may have many rationalizations for doing so. He may say, "I tried to stop, but couldn't," or, "I've cut back from three packs a day," or, "I really don't need to give these up, because two packs a day won't hurt me." Sadly, the children who grow up in that home will model the parent and start smoking. At the very least, they will suffer ill health from secondhand smoke.

The same applies when we drink too much, are immoral, become enraged at other people, gossip, lie, cheat on our income tax, or gamble. We can take our pick, or even add other things to this list. The point though, is simple. When we really care about others who are important to us, we had better model upright behavior for them. We had better be careful not to say, "I can't change my behavior." When we say this, we are communicating two things. One: They will not be able to change either. Two: "I won't change." I have a word of hope for all of us. With God's help, we can do all we have to do in order to be all that we are meant to be.

When we learn from correction, we are enabled to show others "the way of life."[18] This life is full, abundant, and overflowing. When we learn from training and correction, we are learning how to live a full and abundant life.

A God-Shaped Life

Slowly, but consistently and noticeably, all of us who submit to godly correction observe that God, in molding our lives, makes us to be more and more pleasing to Him.

Suppose we have lived an undisciplined life filled with error, failure, and carelessness for many years. Even so, God offers us tremendous hope. The circumstances in our lives may not change overnight, but as we Take-Charge of our lives and start making changes, we will experience blessing in one area after another.

There is an amazing, power-filled reality in the Bible. It teaches us what real change is all about. It is not just the replacement of a bad habit with a good habit. It is the replacing of our old lives with new lives that are made to be like God Himself. This is what happens when we put off the "old self" and put on the "new self."[19]

Our new self is really new! It is created to be like God, and reflect His true character. That's exciting! Godly correction helps to bring the newness of the new self into being. It is new because we actually become more and more like God Himself. At the same time, living as a new person requires that we give everything that we have. We must be willing to commit our energy, our time, and our efforts to becoming what God has made us to be. As we live in this manner, the wonderful fruit of the Spirit[20] is ours in abundance.

As a young believer, I had to work on one area after another in my life. Correction seemed to be needed everywhere. There were times that it seemed endless and impossible. I was wrong. I learned that a true relationship with Jesus that develops more and more as we allow Him to train and correct us, is the greatest joy there is. I obeyed God in spite of how I felt. As a result, God stayed with me through the renunciation in my life of one area of pride and rebellion after another. I understood this to be what many believers call a "surrendered life."

The Bible calls us to "strengthen our feeble arms and our weak knees."[21] It goes on to say, "Make the path you walk on to be level."[22] Earlier, King Solomon wrote the same thing, but added, "Only take ways that are firm and solid."[23] That is, we are not to become involved in doing evil. To explain this further, he added, "Do not swerve to the right or the left; keep your feet from evil."[24]

Ultimately then, living on the firm ground of Bible truth will keep us from doing evil. We will have the strength and wisdom to avoid the snares that come our way. We will seek instead what is true, honourable, right, pure, lovely, admirable, excellent, and praiseworthy.[25] We will be clearly focused. We will clearly know which goals to strive for. We will clearly know what to watch out for. This is the process of training and correction. It is strenuous, but without it our life is chaotic.

God wants us to be changed, because He wants us to be upright. The Bible challenges us to offer ourselves "completely to God, because this is pleasing to God."[26] It then adds that this is our "logical response to being worshipers."[27] We do this as a response to mercy from God that we have received.

The idea develops as we learn how to become pleasing to God. We are pleasing to God when we live a *truly* nonconformist life. As we read, "Do not conform any longer to the ways of this world. Rather, become transformed as your mind is made new again."[28] We are to live in nonconformity to the ways of this world. Our minds are to be transformed to demonstrate a way of living that opposes the consumerism, the commercialism, the lusts, the greed, the anger, and the fleeting pleasures of this world. Instead of conformity, there is to be *transformity.*

Training has a goal of remaking us. Everyone undergoing training knows that only the *results* of our training struggles are visible. These results are seen in our behavior. The contest has already taken place in our minds. What is won or lost in our minds determines what is won or lost in our lives.

We need to ask ourselves if we are living a life of disciplined self-mastery that is taking us day by day and step by step in the direction we want to go. If not, we have no alternative but to begin making changes *now.* We must Take-Charge now.

We must not be afraid of training. The Bible teaches us that "if we love training, we love knowledge." It adds though, that whoever "hates correction is stupid."[29] We need to remember that God has given us "a spirit of power, and of love, and of self-mastery."[30] This means that it is possible for every area of our lives to be transformed.

Such transformation begins as our thinking conforms more and more to the truth.

As we Take-Charge of our lives, we will become more and more transformed to be like Jesus. This is a top priority for us. This transformation is not easy, but it is readily available to us.

TAKE-CHARGE ACTION INITIATIVES

1. *List some of the goals you believe God is putting on your heart.*

   _____

   _____

   _____

   _____

   _____

2. *As you compare these goals to the ways in which you spend your time, what do you discover?*

   _____

   _____

   _____

   _____

   What changes do you need to make?

   _____

   _____

   _____

3. *Which areas of your life would you like to see transformed?*

   _____

   _____

   _____

   _____

In view of this, what steps will you take, starting TODAY, to begin to work towards a transformed, Take-Charge life?

_____

_____

_____

4. *What are the impediments or obstacles standing between where you are now and where God wants you to be?*

_____

_____

_____

_____

5. *In which areas of your life are you willing to receive God's correction? Why?*

_____

_____

_____

_____

In which areas of your life are you not willing to receive God's correction? Why not?

_____

_____

_____

_____

6. *List the areas in which you believe God is training and correcting you. What does He want you to do in each area?*

_____

_____

_____

_____

PART FOUR

The
Challenges
of a Take-Charge Life

12

FACING CHALLENGES IN A TAKE-CHARGE LIFE

It is not what you face but how you face it that is important. Ask the right questions, and develop a godly focus. You will be amazed at how you are able to Take-Charge of even some of the greatest challenges in your life.

It is easy to forget that other people face struggles as tough as or even tougher than ours. They too have to choose whether or not to focus on enabling truths or disabling truths. In many cases, their choices determine the outcomes. To understand the importance of focusing correctly, let's consider the difficult experiences of three people and how they chose to think about their circumstances.

JOSEPH: ABUSED, ENSLAVED, IMPRISONED

Do you remember the account in the Bible about Joseph? He faced a terrible situation. His brothers, whom he adored, loved, admired, and respected, decided to kill him! At that point, his eldest brother, Reuben, did some fast talking, and they hurled him into a deep cistern rather than killing him.

While he was in that cold, dark cistern, Joseph could hear his brothers eating their lunch, making jokes, and scheming his destruction. Then he heard the sound of a caravan approaching. He heard the traders' voices, and his brothers agreeing to sell him for twenty shekels of silver.

Soon Joseph was sold as a slave and was on his way to Egypt while his brothers finished their lunch. Perhaps the last image he saw was that of his brothers holding his multicolored coat (his most precious possession), the coat given to him as a token of his father's love.

We can picture Joseph sometime later standing on the auction block in Egypt as the traders pinched his skin and looked at his fine-toned muscles. Torn from his home and family, facing a lifetime of slavery, he still maintained hope.

What was the good in Joseph's situation? What gave him hope? He was an innocent victim of horrible treachery. Did he have anything left? Yes! Joseph was alive. As the ancient philosopher Cicero said later, "Where there is life there is hope."

Joseph also had a strong faith in the character of God and chose to focus on the truth. He knew that he could depend on God.

Facing enormous emotional pain, virtually forgotten by his brothers, forced to enter a heathen culture, Joseph could have brooded on what had happened to him. He could have wondered what he had done to deserve such treatment, and come to think of himself as a powerless victim. He could have blamed himself and begun to believe that nothing he could do would get him out of his desperate situation. He could have allowed what his brothers did to him to lead him into despair and to control the rest of his life through anger, bitterness, blame, and failure. Joseph could have just given up and pined away.

He didn't. Joseph could have nurtured anger and bitterness, feeding on revenge. He didn't. Instead, he moved from his thoughts of pain to thoughts of hope. He moved from disabling thoughts to enabling thoughts. Joseph made it a point to learn from what had happened to him. He began using that knowledge at his first opportunity. He focused on the positives. He Took-Charge of his thoughts, obeyed God, and drew near to Him.

Joseph was determined to seek a godly direction and to walk uprightly. Like Job who stated, "I know that my Redeemer lives"[1] after losing virtually everything but his life, Joseph also knew that God was trustworthy and faithful. He knew that he could count on God. Even when he was falsely accused and thrown into prison, he continued to trust God. In the end, even while he was in prison, he was elevated to become the second in command in Egypt. Pharaoh alone was above Joseph.

DAVID: THREATENED, PURSUED, DESPAIRING

As a young man, David faced tough challenges that included a murderous attack on his life, pursuit through the wilderness, hunger, loneliness, being cut off from the opportunity to worship God in the temple, and despair. As he wrestles with the fear that God has abandoned him, he writes, "My tears have been my food day and night."[2] This conveys the picture that the tears dripping into his mouth are his only sustenance.

Facing despair, David chooses to redirect his thoughts. Instead of focusing on his circumstances, he directs his thoughts toward God and asks two questions: "Why are you so depressed, O my soul? Why is there such trouble churning within me?"[3] The very act of asking these questions begins to refocus David away from his despair. As he refocuses, he begins to rethink.

David does not deny his present distress. This is important. He does not say, "Wow, everything is great." He admits he is deeply depressed, and he uses the Hebrew word *tsuris*, which means "to be deeply disturbed," or, "to be despairing." He also uses the word *shochah*, which means "troubled," or, "clamorous." His troubles are like a raging noise inside of him.

We can picture David lying motionless on the ground in that darkened cave, crying out as he experiences deep, emotional pain. He hears the echo of his despair bouncing off the walls. He faces deep depression.

In the midst of this, David refocuses his thoughts. In the midst of hurt and despair, he does not just think, *Everything is bad. Nothing will ever be good again. My life is ruined.* He shifts his focus from debilitating thoughts that are destroying him to questions that ask, in effect, *Are things really bad enough for me to allow myself to become so terribly troubled and depressed?*

David experiences a battle of sensations—anger, despair, abandonment, fear—while hiding in the cave. Saul is not standing in front of him at this moment. David is not actually fighting a physical battle with other soldiers. He is fighting a battle in his mind. In the midst of this battle, he chooses God and he finds joy.

God makes it possible for each of us to be filled with joy, even in times of trial. Like David, we are capable of reminding ourselves of our blessings and of responding to our circumstances, other people, and God in ways that allow joy to fill our lives. We who live joyfully are not born that way. We have learned to trust God in all the situations of our lives. "We need to be happy if we have great wealth. We need to be equally happy if we are as poor as a church mouse. We are happy when we learn the secret and know that we can do everything we have to do. We can bear everything we have to bear. We can endure everything we have to endure. We can do it all! We can do it all because Jesus loves us, cares for us, hears us, provides for us, and has given us everything we need."[4]

After David says how despairing his life is, he looks to God and sees a deeper reality: "I will put my hope in God, and I will praise Him once again, for He is my Savior and my God."[5]

Matthew Henry, the Puritan preacher, wrote about Psalm 42, which I quoted above: "The Psalms are a mirror or a looking glass of holy emotions. This Psalm in particular kindles and excites tremendous devotion in us. Grace-filled desires become strong and powerful. Grace-filled hopes, and fears, and joys, and sorrows indeed are struggling here, but joy conquers."[6] In the face of despair, joy and exultation conquer!

As David refocuses his thinking, not only his thoughts, but also his feelings, change. A very important principle is reinforced for us. *It is not the situation that matters, but how we face it and how we respond to it.* For David, the critical issue is not the cave. The critical issue is his understanding of what is taking place in the cave. Even more critical is what he does based upon that understanding. The real issue is how he chooses to live. Does he choose to Take-Charge of his life, or does he choose to allow himself to sink deeper into despair?

Inevitably, how we live will be determined by how we understand, view, and act on the circumstances of our lives. When we face tough situations, we have the opportunity to make them positive and learn something from them. Others, sadly, choose to be deeply disturbed by difficult and challenging circumstances. Both sets of people face the same situation, but respond differently based upon a choice to think and act differently.

As we continue to look at David's situation, we notice that he uses two questions to refocus: "Why are you so depressed, O my soul? Why is there such trouble churning within me?"[7] We need to see the importance of both asking and answering these kinds of questions.

Notice that David does not just ask *questions* when he is depressed. He asks the *right questions*. In effect, he asks this motivational question: "What is it that has me depressed?"

David could have asked, "I am chosen by God, so why do I have to face this kind of treatment? How can this be happening to me?

Why am I alive? Is life worth living? What good is anything?" If he had asked those kinds of questions, his despair would have deepened. Instead, he asks the right questions, and they lead to the renunciation of his depression. He chooses to change his response to the terrible situation in which he finds himself. He knows that he cannot change his situation, but that he does have the ability to Take-Charge of his response!

What does David do next? He focuses on the reality of God. He takes an inventory of the blessings of God in the *midst* of his suffering: "By day the Lord directs His love towards me. By night His song is with me. His song is my prayer to Him. He is the God of my life."[8] David focuses on the positive realities in his life.

There is tremendous power in positive thinking, just as there is tremendous power in negative thinking. The Bible offers us more than just positive thinking without a basis in reality. It offers us the positive reality of God. It directs us to focus our thoughts on the reality of truth, not just wishful thinking. We can think positively because our thoughts are based on the character of God.

David wrote, in effect, "Your song is a prayer from me to You." On the basis of this positive truth, David is able to recognize that although he *feels* abandoned, God is with him. David realizes that his feelings of abandonment will pass, and that God will lift him out of the pit of despair.

In the end, David faces his present difficulties and can say to those who are in similar circumstances, "Put your hope in God."[9] This is his encouragement for himself even through the presence of depression. David gives the reason: "I know I will yet praise Him in the future, for He is my Savior and my God."

Does this mean that simply asking the right questions will change our lives? Of course not. However, not asking the right questions during those times when they are necessary to be asked can be disastrous. Asking the wrong questions can lead to despair and even death. We need to ask the right questions, and give ourselves the right biblical answers. We need to do this based upon who God is and what He has done for us. When we do this, we will find ourselves able to quickly get started in the right direction, in the direction we need to go. We are enabled to Take-Charge of the situation, even when our actual circumstances have not changed.

Dying to get Out of Auschwitz

Everything depends upon the quality of our questions and the truthfulness of our answers. Here is an account that illustrates this principle. During World War II, millions of Jews perished in concentration camps. One Jewish man, however, refused to give up. After watching the slaughter of his family, he did not ask, "How could something like this happen?" or, "How did I get into a place like this?" Rather, he asked, "How can I get out?" When the answer came to him, he placed his naked body among the distorted, tangled bodies of murdered Jews and was at day's end dumped outside the camp!

Apollo 13: An Impossible Situation, an Impossible Solution

Here is another example of how asking the right questions led to the right answers and saved several lives. The crew of *Apollo 13* was doomed to orbit endlessly in space unless NASA scientists could eliminate the deadly carbon monoxide in the crew's quarters. They faced this incredible question: "Given the materials the astronauts have on board, how can a square pipe fit into a round hole?" The question demanded an answer, and if they had looked at its impossibility, they would not have even asked the question. Instead, these men knew they had to Take-Charge of the situation or the astronauts would die. By asking the right and only question, they arrived at the impossibly right answer, and the astronauts' lives were saved.

ALVIN YORK: ALONE, SURROUNDED
BY ENEMIES AND DEAD FRIENDS

An example from World War I reveals again how important it is to face our challenges, ask the right questions, and focus our thoughts on the right answers.

Alvin York was a committed follower of Jesus. He became a soldier during World War I after deep soul-searching before God. After just two weeks in battle, his regiment found itself in some of the bloodiest fighting of the war. He and the other Allied troops were surrounded by thirty machine gun nests. His battalion had been virtually wiped out, and he found himself in an exposed position at the bottom of a hill.

"Thousands of bullets kicked up dust all around me," he wrote, but he was not injured. He describes feeling "completely protected," certain he would not be hit. *I can't hit any Germans while I'm lying down on the ground with everyone around me shot to pieces*, he thought. So he asked himself, *How can I possibly handle this situation?*

He answered his question by standing up. Using his rifle, he began shooting at the machine gunners. One by one, he silenced them, but his rifle became too hot to hold and he was forced to drop it. At this point, six Germans leaped out of a trench and ran toward him shooting. All he had was his six-shot pistol.

I'm in a terrible situation, York reasoned. He asked himself, *Do I know anything that will get me out of this?* Then he fired at the last man first, remembering turkey shoots back home. As he put it, "You see, we don't want the front ones to know that we are getting the back ones." He ended up shooting all six soldiers.

Completely demoralized, the remaining Germans were afraid to shoot for fear of revealing their positions. So York picked up his rifle and shouted for the entire German battalion to surrender. Then, as he put it, "I had the feeling that someone was shooting at me from behind. I turned and saw a German major standing behind me with an empty revolver in his hand. He had missed every time."

York commanded the major to call out all the nearby German troops and then asked him the easiest way back to the American lines. After he received directions, he departed in exactly the opposite direction, forcing the major to order more Germans to surrender along the way. York returned to the American lines having shot 25 Germans and single-handedly capturing 132 more! Later he was given the French Legion of Honor and the Congressional Medal of Honor.[10]

How did York live through that situation and accomplish so much? Of course, God protected him. Of course, God was a shield about him. Of course, he could have responded, "I am overwhelmed, I am in despair, and I surrender." He didn't. He asked the right questions. Although the difficult answers required bravery and courage, acting on them saved his life. Based upon the answers, he stood up, did what seems impossible, and received unparalleled honor for his actions.

What else did York do? He did not allow his fears or hesitations to dominate or stop him. He acted decisively. He was a Take-Charge man, and he won a decisive battle single-handedly.

Each one of us has a similar choice today! We may not have to stand up alone against hostile soldiers, but each and every day we are called to stand up against the fears, anxieties, and despairs of life. It is not what we face but how we face it that is critical.

Can any of us think of anything that should ever be allowed to keep us from "standing up"? By God's grace, we are enabled to Take-Charge of everything that would hurl us down. God empowers us to stand up and be the Take-Charge people He wants us to be!

If we have not used our mind properly, God will redirect us. If we have abused our mind, God will heal and renew it. If we have not yet learned how to train our mind, God will empower us to do it.

The "secret" of trusting Jesus is open to everyone. We are able to Take-Charge of every situation in our life, representing it in a way that will lead to joy or to despair. The decision is up to each of us.

TAKE-CHARGE ACTION INITIATIVES

1. *If you were Joseph, how do you think you would have responded to being on the auction block?*

   _____

   _____

   _____

2. *Read Genesis 50:15-21. What do these verses reveal about Joseph?*

   _____

   _____

   _____

   What do they reveal about God's work in your life?

   _____

   _____

   _____

3. *What was the secret of David's ability to handle all the suffering that came his way through no fault of his own?*

   _____

   _____

   _____

4. *In Psalm 42:5 David wrote about hope in God. What does it mean for you to place your hope in God?*

_____

_____

_____

5. *What questions might you ask in order to more effectively Take-Charge of a difficult situation in your life?*

_____

_____

_____

13

POWER BELIEFS OF
A TAKE-CHARGE LIFE

What you believe influences what you think. What you think influences what you do. Take-Charge of your beliefs, because your life depends upon it.

What we believe is the key to how we live our lives. What we believe heavily influences our ability to Take-Charge of our life. When we pursue right beliefs that are rooted in the Bible and in the character of God, we experience blessing and joy. When we pursue wrong beliefs, not only do we do what is wrong, but we are also miserable and create negative consequences in our lives.

Many of us cannot articulate what we believe, even though what we believe affects everything we think and do. Others of us try to articulate our beliefs, and have a difficult time doing so.

Some people claim to be *"un"*believers. They believe that nothing can be believed, and yet they believe their unbelief is true.

Other people believe in "chance." They say, "Randomness, nothingness, meaninglessness, and hopelessness rule all of life." They too suggest they believe nothing. They nonetheless communicate this "non-belief" to others with evangelistic passion. They go so far as to treat other beliefs as foolish, because they believe there is nothing to believe in.

Still others believe in "luck." Although this belief system is not much different from a belief system built on chance, the behaviors connected with it are often quite different. "If only I get lucky," a proponent of this belief system may say, "everything will be different." They do not know that they are giving away responsibility for their lives to a system they call "luck." They go after the things of this life, hoping that in the process they will "get lucky," and in so doing secure happiness. Luck is their road to happiness.

Sadly, wrong belief systems can empower people to take wrong actions. The beliefs of Buddhists empowered them to burn their bodies during the Vietnam War. The beliefs of Nazis empowered them to kill millions of Jews during World War II. The beliefs of racists empowered them to enslave millions of Africans in the United States.

TWO BELIEFS, TWO RESPONSES

Not long ago, Al came to me for help. He exuded rage and told me that he hated God. "I hate God because my brother was killed in an accident and, at almost the same time, my mother died from cancer. It's God's fault. He's responsible. He did this to me. He could have stopped all this from happening."

Phil had a different set of beliefs. "My four children were killed in a devastating accident," he said, describing the torment of his grief. "God has encouraged me in the midst of all this. I'm a believer, and my children were believers. God has encouraged me, reminding me that we will all be reunited in heaven. I have something to hope for. This life isn't all there is." From that time on, he committed his life unswervingly to the service of God. He now lives a Take-Charge life.

These men each faced tragedy. They had two completely different responses based on two completely different belief systems. The events themselves did not create the different responses. Their basic beliefs concerning these events, however, did. Al and Phil held to basic beliefs about life and death. These beliefs determined how they faced, interpreted, understood, and lived with their tragic circumstances.

If we, like Al, come to believe that life is meaningless and that God is evil, our core beliefs will lead to a set of thoughts and actions completely different from those of us who believe that our lives are governed by a loving, personal, perfectly good Creator. Our beliefs determine the focus, passion, and significance that we attach to who we are and what we do.

Victor Frankl was an Austrian psychiatrist who wrote a book titled *Man's Search for Meaning.* He and his family had been taken to Auschwitz, a German concentration camp. There, the Nazis killed his family and many others he loved. Even so, he worked hard to encourage people in the camp who had lost all hope. He watched them dying from personal loss, tragic situations, and physical debilitation. He urged them to continue to have meaning in their lives, to believe in something.

One woman Victor Frankl writes about attached meaning to a branch that she saw through the bars of her cell in the barracks. Other prisoners in the camp attached meaning to different kinds of things. Those who believed something had a higher survival rate than those who had lost all belief and all hope. Those who survived the camps still faced incredible difficulties following their liberation. Many of them discovered that the things to which they had attached meaning—a husband, a wife, a child, a parent, a friend, a hometown, a building, a job they hoped to return to—were no longer there. People had vanished. Cities had been destroyed. In some instances, virtually everything from their past was completely gone.

What happened to these survivors? Some of them experienced even more grief after their release from Auschwitz than they had experienced in the camp. Why? What really matters is not just believing in anything. What really matters is what we believe. If we hold to a false belief, its consequences can be disastrous.

BUILD ON BIBLE BELIEFS

I have met and spoken with thousands of believers. Regardless of the distinctions that mark their particular expression of the faith, they share a core of between seven and ten beliefs that strongly influences how they live their lives. The problem is that although many believers know that they hold certain core beliefs, they do not pay much attention to them. Those who do not consciously use their beliefs to help them understand and triumph over life's difficulties, find themselves floundering in the sea of life. It is as if they know there is a life raft nearby but will not climb into it.

In the rest of this chapter, we are going to focus on eight core beliefs which can anchor our lives. Using these beliefs will help us to Take-Charge of our life. When we consciously embrace them, we are taking a giant step toward a Take-Charge life. We are changing our thoughts, our attitudes, and our behaviors. As our beliefs become more focused, even previous hard to change behavior will change as God empowers us.

The following eight core beliefs are based upon thousands of hours of counseling experience, knowledge of the Bible, and invaluable life experiences. Build on these beliefs. Rephrase these beliefs. Add beliefs in addition to these. I am confident that these eight beliefs, applied in our life, will help us apply biblical truth and Take-Charge of our life.

BELIEF #1: THE AUTHORITY OF THE BIBLE.

Believing in the Bible is foundational to every other belief we will see in this chapter. We have an error-free Bible that cannot fail. The

Bible says of itself that it is "breathed out of the mouth of God and useful for teaching, instructing, correcting, and training us to do what is right. It helps us to become fully prepared for every good work we have to do."[1]

Bible truths guide us. They impel us to love, pursue good deeds, and live a joyful Take-Charge life. These truths do not change. We may change, but they remain the same even if we no longer accept them and live by them. Bible truths, as we will now see, are life changing.

BELIEF #2: WE BECOME NEW.

We are entirely changed when we enter into a personal relationship with Jesus. We are changed in our *entirety*, not just in our behaviors, attitudes, and thoughts. When we receive Jesus as our Savior and Lord, and confess our sins, we are spiritually reborn. We read, "In Jesus, the old things really have passed away. All things really have become new."[2] Our transformation in Jesus enables us to live a truly Take-Charge life.

Jesus teaches the centrality of our new life. He says to a seeker, "You must be born again."[3] He shows us clearly our need to become totally new people. We are to be spiritually born from above, from heaven, by the Spirit of God. We are radically new!

Without this radical spiritual rebirth, we can still change all kinds of thoughts, attitudes, and behaviors. People do that all the time, but such changes often do not last and are based on the wrong things, such as selfishness and self-protection.

The Old Testament rules and regulations oriented Pharisees demonstrate what happens when people who have not been spiritually reborn make moralistic changes. These religious leaders complain that Jesus spends too much time with immoral people: "If you really are upright, you would only spend time with people like us."

This, in effect, is their message to Jesus. They are hard hearted, and Jesus does not hesitate to let them know how far from a new life, a Take-Charge life, they actually are.

BELIEF #3: WE BECOME DIFFERENT.

The Holy Spirit helps us to Take-Charge of our lives. He guides us into all truth. He is with us, even as we struggle. He is there when we feel abandoned. He is our advocate with the Father. He is sent by the Father and the Son to enable us to see ourselves accurately, to restore our lives, and to renew our hearts. We are not facing troubles on our own. We are not changing ourselves by our own strengths. We are being guided by the Spirit.

As Jesus prepares to face the cross, His followers and friends are frightened. Jesus encourages them and comforts them when He says, "I will ask the Father, and He will give you another Counselor to be with you forever—the Spirit of truth. The world cannot accept Him, because it does not see Him or know Him. But you know Him, for He lives with you and will be in you."[4]

We believers have an intimate relationship with the Holy Spirit. He walks alongside us. He defends us. He helps us as we live Take-Charge lives for Him.

BELIEF #4: GOD LOVES US.

God's love is the overarching message of the Bible. It is best captured in what is called the most loved verse in the Bible, John 3:16: "For God so loved the world that He gave His one and only Son, that whoever believes in Him shall not perish but have eternal life." God sent His Son to claim a people as His own forever. This is a wonderful truth, and should make us glad, thankful, and grateful.

There is nothing more foundational in our experience than the love of God. When Jesus enters our lives, He is not a passive guest.

He Takes-Charge of our lives and empowers us to Take-Charge of all that He desires to bring into conformity with Himself. What is most amazing is that He does it through love.

Francine came to me seeking help. Her father had sexually abused her for years. She had loved him, and he had betrayed that love. To Francine, a father meant evil, pain, and betrayal. Gradually, her focus came to rest on her heavenly Father who *really* loves her. Accepting God's love has not been easy for Francine. She has come to realize that her Father in heaven is more real, more significant, and more close to her than her earthly father could ever be. It is God's true love for her which has changed Francine's life, and can change us as well.

BELIEF #5: GOD RULES.

Years ago Rabbi Kushner wrote a best-selling book titled *When Bad Things Happen to Good People.* In this book, which deals with God's rule, Rabbi Kushner concludes that God rules over good things but has nothing to do with the bad. The book was a huge bestseller because people like to think that God's rule is very limited. There is a problem in this thinking. If God has no power over evil, who does?

Job is a man in the Bible whose life is filled with trouble. He is a good man, yet he faces unimaginable suffering. In his suffering, people come to help him. Here is what they see. His children are dead, his wealth has evaporated, and his body is covered with oozing sores. They conclude that Job is evil because they believe in God's rule. God, they believe, would never allow such tragedy to happen to a good man. These counselors have a fairly reasonable view of God's rule, but they misapply their understanding to Job's situation.

Job's misfortunes come to an end. Job finally comes to understand the far-reaching power and rule of God, even as it applies to his own life and family. He sums it up this way: "Now I know that You can do all things. No plan You purpose can be stopped."[5]

Job is speaking from the depth of his heart. His new-found appreciation for the rule of God has changed his life. He asks God's forgiveness for his anger towards God. He realizes that God has meant all the things that have happened to him for good. He knows that even the evils that have come upon his life are under the rule and power of God, and are being used by God to bring about good.

Thousands of years later, a well-known follower of Jesus wrote a letter to encourage the persecuted followers of Jesus. "We know that in all the things we have to face in our lives, God really does work them out for our good."[6] We can know with certainty that God is good, no matter what.

Will God allow only good things to happen to us? No! He allows many things—good and bad, blessings and evils—to forge and build up our characters. He strengthens us so that we follow Him with a sure faith regardless of external circumstances.

Jesus faced incredible difficulties. He was alone. He was scorned. He was scourged. He was mocked. He was pierced through His hands and feet with sharp nails. He carried our sins. He endured it all. He wants us to trust in a loving God who rules. We need to remember that what we face is insignificant in comparison to what Jesus faced for us.

The Bible tells us of Joseph. What a situation he faced! His brothers envied him and were going to kill him. They decided instead to sell him into slavery. Joseph spent many years as a slave. Some of those years he was imprisoned because he remained upright. One day Pharaoh made him second in command over all of Egypt.

Much later, Joseph and his brothers were reunited. When his brothers realized who he was, they were terrified. Joseph saw their terror and said to them, "Do not be terrified because of what you did in selling me into slavery. This was the plan God used to save people's lives."[7] Joseph was stating the principle that would come to be a central teaching in the New Testament. God rules over everything, and uses the good and bad to bring blessing.

Nothing is impossible with God. He rules over all things. When we believe this, we can face anything that God allows to cross our path. We not only possess a Take-Charge life, we possess as well a Take-Charge character.

BELIEF #6: FOLLOW CHRIST.

Believing in Jesus is not simply accepting doctrine. Believing in Jesus is our life. Jesus says, "If anyone desires to come after Me, he must say *No* to self interest, he must take up his cross daily, and he must follow Me. Whoever wants to save his life will lose it, but whoever loses his life for Me will save it. What good is it for a man to gain the whole world, and yet lose his true self?"[8]

A Take-Charge life is marked by saying *no* to self, bearing our cross, and following Jesus. There is trouble that comes upon us because of our identification with Jesus, yet our relationship with Him grows deeper and deeper the more difficult our suffering is.

What Jesus spoke about touches our hearts. How often we exalt ourselves rather than saying *no* to ourselves. How easy it is to let ourselves take precedence over Jesus. As a consequence, our lives reflect self absorption. We could never imagine it, but we have fallen prey to one of Satan's tools to control our lives and rob us of a Take-Charge joy.

BELIEF #7: LIVE!

We are to live like Christ. We are to become more and more like Him. We are to live in such a way that nothing can ruin our lives. As we live a Take-Charge life, we are triumphant even in death. Guided by our beliefs, our lives will become more and more given over to Jesus.

We will not be driven by self-interest. Our faith will not be a creedal statement. Our faith will be a *living faith.*

Let us not separate what we believe from day to day living. Let us build our lives around an active engagement in a change process that is built on a living Word.

A common concern is why so many children do not grow up sharing the beliefs of their parents. There are many reasons for this, but one thing is clear: If parents say one thing but live another, the children are not duped. They realize that the faith they are called to embrace is not a vibrant dynamic faith in their parents' lives. They often wonder, *Why should I assume it should be dynamic for me?*

Some parents strongly attempt to instill certain beliefs in their children in order to keep them away from drinking, smoking, drugs, and sex. This is not the goal, direction, or purpose of our faith. As a follower of Jesus, we are empowered in a Spirit-filled life to glorify God in all that we are and all that we do. By living such a Take-Charge life, the glory and power of God is ever present in our lives. On that basis, we stay away from evils that surround us.

The living beliefs that we possess are the essence of God Himself. These beliefs do not simply guide us toward our goals. They are filled with power. They guide us on our way through life. They are foundational to our lives and allow us to live bravely and courageously. As we live this Take-Charge life, we reject all the fears that keep us from courage and from living with determined abandon.

Some children believe with great seriousness. Such faith can be disturbing for their parents. Shortly after her seventeenth birthday, our oldest daughter said that she wanted to serve as a missionary in Africa that summer. Soon after this, close Christian friends who knew of her interest began telling us why we should not allow her to go and face danger. My wife and I decided to allow her to go because what we believed demanded living out.

As it turned out, our daughter did face dangers, but God delivered her. Her faith was strengthened. After her graduation from university, she decided to do missionary work in Bangkok. Again, there were various warnings. Again, we had to ask, "Is our faith big enough to trust God with our daughter's life no matter what might happen?" Again we supported her decision, and she learned that acting on her faith does not preclude the possibility of danger, but that she can trust the Lord in the dangerous situations.

BELIEF #8: TAKE-CHARGE!

Certain beliefs empower us to fulfill our life's callings. Other beliefs limit us. All sorts of things that we allow to rule and dominate our lives are nothing more than self-imposed limitations to which we tenaciously cling. These can include, but certainly are not limited to, negative and destructive beliefs about who God is, what He will do to and through us, what are our gifts and talents, and so on.

Beliefs that limit our lives, our walk with God, and our relationships with other people must be changed. We do not have to hang on to beliefs that keep us from becoming the men and women God wants us to be. We need to be willing to throw aside any false belief, even if we have held it all our lives. We must allow Bible-based beliefs to take over and redirect our lives.

I know that you want to Take-Charge of your life. We all do. The Bible is pivotal in accomplishing this. It equips us to do all that God calls us to do. In a few moments we will see how the Bible functions as an anchor for the changes in our lives. This will make all the difference in the world for us. The issue is not what we have or do not have. The issue is this: Will we Take-Charge of all that God has given us?

TAKE-CHARGE ACTION INITIATIVES

1. *What are your core beliefs?*

_____

_____

_____

_____

To what degree are they built on the foundation of the Bible?

_____

_____

_____

2. *How do your core beliefs influence the way you think?*

_____

_____

_____

_____

The way you feel?

_____

_____

_____

_____

The way you respond?

_____

_____

_____

_____

3. *In what ways have your core beliefs influenced the way you responded to a recent problem?*

_____

_____

_____

4. *Which of the eight core beliefs in the chapter are easy for you to apply? Why?*

_____

_____

_____

_____

Which ones are harder to apply? Why?

_____

_____

_____

_____

5. *Describe a time when God used a difficult situation in your life to bless you or to bless another person.*

_____

_____

_____

14

THE ANCHOR OF A TAKE-CHARGE LIFE

When you want to make changes in your life, you can look with confidence to the Bible. It has the answers for all your problems. God will help you to accomplish all that He gives you to do.

After I spoke at a seminar, a woman approached me. "Okay," she said, "I have thought about what you've said. I know my core beliefs are important. I'm trying to bring those beliefs into line with the Bible's teaching. It's hard to do so. It seems as if my beliefs are different than my emotions. I need something to help me deal with my practical everyday circumstances."

This woman is right in knowing that she needs to bring the Bible more fully into her life. When we want to Take-Charge of our life, we need to look first to the Bible. It has the answers we need. It is our anchor. Many of us though, do not really believe that it is relevant for us today. Many pastors who teach from the Bible fail to apply its truths because they too, in one way or another, doubt the Bible's relevance. They have even been taught to preach this way.

One pastor told me, "We're not supposed to do application. My seminary taught me that. I heard it again when I took counseling courses." He is really saying, "It is my job to teach people truths they can store in their minds. They have to decide how to use those truths on their own, because the Bible is not meant to be applied in my teaching to the practical realities of daily life." This perspective is wrong. This perspective is harmful to people!

The Bible strongly and forcefully addresses this. A letter in the Bible written to Timothy decidedly anchors the first core belief we examined in the last chapter. This letter says that the Bible is "breathed out of the mouth of God and is useful for teaching, instructing, correcting, and training us to do what is right. It helps us to become fully prepared for every good work we have to do."[1]

This is a wonderful truth! The entire Bible comes from God. Not just one verse. Not just one particular book. Not just the New Testament. Not just the Old Testament. *All of it* comes from God. God has given it to us. It is His gift to us. Why? He wants to equip us, prepare us, and make us adequate for every good work we are called to do.

In our efforts to find meaningful answers to the important life-related issues that we face, we need to ask a specific question. That question is this: *What information do I need to know?* Finding the answers we seek is not a matter of obtaining more intellectually-based information. The answers to our everyday situations open up to us as we apply what God has shown us in His Word. We need to put the Bible into practice.

The Bible itself teaches us this principle. It states: "God's power has *already* given us *everything* we need to live a good and upright life."[2] In our relationship with Jesus, we have everything we need for good living right now! The issue is simply this: Will we use what we have from God to Take-Charge of our life?

Set Your Sights High!

The Bible is always before us, always above us, always giving us more to strive after. David wrote a beautiful song that sums up this principle: "With everything that is perfect I can see imperfection, but Your commands are limitlessly perfect."[3] We can never reach the stage of perfection to which the Bible calls us. Even so, Jesus encourages us *to set our sights high.* "Be perfect, therefore, just as your Father in heaven is perfect."[4]

One reason we find it so difficult to Take-Charge of our life is because we set our sights too low. We settle into mediocrity. Mediocrity gets us only halfway to the goal. Mediocrity is an awful thing to settle for, but many of us still say, "I'm halfway there," or, "I'm getting there slowly." Many of us do not really mean that. What we really mean is, "Halfway there is all that I'm doing. I'm satisfied. Why strive for more?" What we do is excuse ourselves from Taking-Charge of our lives with a wholehearted engagement of life today. We really do not want to make the effort to know God most deeply, most personally, and most intimately. We are not persuaded that the study of the Bible, with its day by day application, is precious.

A number of years ago, I taught at a Bible school in the Swiss Alps. The school was not just in the Alps, but was located on the Matterhorn. Nancy and I hiked up a trail on the mountain, and we reached a spot where I thought we were on top of the world. The view was incredible, and I just wanted to stop and exult in our surroundings. I started to do that, until Nancy said, "Maybe we haven't reached the top."

I was sweating and feeling too tired to go on. I told Nancy, "How could we not have reached the top? Look where we are! This is amazing. We have to stop here." She said, "No. Let's keep going. I am sure there is something beyond." We walked farther and realized that the real peak was some distance away. As the sun was setting, Nancy said, "Let's come back tomorrow."

The next day, Nancy and I walked several miles farther up a mountain path. We saw wild mountain goats. Beautiful wild flowers were growing out of the sides of the rocks. Then we reached the top, the real top of the mountain. I felt as if I had been carried to the heavens, it was so magnificent. *What if I had stopped back there and never gone farther?* I thought, *I would have missed all of this.*

Many of us live our lives in a comfort zone that seems pleasing enough. Just as it is on the mountain, so too it is in our relationship with God. We miss the real beauty of God because we have not gone far enough with Him.

God has more in store for us than we can imagine. His boundless perfections await us. He has things for us just beyond our sight and our reach. It is great to be able to stop, to look around, and appreciate the place where we have arrived. We can most assuredly say, "God has certainly done a lot for me. Look at how far He has brought me." God though, calls us to keep walking. He calls us to Take-Charge by "energetically pushing ourselves toward the goal, so that we will win the prize that God has for us, as we get closer and closer to heaven through our life in Jesus."[5]

Whether a committed, disciplined runner is involved in the Olympics or in a high school track meet, what is his goal? Hopefully, it is to run the best possible race, and perhaps cross the finish line ahead of all the other competitors. At the same time, if the runner runs a great race for 99 percent of the distance and then decides to stop running, he will not finish his race.

Matt Biondi provides a perfect example. In the Seoul Olympics of 1988, he swam in seven events and won gold in five. What is interesting is the 100-meter butterfly event in which he competed. Matt led all the way, but in the last two meters he failed to do what he had to do. He failed to take the last stroke and crash into the wall. The result was that he was beaten by Anthony Nesty of Surinam by a centimeter.

It is important for each of us as we run our race each day to learn how to run so that we can keep going from the beginning to the end. This running involves pressing on, reaching forward until the very end, and not getting bogged down.

Decide to Commit

In order to Take-Charge of our life and see changes occur, we must decisively commit ourselves to implementing biblical principles. The Bible challenges us to live outwardly as well as inwardly. It offers us solutions to life's practical problems. The Bible shows us how to deal with anxiety, worry, envy, and jealousy. It shows us how to face problems and suffering in biblical, God-honoring, Take-Charge ways. It shows us how to deal with destructive habits. For example,

- ▸ What is the answer to fear? "Perfect love drives out fear."[6]

- ▸ What is the answer to guilt? "If we confess our sins, He is faithful and just, and He will forgive us our sins and cleanse us from all that is wrong in our lives."[7]

- ▸ What is the solution to conflict? The Bible teaches us to get right with anyone who has done anything wrong against us.[8]

We cannot just Take-Charge of ourselves by our own power. We cannot expect time to bring us to a Take-Charge life either. We need to allow God and His Word to make us into Take-Charge people. Change in our life comes about as a result of our decisive commitment to God and our determined obedience to do what pleases Him.

Suppose a person comes to me and says, "My marriage is rotten. I have seen it going downhill for years. I am fed up with my spouse...." They go on and on.

No matter what shape their marriage is in, if they are not willing to make changes that will show love and respect, the marriage will not improve. Time alone will not make it better. Each spouse must be willing to change. Each must be committed to applying biblical principles to their lives and to their marriage.

Listen to the depth of commitment to biblical principles that is required of us:

- ▸ "Count yourselves dead to sin but alive to God in Christ Jesus. Therefore *do not let sin rule you,* so that you obey its evil desires."[9]

- ▸ "Offer yourself as a living sacrifice. God is pleased with this. This is a logical part of worship. *Do not live like the world,* instead experience what transformation is really like when your mind is made new again."[10]

These are decisive commitments. We count ourselves dead to sin. We do not let sin have any power over us. We offer ourselves fully and sacrificially to God. We do not live like the world. These are life changing principles! When we live by them, we will have a Take-Charge life.

No Excuses!

We often think, *I would love to be able to make a commitment that would enable me to Take-Charge of my life, but I don't really feel up to the challenge. Because I don't feel up to it, I guess I can't make the commitment.*

This is just a rationalization. Making a decisive commitment to Take-Charge of our lives goes beyond our feelings. If we wait for feelings, we may wait a long, long time, because doing the wrong thing often feels really good. The Bible does not say that it feels bad to do the wrong thing, it simply says that doing the wrong thing is just plain wrong.

We need to Take-Charge by doing what is right whether we feel like it or not. As believers, we know that "the One who is in us is greater than the one who is in the world."[11] This means that we are empowered by God. The devil cannot make us do anything we do not want to do. He is not the one to blame.

We need to Take-Charge responsibly. We need to make the kinds of commitments that will enable us to live as the Bible calls us to live. We need to confess whatever we do that is wrong. Let's Take-Charge of our lives and hold nothing back.

When I teach this, invariably I hear, "Rich, I hear what you are saying, but I can't be a hypocrite. I will not stop doing something just because it is wrong to do. If I am going to do the right thing, I will do it because my heart tells me to, not because my head tells me to."

That sounds good, but it is really another excuse. If we wait until we feel right about everything we do, the chances are that we will not do the right thing. Doing something we do not want to do does not make us hypocrites. We are hypocritical when we do something we do not want to do, but tell others, "I wanted to do it."

The point is this. We do not have to really want to do everything that we do. We need to say, "I want to do what God wants me to do whether or not I feel like doing it." In other words, this kind of decisive commitment will lead us to say, "My commitment to God is much stronger than my commitment to those things that give me wrongful pleasure. I am giving up all wrongful pleasure because the greatest pleasure is to do what God wants me to do."

It is so easy to allow "feeling" words or intellectual arguments to keep us from taking the decisive Take-Charge actions that the Bible commands. As parents, we know that our children often do wrong things. Have any of us ever said to our children, "I want you to *feel* like doing what I want you to do"? As parents, we simply say, "I want you to do it!"

Every time we do something wrong, what we have done is to give in to what we feel like doing, instead of doing what we know we are supposed to do. Sadly, we are a feeling-oriented society. We try to live by our feelings. The Bible, though, presents a totally different picture. It calls us to obey God by living according to the Bible.

As a leader of the Israelites, Joshua assembled all the tribes of Israel. He challenged them to make this decisive commitment to God: "Now honor God and serve Him faithfully with your whole being." How is this to be done? "Throw away your idols and serve the Lord. If serving the Lord seems undesirable to you, then today make a choice whom you will serve. As for me and my family, we are making our commitment to God, and we will serve the Lord."[12]

This is the kind of commitment God calls us to make. This is the kind of commitment we are to live and demonstrate. We are to serve God. We are to do the right things. We are to worship God. We are to do what pleases God. We are to train our children to follow God. In short, we are to live according to the Bible.

DECISION TIME!

There is nothing more exciting than following God and living an upright life. If we are not living this way, what is keeping us from being the people God wants us to be? What is standing in the way of a decisive commitment to Him?

It is so easy for us to make excuses for not living Take-Charge lives. We wonder if such an energetic Take-Charge commitment will ever really change anything anyway. We know how easy it is to just keep putting off making changes. We tell ourselves it will make no difference. We suggest to ourselves that such a difficult change of attitude or behavior may not work anyway. We tell ourselves that what we are facing is too difficult or unique for the Bible.

Herein lies the problem. We do not see that making changes in our commitments, making changes in the energy we put into our lives *already* means something, regardless of what happens afterwards. Living a Take-Charge life matters, regardless of the outcome.

What is really keeping us from making the decisive commitments to a Take-Charge life? Are we too proud to admit that we make excuses? Are we allowing our emotions to dictate which beliefs we will cling to today?

There are four reasons we do not wholeheartedly commit ourselves to living Take-Charge lives before God. First, we love the things we do that are wrong. It is absolutely necessary for us to admit just how much we enjoy the things we do that are very wrong. We also need to admit that we often persist in doing the wrong thing because we are not concerned about God's anger, nor are we concerned about pleasing God. We need to admit that our wrongful pleasures are keeping us from making a decisive commitment and finally coming to Take-Charge of our lives.

Second, we so readily feel like failures. When we have not been successful in making changes in our lives, we want to give up trying. It can be tough to have what seems to be such meagre success when we so desperately want to change.

Third, it is just plain tough to persevere in the race of life. We see life as a long distance cross-country run. We want to just hide in the bushes and not have to face all these people and all their problems.

Fourth, our race is sabotaged, and our best efforts are ruined despite the amount of work or diligence on our part. This happened to my daughter during a junior high school cross-country race. Someone was planted in the woods to direct her to go in the wrong direction, since they knew that she would be in the lead. She took that wrong path for about .5 kilometers before she realized the treachery that had been done to her. All her preparation, all her training, amounted to nothing. She thought about giving up, but decided to run her race anyway, even though she had to go an extra kilometer. She ended the race in seventh place, but her determination to finish was gold medal quality.

Once we have made our commitment to do the right thing, we must not expect a trouble-free path. Our goal is to endure in spite of the obstacles or difficulties.

Perhaps we have run our hearts out and have not yet achieved what we had hoped to achieve. Perhaps we have put all our heart and energy into it, and can only say for all the effort, "I am exhausted." We must not give up. Maybe we have actually made a great deal of progress, even if we can only see how far we have yet to go. When we have committed ourselves to God, we need not worry about the remaining distance. He will get us there.

At some time or other we have all felt like giving up. God understands that, continues to stand by us, and will give us the strength necessary to make it to the end. Jesus is so encouraging. "Surely I am with you always, right to the very end."[13]

Take-Charge Action Initiatives

1. *Determine a basic change in your life that you would like to make. Several examples to help you get started are listed below. How do you intend to implement this change?*

   ▸ *"I would like to make time to read the Bible and pray every day."*

   ▸ *"I would like to seek forgiveness from my daughter."*

   ▸ *"I would like to quit my daily drinking of alcohol."*

   _____

   _____

   _____

   _____

2. *Using a concordance, what Bible passages deal with the particular changes that you would like to make? Write them here, and state how they directly apply to the changes you wish to make.*

_____

_____

_____

3. *Now set a standard related to the change that is possible for you to reach. Make it something attainable. The following are examples:*

   ‣ *"To start, I'll read a paragraph of the New Testament every day and then pray for a few minutes."*

   ‣ *"I'll call my daughter and ask her if we can get together next week at a time that will work for her."*

   ‣ *"On my way home, I won't stop at the liquor store anymore. When I get home, I will change my clothes and do some work on the house."*

_____

_____

_____

4. *Now pray and ask God to help you meet your commitment.*

5. *On a separate sheet of paper, write out your decisive commitment to start making that key change in your life. It might read something like this:*
   "I desire with all of my heart to please God, to do this for His pleasure and not my own. I am committed to [being a better _____, completing _____, crushing a particular sin, and so on], and I purpose that with the help of God, I will _____."

6. *Sign this commitment and tape it up someplace where you will see it regularly until it has been completed.*

7. *Tell someone close to you about your decisive commitment to make that change and ask them to follow up on your progress toward your goal. It is important to be accountable to someone.*

8. *Read your commitment every day and change it as needed to keep up with your progress and the new changes you would like to begin making.*

9. *Realize that change can take time and that it is better to start somewhere than never to start at all. Edith Schaeffer has used this expression: "If you want perfection or nothing, you are going to have nothing every time."*

10. *Pray every day that God will guide your thoughts, your words, and your actions. Pray as well that He will empower you to remain decisively committed to Him and to the goal(s) you have set for yourself.*

15

TAKE-CHARGE NO MATTER THE CIRCUMSTANCES

When you feel that your life is Taking-Charge of you, cling to God, who has proven His faithfulness. As you wait upon Him, you will find that His promises will never fail you. He will not leave you to just make it through life. His power will enable you to Take-Charge of your life, even through some of the most difficult and confusing times.

The lines on Marcia's face were etched from years of difficulty. She knew the meaning of suffering and confusion. For years she had lived in a relationship with an abusive man. She had not married him, and could have left him at any time. Finally she did leave him. Soon after that she became a believer. She kept asking herself over and over, *How did I ever get myself into that situation with him?* She would ask me, "Will I ever be free from all this guilt? I can't forgive myself."

Marcia was experiencing more than just regret and the consequences of her decision to live with that man. She was experiencing the deep regret of having done the wrong thing. Before she was a believer, she did not question her lifestyle, nor did she struggle with guilt. Soon after she came to faith in Jesus, she came to understand that she had been living a life that was displeasing to God. As she looked at her life from the perspective of the Bible, she was saddened at the way she used to live. Only as she came to understand the power of God's forgiveness, did she experience the peace she had never before known.

Most of us can relate to Marcia's struggles. Even as believers, we often continue to act in ways that go against what God wants for us. We think wrong thoughts. We fail to meet the standard that is revealed in the Bible. The result is that we continue to experience guilt and regrets that seem to linger perpetually.

We are at times almost disabled by a thought or circumstances over which we seem to have no control. We feel helpless. We feel as if our life has Taken-Charge of us. Maybe an important relationship has ended. Maybe we have suffered financial reversal. Maybe we have lost a job after many years of dedicated work. Maybe someone close to us has just been diagnosed with cancer. Maybe we feel that what has happened to us is not only a disaster, but a permanent disaster. Maybe we find ourselves sinking deeper and deeper into depression. We all know how this feels. Take heart. For those of us who can identify with this, we have a choice.

Consider two people who work in the same office and who lose their jobs within several days of each other. The first says, "I will never find another job. I am too old. Who will ever hire me now? It took me so long to find this job, I can't imagine finding another." A coworker assesses her situation differently. "This is just the push I need to get a better job," she says. "God provided this job in the first place, and I really do need to work for a while longer. Even though I do have talent, ability, and experience, it may not be easy finding a job I like as much as this job. However, God knows, and He has taken care of me up to this point. I am sure He will keep on doing so."

The truth of the matter is that the man who views his situation as hopeless may be right. Maybe there are no jobs for him out there. Maybe he is too old. Maybe no one will want him. At the same time, if there is a job opening, who do you think will get it? Will it be the person who says, "You probably don't want me. I was laid off my last job, I am not really capable, and I am too old"? Or will it be the person who has confidence in her abilities and talents, and possesses a hopeful confidence in the God who direct her paths?[1]

Both the attitudes that we have towards the difficult circumstances that challenge us, and the core beliefs that stand behind our attitudes, are vitally important. As believers in Jesus, we have more than just the ability to choose positive attitudes. We have God standing with us! He protects us whenever we are in trouble.[2] He hears us when we call to Him. He offers us a firm place on which to stand, no matter how helpless we feel or how challenging our circumstances. He offers us solid ground upon which to stand, no matter how shaky our lives seem, no matter how impossible it seems that we might ever be able to go on and Take-Charge of our lives.

CLING TO GOD

King David lived 3,000 years ago and knew what it was like to face trying circumstances. He battled depression. He faced hunger. He fled for his life. He was often alone. Through it all, he held onto certain key beliefs that deepened his relationship with God.

David describes his experience of life beautifully: "I waited patiently for the Lord. He turned to me and heard me crying. He lifted me up out of slime, out of mud, and out of mire. Even while my life was a total mess, He got me going again. He set my feet on a rock and gave me a firm place to stand. He put a new song in my mouth, a song full of praise to our God."[3]

As David remembers the great things that God does for him, he knows that God will continue to get him out of trouble all his life. He knows that God will enable him to Take-Charge of his life, even in the midst of life shattering difficulties. Marcia, on the other hand, allowed all that had hurled her into a bog of muck and mire to continue dragging her down. Her eyes were not looking to God. She had forgotten about His forgiveness and faithfulness. She was consumed with only her troubles.

It is sad how many of us respond to difficulty more like Marcia than like David. We feel helpless and trapped in the mire of life. We feel as if there is no way out of it. We forget that God is willing and able to help us face all our challenges, no matter how difficult they may be.

Often the problem is one of experience. We have not learned that life does not become easy just because we trust in Jesus. We need to learn how to refocus. We need as well to remember all the wonderful things that God both has done and is doing for us. We must not forget to remember that He is capable of lifting us out of the mire, of setting our feet firmly in place, and of establishing us on the way that we must go. We must be less concerned with our troubles. We must not forget God and His life-changing power.

David went on to write songs that reflect life the way it really is. These songs have helped hundreds of millions of people for over three thousand years. These songs deal with our troubles, our hopes, our joys, and our sadness. These songs also reflect upon what happens when we focus on our troubles rather than focusing on the character of God. These songs go even further. They teach us how to emerge from depression, from anxiety, from rage, or from bitterness. They teach us how to focus on what will help us in our lives. They teach us how to Take-Charge of our lives.

David collected these songs and they became a book, which he entitled *David's Songs*. When we read them and sing them, they become ours as well. It is sad how few of us avail ourselves of such a great treasure.

OUR ROCK OF CONFIDENCE

There are those who think they are firmly standing, based on confidence in themselves alone. This is very different from those of us who live Take-Charge lives. Our confidence is in the God who is our Rock.[4] Those whose confidence is in themselves alone often tenaciously cling to such a superficial confidence, even while they are sinking into quicksand. They have nothing other than themselves. If they give up confidence in themselves, they have nothing else. At the same time, we believers often think and talk as if we are in quicksand, while we are actually standing on the Rock!

It is one thing to be trapped in quicksand, struggling to survive. It is quite another thing to build our lives on the Rock, but to keep living in a past life that is choking and killing us. Why are we so like Marcia, transfixed by our past, often devastated, lives? Why do we fail to see that we are to "forget what is behind us and push forward to what is ahead"[5]?

When the songwriter David faced a situation of terrible torment, he had to choose how to respond. One of David's songs reveals his decision. He says, "I cried out to God for help; I cried out to God to hear me. When I was in distress, I cried out to the Lord. Throughout the night I stretched out my hands even though my soul refused His comfort."[6]

David goes on to say, "I think of the good old days, the days that ended long ago." He continues by presenting a number of questions in rapid-fire order. These questions clearly reveal the focus of his mind. "Will the Lord reject me forever? Will He never show me His favor again? Has His unfailing love vanished from me forever? Have His promises permanently failed me? Has God forgotten to be kind to me? Is God so angry with me that He has no compassion left for me?"[7] David is focusing on his calamity. He is saying, in effect, "I don't see anything good in my present circumstances."

Dealing with the Darkness

Most of us can relate to this. Most of us have felt like this. Most of us have experienced times in our lives when nothing seems right. Most of us have gone through seasons where everything seems confused and bewildering. Most of us have experienced terrible doubts. This is what provoked David to ask, "Has God's unfailing love vanished from me forever?" David's calamity initially turned him so inward that all he could see is the darkness of his own troubled soul. After all, if he had been thinking clearly, he would have realized that love which can never fail can never vanish forever.

We are not alone with these questions. They have been asked throughout the ages. They lead to despair. When we come to believe that God has totally and permanently rejected us, where else can it lead us? When we come to believe that God who promised to love us forever has rejected us, we are then left in utter despair. Why? Because His promises are our only hope for this life and the next. If in this life His promises fail us, what hope is there for the next?

Suddenly, however, David refocuses his thinking. "Then I thought . . . ," he writes. After asking questions that can hurl him into utter despair, he begins to refocus his thinking. He realizes that his thoughts have been untrue, unfaithful, and uncharitable about God. He sees that they lack good judgment and accurate thinking. As he comes out of this despair, he asks, in effect, "What kinds of questions am I asking? When I ask questions like these, they show me what's wrong with me, not what's wrong with God."

David continues: "I will appeal to the power of the Most High God. I commit myself to remember the deeds of the Lord, even His miracles that happened ages ago. I will meditate on all His works and consider all His mighty deeds."[8]

It is clear what David does. He focuses in on a single reality: God does not change. He then remembers God's deeds and miracles that have taken place years earlier. He recalls to himself what God is really like. His situation has not changed. All that has hurled him into anguish is still there, ready to eat him up and spit him out. Something has to change! God does not change. The situation probably will not change, at least not immediately. What is left? David is left. That's all. If he does not make the right kind of changes in his thinking, he is going to be destroyed.

David's attitude is changed, because he remembers that in his life of trouble and terror, there is something unchangeable. It is God. David makes a choice. Rather than dwell on himself and his miserable situation, rather than self defeating question after self defeating question, he makes his focus God.

Think for a moment about our lives. Think about what it is like to focus on the changelessness of God. Think about what it means to move mentally from our present distress to the eternity of God. This is a huge move. Our souls are strengthened. We believe what is written: "Our light and momentary troubles are achieving for us an eternal glory that far outweighs them all."[9]

What are those words referring to? Which "light and momentary troubles" did the writer of those words, the Apostle Paul, face? He was shipwrecked, beaten, stoned, left for dead, imprisoned, and ultimately beheaded. If these are "light and momentary," I would like to know what some of the more difficult ones are!

Paul is saying in effect, "This is how I have come to view the afflictions in my life when I compare them to the eternality, the changelessness, of God. Everything that happens to me is temporary and superficial, even getting beaten and thrown into prison for my faith. In fact, I do not even think they are worth making a comparison with when my hope is in the presence of God."

TRANSFORM YOUR MIND

An amazing change of perspective occurs in Paul's mind. That is why, when he writes about life, he says, "Be transformed [metamorphosed] by the renewing of your mind." Then he adds the reason for this transforming renewal. It is so that "we will be able to test and approve the purpose of God for our lives—all that is good, and pleasing, and perfect."[10]

What an amazing opportunity God gives us! Almost everyone I know would love to be made new. Renewal of our minds and transformation of our lives is readily available. Living a Take-Charge life is open to us TODAY. This wonderful transformation seen in a Take-Charge life begins in our minds. It begins in the way we think. This transformation engages us in the way we use our minds. When we are in situations in which terrible things are happening to us, how will we choose to respond? In which direction will we focus our thoughts?

Much of the time, we use our mind—this precious gift—just as David did when he asked one question after another that immersed him in despair and self-pity. It is so easy for us to use our minds this way. Instead, we need to use our minds to focus on God's changeless character, and on what He has done for us, regardless of the temporary, momentary troubles.

When we cling to God's changeless character, we are able to face life without anxiety. We can remember that we do not live in the past. We can remember that God has extricated us from often terrible and frightful pasts. We can know with confidence that God will continue to work, helping us to Take-Charge of our lives every step of the way.

When the Israelites crossed the Jordan River, they set up twelve stones as a memorial. Why did they do that? They wanted to look back—not to the miserable times they had experienced in the wilderness, but to God and the fact that He had taken them *from* the wilderness into the Promised Land.

I want us to understand this point. *It is okay to look back. What matters is what we look back to.* The Israelites' stones were not a call to look back and focus on forty years of disobedience. They were a call to look back and focus on forty years of God's deliverance. He brought them into a land overflowing with milk and honey, in spite of themselves.

David is no different in this sense. He needs to focus on what God has done for him, because he does not see God doing anything to ease the misery of his present situation. We have all faced situations like this. David realizes that he must remember God's deeds from the past. He must remember God's deeds that reveal His mercy, His love, His favor, His compassion, and other aspects of His unchanging character. David knows that he can apply these truths of God to his present situation, and that they will help see him through his crisis.

David needs help to get through the pain. He reviews God's expressions of love, mercy, compassion, and grace to him in the past. Although David is not visibly experiencing God's work in his life, nevertheless, he is able to affirm, "I know He is at work. He has helped me in the past. He does not change. He will help me now, because my God is a Take-Charge God."

David goes back through thousands of years, recalling all that God has done. What he recalls gives him hope in the face of despair. Amazingly, although his situation does not change a single bit, he is no longer hopeless. He realizes that trusting God and living hopelessly is a complete contradiction.

REVEALING THE POWER OF GOD

David helps us in yet another way. He appeals to "the years of the revealing of the power of God."[11] How does David do that? How does he know so assuredly this power of God? It is because David knows that God is a God of deliverance. The only way he can know this, is because the Scriptures teach this. If we want to know God's power, we too need to know the Bible.

Jesus gives us another example of this when He condemns the Sadducees, the religious leaders of His day. These men had head knowledge, but no relationship with God. In His frustration with them, Jesus said, "You do not know the Bible or the power of God."[12]

The Bible contains a mountain of truth that can negate any negative psychological state we may be in today, or may find ourselves in tomorrow. This includes despair, anger, anxiety, loneliness, and so on. The truth demands a verdict! The problem for us as we face this is simple. If we do not know the Bible, we lack the ability and knowledge to counter disabling thoughts. David knows that the Bible teaches him that his present distress is not meant to be his ultimate focus.

Today, we need to remember the deeds of Jesus. We need to remember that He loves us with an unfailing love.[13] We need to remember that He shows us that love on the cross. We need to remember that He has delivered us from slavery. We need to remember how great our redemption is. We need to remember that we live today in the age of "something better."[14] Better than what? We have something better than anything the Old Testament provided or possessed. We have something better than even God's deeds in Israel's history to which David looked. These deeds changed David's life. How much more can the deeds of Jesus change us! Knowing this, why do we let ourselves remain even for a moment in despair, confusion, fear, anger, or anxiety? How can we possibly justify remaining in those states when we have Jesus? We have the cross! We have the fullness of redemption!

Exercise Your Mind

David is not finished yet. "I will think about all of Your works and consider all the mighty things You have done."[15] David was able to meditate on creation. David was able to meditate on the Flood. David was able to meditate on Abram leaving Ur of the Chaldees to go to Canaan. David was able to mediate on the establishment of Israel. David was able to meditate on the Israelites' deliverance from slavery. David was able to meditate on the giving of the Law and the defeat of Israel's enemies. David was able to meditate on the establishment of the temple and the worship of God.

When we experience challenging, distressing times, we can choose to exercise our minds in the right direction or in the wrong direction. God has given us enough works of His power so that we can meditate on them for a lifetime and not run out of material! He has given us truths that will give us comfort, encouragement, and hope. However, like a weightlifter, we cannot expect our muscles to grow stronger just because we place a set of weights in our room. Having dumbbells in the room with us while we sleep will not make any difference either. We need to use these weights and exercise our muscles with them. Likewise, in order to live a Take-Charge life we must exercise our bodies, we must exercise our minds, and we must focus on the changeless character of God.

Notice where David moves next. From having doubt-filled questions about God, he comes to a place of great faith in God. "Your ways, O God, are holy. What god is as great as our God? You are the God who performs miracles. You display Your power among the peoples. With Your mighty arm You redeemed Your people."[16]

What is wonderful is that David does not say, "Your ways, O God, are good," "I can accept Your ways," or, "I'll bear with these things as long as I have to, but I hope I don't have to put up with them for long." Instead of all of this, David says, "Your ways, O God, are holy."

David moves from wondering whether God has removed His love forever from him, to asking, "What god is as great as our God?" His rhetorical answer is, in effect, "No god is as great as my God, the God who redeems His people."

I want us to see the transformation. Within just a few verses, this man moves from despair and devastation, to deliverance and dedication. He is blessed by the redeeming power of God. Likewise, if we want to break the patterns of despair, fear, terror, and lostness, we need to focus on the work of Christ. When we focus on the redemptive work of Jesus, our focus is salvation. This is the greatest work of God since time began. In redemption, we are focusing on the greatest deed expressed by the character of God. It is an ultimate memorial to His mercy, grace, and love.

David recounts how God led His people through the waters of the Red Sea: "Your path led us through the sea, Your way led us through the mighty waters. We knew You were with us, even though Your footprints were never seen."[17] David reveals that when we find ourselves in trouble we must not look around us and focus on the trouble. If we do that, it will cause us to become more depressed, and even experience other types of pain.

Rather than living by what we see, we are to live by faith. We are to live the same way David lived. We are to live the same way the Israelites lived. The entire nation had asked, "What is going to happen to us when the chariots of Egypt catch up to us?" They had their answer as they crossed from one side of the Red Sea to the other through the parted waves. God took them through, and no one saw even a single footprint from Him.

David finishes his song by saying, "You lead Your people like a flock by the hand of Moses and Aaron."[18] Instead of questioning whether God will ever love him again after what he has done, David deepens in his understanding of God's tender, shepherding care for His flock.

There are strong parallels between David's situation and responses, and our situation and responses today. The evidence we have of God working in our lives is our deliverance; the salvation we have in Jesus. God delivers us through the cross of Jesus. This cross is the centerpiece of our life and our joy. As we learn to look to Him and to look away from our difficult situations—both past and present—we will find the resources we need in order to live a Take-Charge life.

A GREATER FOCUS

As we rest in the character of God, our lives will be filled with so much that is good. We will not have to manufacture hopeful outcomes. We will not have to survive difficulties and challenges on our own. We will not have to depend on ourselves or others to get us through. We will come to learn that we can depend on God. He is dependable because His character of love and uprightness never changes. In the strength of His power we can take step after step in the direction of a Take-Charge life.

In spite of our past, in spite of our present, in spite of our doubts and our fears, we can always focus on God. We have His evidence. He has saved us. We will not see His footprints; we will only see the result of His great work in the hearts of hundreds of millions of people around the world.

In his letter to believers, Peter wrote, "Though you have not seen Jesus, even so you love Him. Although you do not see Him now, even so you believe in Him and are filled with an inexpressible and glorious joy, for you are receiving the goal of your faith, the salvation of your souls."[19]

When we have learned to place our faith in Jesus and trust in the character of God, we will find the resources we need to live the way

God intends us to live. We will not only make it through life, but we will also Take-Charge of our life through His power and grace.

TAKE-CHARGE ACTION INITIATIVES

1. *Which thought or circumstance in your life is particularly troubling to you right now?*

   _____

   _____

   _____

2. *How have you responded to it? Has it been with a positive or negative attitude? Be honest.*

   _____

   _____

   _____

3. *As you think about this chapter, which aspects of God's unchanging character help you deal with the difficulties that you face in your life?*

   _____

   _____

   _____

   What hope does God's character give you?

   _____

   _____

   _____

4. *David remembers what God has done for him when times get tough. What has God done for you?*

   _____

   _____

   _____

5. *Why does being rooted in who God is and in the Bible offer a much stronger foundation than just positive thinking?*

---

6. *What does Jesus' sacrifice on the cross for you reveal about His love for you and His plan for your Take-Charge life?*

16

AN UPRIGHT TAKE-CHARGE LIFE

Instead of feeling powerless, avoiding pain, or blaming other people or circumstances when life is tough, a Take-Charge life is an upright life. Become the person God calls you to be and experience His joy. Allow Him to use your challenges to accomplish His will in your life and in the lives of others.

I counsel people who have all kinds of problems. Invariably, they believe that if an unpleasant colleague or an unfair boss or a tyrannical parent or an unkind spouse were removed—if people would only do what they want them to do—then they would have better lives. I suggest that this type of thinking is inaccurate and avoids the real issues.

How much good does it do, for example, if we focus on what we believe other people's faults may be, and blame them for how we are feeling? Imagine if all the people who cause us problems suddenly caused us no problems whatsoever. Here is the question: Would our life be better? The answer is that the quality of our life never depends upon how other people treat us. Quite the contrary. If we believe that our enjoyment of life is based upon how others live, we are in for a pretty rough life. We are implying that they, not we, are responsible for the degree to which we experience quality of life. Do we *really* believe that we are simply the victims of other people's behavior? Or are we willing to work instead on ourselves; our attitudes, our weaknesses, our lack of love, and so on? We will always face relational and circumstantial difficulties, yet our enjoyment of life can and must continue in the midst of them.

The Apostle Paul demonstrates a firm commitment to work on himself: "I beat my body to make it my slave, so that it works for me and not against me. I do all that I have to do so that I will not miss out on my prize."[1] "I have applied these things to myself."[2] Paul does not take anything for granted, not even things about himself. He tries to do everything he can do to become a person who does not live presumptuously, but by faith. He is aware that we cannot take ourselves for granted before God.

Rather than trying to straighten out everyone else first, Paul commits himself to Take-Charge of his own life so that the path to which he calls others will be filled with uprightness and truth, not strewn with the debris of a wrecked life. He seeks to do this living as a man who is changed and dominated by God. He is not controlled by circumstances, nor by others, nor by his emotions. He is ruled by God alone. He lives by grace through faith in Jesus alone. He takes step after step for God and is willing to live fully for Him.

TAKE THE FIRST STEP

As we saw in the last chapter, it is important for us to focus on the character of God and what He has done, and continues to do, for us. This is just a part of the process. The other part involves our decision to take a positive first step, and then other steps. Taking that first step is vital. In fact, many people have moved out of severe depression just by beginning to do what needed to be done!

God rules, governs, and sustains our universe. God empowers us to be radically different than the moaning, grumbling, complaining individuals all around us. We are not to blame how we feel on anyone else. We are to be radically different than people who view themselves as powerless because the difficulties of their lives seem so overwhelming.

Paul writes of this radically different person: "I pray that you, being rooted and established in love, may have power, together with all the believers, to come to know just how wide and long and high and deep is the love of Jesus. I want you to know this love that surpasses knowledge. I want you to know this love so that you may be filled to the measure of all the fullness of God."[3] Paul goes on to teach us how to accomplish this, when he says, "Put off your old self, which is corrupted by deceitful desires. Instead, be made new in the attitude of your mind."[4]

As we consider these verses, we realize that when we are made *new* in Jesus, we begin learning new ways to think that fill our minds. As we Take-Charge of our lives, God works in us to change our former attitudes and replace them with new, godly ones.

Paul continues by listing our new behaviors. We are to:

▸ "Put off lies and speak the truth."[5]

▸ "Do not let anger get the upper hand and provoke you to do the wrong thing."[6]

▸ "Stop using your hands to steal. Instead work, and do something useful with your hands."[7]

▸ "Never let any unwholesome talk be part of your conversation. Only say what is helpful for building others up according to their needs."[8]

▸ "Get rid of any hint of bitterness, rage, anger, brawling and slander. Make sure you also eradicate malice."[9]

▸ "Be kind and compassionate to each other. Forgive each other, just as in Jesus, God forgives you."[10]

Recognize What is Good

When we live our lives as those whom God has called us to be, it is revolutionary. We are transformed. Not only will we change, we will help others to change as well. We will love, give, speak kindly, and be gracious and forgiving. Never does empowerment become so humbling as when we see it within the context of our life in the Lord. We come to realize that no matter how challenging our situations may be, not only can they work for good in us, but they can also work for good in other people as well.

Paul often challenges us to recognize the blessing of affliction. He desires us to see the possibilities for good in life's very difficult situations. Paul is not an armchair philosopher waxing eloquent on elitist ideals. Every day Paul faced great adversity. When his dreams were smashed, wonderfully, he saw greater dreams realized. His life, his attitude, his situation, his thinking, speaks clearly to us even today.

Paul's dream was to go to Rome and spread the Gospel in the heart of the Roman Empire. He seemed always to be on the move. In his far reaching journeys, he planted churches everywhere.

We need to consider what it was like for Paul when, instead of ministering in Rome, he ministered in a Roman prison cell. In case his cell was not enough to restrict his movements, Rome assigned two guards to be with him at all times!

What would we think if this happened to us? *How can this be happening to me? How can God really be in control? How can any good come out of this?* If we look at Paul's situation simply in terms of how the circumstances appear, what other conclusions could we draw? Paul though, does not just make his conclusions based on his circumstances. Paul knows that if God has narrowed his field of evangelism from the whole city of Rome to a cell with two soldiers chained to him, then he will have to adjust his mission field.

Paul never bemoans his fate. Instead, he shares the grace of His Lord and Savior with the soldiers. Paul does not whine and complain that he is in chains. Instead, he uses this opportunity to the fullest measure. Later, Paul writes another letter to the churches. Not only does he greet his readers, so too do the soldiers who have been guarding him![11] They are now believers! Paul views his hardships as opportunities. Even soldiers and palace officials are coming to believe in the Jewish Messiah that Paul is preaching.

It is easy for us to use our hardships as excuses and complain that we are victims. We love to immerse ourselves in self-pity. In comparison, look at Paul. While he was imprisoned, he wrote four letters that have become some of the most important writings in history. These writings are known as the letters to the Ephesians, Philippians, Colossians, and Romans. Paul's dream was to start a dozen churches in Rome. He could have cried and whined about his misfortune while he was in prison. Instead, he redirected and refocused his efforts, and turned a personal disaster for him into a world-wide blessing for us. It is hard to imagine the world without these four letters from Paul in the Bible.

Paul never assumed that his life or his work would be better if he was no longer in prison. He was not thinking that a different external situation would make his life better. He did not waste away in prison. His firm belief was that his responsibility before God is to trust God throughout his situation, no matter what it may be. As a consequence of such determination, hundreds of millions of people have been blessed during these last two thousand years. In addition, there has probably been over one hundred thousand commentaries written on these four letters during this time. The impact of Paul in prison is impossible to calculate.

Choose Joy

Why is Paul's life so fruitful? For one thing, he is dominated by a living faith in the core of his being. Everything he desires to do is surrendered to God. Instead of basing his joy on his circumstances or on his accomplishments, Paul's joy is deeper than either of these criteria. His joy comes from being where God wants him to be, and doing what God wants him to do in that place and in that circumstance.

How can we, like Paul, avoid being trapped by worry, depression, fear, or other negative states when we face difficulties? How can we receive the type of joy that Paul experienced when our circumstances, like his, are awful? How can we move from deeply negative emotional states to a Take-Charge life? How can we stop blaming these disturbing emotional states on other people and circumstances?

Years ago the first Vietnam war movie, *The Deer Hunter* was released. The main character is an American prisoner of war in North Vietnam. The plot revolves around a game of Russian roulette that the North Vietnamese forced the American prisoners to play against each other. After the war ends, the main character continues to play the game. His obsession with this game ends in the only way that it can: Death by a bullet to his brain from his own gun.

Why didn't he stop? He could have stopped at any time. It is easy for us to think that if we were in the same situation, of course *we* would stop playing. Here is the difficulty. Countless people continue to act out patterns that are killing them. For example, when someone says, "I'm depressed," what he is really saying is, "I don't have anything to do with this depression. It's just here. How did it get here?" The lives of these people are truly filled with pain. It adds to the pain that they live as outsiders to their pain. They live as if what they experience is completely beyond their control. They live as those whose lives are

Taking-Charge of them, rather than living as those who Take-Charge of their lives.

It is easy to fall into this trap. We do not even think of transformation for our lives. We live instead under the principle of victimization. We think we are simply pawns, both of other people and of circumstances.

Some of us remember the comedian Flip Wilson. He was popular because he created a television persona, Geraldine Jones. Geraldine was always getting into trouble. She would do one wrong thing after another. Following her misbehavior, she would strut on the stage, look you in the eye, and say, "The devil made me do it."

Throughout our lives we experience all kinds of situations, both good and bad. We cannot protect ourselves against external circumstances without isolating ourselves from the world. Even if we did that, we would still have to deal with despair, loneliness, alienation, and so on. As human beings, we can never entirely avoid difficulties. At the same time, we can Take-Charge of our lives when we choose the right way to respond to our difficulties. We can create the emotional and mental states in which we desire to live.

Let's say that something sad happens to us or to someone we love, and we experience grief. It is one thing if we grieve for a while. It is quite another thing to choose to be depressed for the next three years. We rarely realize that so much of this actually is a choice. Today we have the power to be depressed for the rest of this day. Today we also have the power to choose joy for this day.

Paul did not write, "Catch the Spirit," "Catch the joy," or, "Catch a joyful feeling when you are out of control." He wrote, "Rejoice in the Lord always. I will say it again: Rejoice!"[12] He urges us to demonstrate that we are responsible individuals who choose to Take-Charge of our lives and live with obedient joy before God. It may be hard to appreci-

ate, but God desires that we actively rejoice no matter how challenging our life may be.

FACING PAIN

Every time we become angry, fearful, anxious, or depressed, that
emotion has been triggered by something that affects the neurochem-
ical pathways in our brain. Perhaps some thugs beat you up badly. As
they left you they said, "We promise that we'll do worse things to you
next time." Now you live in fear.

Maybe you study day after day for examinations in university.
Your study is important. So too is your attitude when you study. If you
tell yourself, *I'm so stupid. I can't learn anything. I know I'm going to
fail*, this has a huge impact. Every time you enter a testing situation,
the association your brain makes with a test is anxiety and failure.

Maybe you were mistreated by other children when you were a
child. Their mistreatment hurt and disturbed you. You determined to
prove to them that you have worth. It may be many years later, but
today you are still trying to prove your worth to other people.

Maybe your parents did not love you. You now habitually asso-
ciate the belief, *I'm not loved*, with every important relationship in
your life. Whenever something or someone reinforces that belief, it
is as if a button is pushed and the old song is played. The lyrics are
simple: *I am worthless and do not deserve love.*

Maybe someone has hurt you deeply. Now, you wind up hating or
avoiding everyone. You avoid not only the person who hurt you, but
anyone else who *may* hurt you. You think to yourself, *That person is
getting too close to me. He is going to hurt me. I won't let that happen,
because I will never let him get close enough to hurt me.*

Maybe you are depressed, but you do not let yourself feel miserable. Instead, you become angry. You tell yourself, *I'm not depressed*

because of myself. I'm depressed because of how everyone treats me. I hate them for doing this to me.

The strange irony in all of this is that when we respond in these or similar ways, we are choosing to hurt ourselves. Do we want to hurt ourselves? Do we want to do or think what will make our lives much worse? Of course not. Everything we do is designed to make ourselves feel better! We live to maximize our pleasures and minimize our pain, even though what often happens is that we have maximized our pain and minimized our pleasure.

For example, the person who takes crack cocaine is destroying his life. He will tell you that if you ask him. Every crack addict I have ever worked with tells me that. Why then do they continue doing crack? It is simply because crack gives them everything they want in that moment, and everything they want includes nothing more than themselves and their immediate gratification. So too whether it is people using alcohol, or getting involved in extramarital sex, or gambling away the mortgage on their home. None of these people do these things to destroy their lives. The problem is that at the end, having entered these roads, they are inevitably and invariably destroyed.

The huge challenge we face is to move from instant gratification to a Take-Charge life. This means that we move from being a baby to being a mature adult. We need to move from wanting what we want when we want it. We need to move to being able at every moment to be those who truly live a God-principled life. These principles are designed to help us consider the destructive consequences of our actions and keep us always on the right path.

We are to be principle oriented rather than pleasure oriented. Because of our unalterable inclination to pleasure, let me put it in a slightly different way: Our greatest pleasure is following God's greatest principles. David, whom we spoke of in the last chapter, exemplifies this approach when he says, "I treasure Your laws, for they are my heart's deepest pleasure. I am determined to keep Your principles, even forever, to the very end."[13] This is principle centered living. It is not the absence of pleasure, because the real pleasures are the treasure principles that come from God and that enable us to delight in Him with our hearts.

To live such a treasure filled, principle centered life is to live a relationship centered life. This is found in living in relationship with God. When we live this way, we truly realize that we are not alone. The sense of aloneness permeates our culture. Why? Because we *are* alone. We have abandoned God. Our credo could be: "We are alone in the universe."

The idea of being in intimate relationship with God is unimaginable to much of our contemporary culture, because it makes them feel helpless and dependent. We do not like to think of ourselves as being dependent, but we are! All of us by nature are dependent from birth onwards. As we grow older, we still remain dependent on others, at least to a degree. When we are really old, we are back once again where we started.

People casually say, "We must never be dependent," "We are autonomous," "We are alone in the universe," "We must be our own best friend." The idea of dependency offends us. We do not like to think of ourselves as being dependent, but we are! All of us by nature are dependent from birth onwards. As we grow up, we still remain dependent on others, at least to a degree.

Some of us remember these lyrics of a Simon and Garfunkel song: "I am a rock. I am an island. And a rock feels no pain. And an island never cries." Which of us is really a rock? Which of us is really an island? Which of us does not cry? We can put up self-protective walls and seek autonomy. The price we pay is the increasing loss of the ability to feel—to experience pain, courage, fear, joy, and so on. We become unable to receive the blessings that God has stored up for us. We blame others instead of looking to and trusting God.

We can make a different choice. God loves us and delights in forgiving us. He sent His Son to die for us. He now lives for us. He delights when we are in a deep, loving relationship with Him.

Why not reach out for God? He delights in helping us. Why seek out other people and all those things that only cause us to feel better now, but will ultimately hurt us and others as well?

We have the opportunity, starting TODAY, right NOW, to choose abundant life. When we seek to find satisfaction and pleasure apart from God, we may hope to minimize or eliminate our pain. Sadly, we don't. That is why psychologists and psychiatrists are so busy (and so wealthy). We choose ultimately self-destructive ways of thinking and acting in order to feel happy, or to feel good, or to escape pain momentarily. Such choices create bigger, deeper, and far greater pain later on. At times, people often commit suicide because they have gotten themselves into such terribly deep pain by trying the wrong ways to feel good and experience pleasure. Death appears to them to be the only way they will truly feel better.

We can choose to draw close to God and put aside all the temporary pleasures we have used to bring about a momentary comfort. Instead, we can rejoice in God. Instead, we can rejoice in living by God's principles. Instead, we can rejoice in the pleasures He holds out for us.

Feeling good is not the ultimate goal of mankind. It does not matter even if everyone we know arranges their lives around this belief. Rather, our chief end is to glorify God, as we enjoy Him both now and forever.

Almost everyone today seeks loving relationships of one kind or another because it really eases the pain when someone seems to offer love. The big problem is that we cannot make people love us, especially when we need love the most and are unhappy.

For example, in many marriages today, a husband who should be expressing love often does not. This lack of love hurts his wife deeply. For her part, as a self-preserving response, she withholds her love from him. It does not take long for this relationship to become loveless. How quickly we become disappointed when the love we desire is not given. How rarely we think, *Perhaps the problem is that I have not loved first.* Remember how God puts it: "This is what love is all about. Not that we have loved God, but that He loved us first."[14]

Dependable Truth

We all know that wrong thinking accomplishes just one thing—it facilitates coping with life's difficulties in the wrong ways. This being the case, it makes sense that right thinking helps us deal with our difficulties in constructive ways. Let me offer us a starting place. It is a truth that keeps us, protects us, and defends us when we are hurting.

Here it is: *God loves us, has always loved us, will always love us, and is committed to taking care of us.* If we believe this, then acting on this truth protects our hearts and minds during even the most difficult troubles. We can depend upon God above all else to help us handle the difficulties of our lives. There is no one that can provide for us what God provides.

Even when we know that God loves us just as we are, we seem to forget that. Instead, we find it so easy to focus on His punishment and judgment. This is sadly so, even when there is nothing of punishment and judgement happening in our lives. I have found this to be especially true in the lives of deeply depressed people who feel worthless.

I remember a blizzard that dumped two feet of snow in our area. I had my boots laid out and warming up as I prepared to conquer the snow and release our car from its frozen tomb.

Our daughter Micaiah awoke, saw the snow, hurled herself into my boots, and ran outside without even putting on her coat or socks. A little while later, she came in covered in snow and dripping wet. Every step left melting snow behind her. When she removed her feet from my boots, she left my boots filled with snow, slosh, and slush.

When I was ready to leave, I could not find my boots. I called out and asked if anyone knew where my boots were. I soon learned that Micaiah had fled to her room when she heard that question. Then I found my boots, soaking wet and containing about three inches of water.

I was angry as I went looking for Micaiah. I saw my wife first. "Make sure she knows you love her anyway," Nancy reminded me. By the time I found Micaiah, she was sitting in her room with a panicked look on her face, expecting the worst. I walked up to her, looked her in the face, and said, "Micaiah, I love you anyway."

Micaiah looked at me and beamed. I, in turn, experienced one of those rare opportunities to affirm her when she was not prepared to be surprised by love. She had been thinking about judgment and punishment, but I was thinking about love— especially thanks to a little reminder from Nancy.

This simple illustration reveals a profound truth. Just as Micaiah needed to be reminded of my love, we need to remember God's enduring love and compassion. We do not need to be reminded about punishment and judgment because we are already predisposed to think about them. We need to remember that God will continue to love us despite the fact that we may be thinking, *No one could ever love me.*

When we respond to God's love, He will see us through our darkest moments. He will empower us to Take-Charge of our lives. He will enable us to make responsible choices. He will help us to experience life fully and to face our difficulties with joy. He will give us the courage to make godly decisions instead of allowing people and circumstances to unduly influence us.

TAKE-CHARGE ACTION INITIATIVES

1. *Consider this statement: "If we believe that our enjoyment of life is based on what people say to us or do to us, we are implying that they, not we, are responsible for the degree to which we experience a joyful quality of life." Do you agree or disagree? Why?*

   _____

   _____

   _____

2. *If you are allowing other people to affect your enjoyment of life, what are you prepared to do to change that?*

   _____

   _____

   _____

3. *Read Ephesians 3:17-19. What do these verses say about God and your relationship with Him?*

   _____

   _____

4. *Do you believe that God loves you and cares for you? If not, why not? If so, how is this influencing the way you live?*

   _____

   _____

   _____

What changes do you need to make in the way you satisfy your needs?

_____

_____

_____

5. *Do you think it is important to obey God in all situations? If so, why? If not, why not?*

_____

_____

_____

What are the situations in your life in which you should respond differently, starting TODAY?

_____

_____

_____

_____

6. *Why do people respond as if they are powerless victims, instead of allowing God to help them Take-Charge of their lives?*

_____

_____

_____

If you are living as a victim, how might you begin to change this NOW?

_____

_____

_____

_____

7. *What thoughts and feelings are provoked in you by Philippians 4:4?*

_____

_____

_____

_____

8. *Have you ever been dependent on anyone or anything other than God that you knew was standing in the way of your relationship with God? What allowed such dependence? Did you find that it helped your life or harmed your life? How? Would you do things differently now?*

_____

_____

_____

9. *Are you committed to living your life in dependence upon God? How do you define this dependence? Give some concrete examples of your dependence in action.*

_____

_____

_____

_____

10. *What changes will you make in your relationship with God, starting TODAY, so that your life is a Take-Charge life?*

_____

_____

_____

_____

17

THE SONGS OF A TAKE-CHARGE LIFE

We all have songs in our lives. Some of our songs crush us. Some of our songs set us free. When we sing God's songs, they transform us and lead us into a Take-Charge life.

Music is powerful. Images are powerful. When we see an image and hear a tune at the same time, it is doubly powerful and deeply embeds itself in our memory. Advertisers, for example, take advantage of this through the use of television commercials. They know the potential for seeing and hearing powerful images and powerful words simultaneously.

Our ability to remember is enhanced when images and sounds are joined together. Let's take a look at one aspect of this for a moment. Think about the music we enjoy. We remember many of our favorite songs and music because they are indelibly linked with events or people that are important to us from the past, even from a seemingly long forgotten past.

Here is a personal example of what I am talking about. *Whenever I hear the song Satisfaction by the Rolling Stones, I see myself driving my car as a teenager on the New Jersey turnpike.* I was driving back from my summer work as a waiter in the Catskill Mountains, and was really anxious to see my girlfriend of the week. It was at that moment that I heard the song for the first time. It hit me so powerfully that I pulled my car over to the side of the road rather than risk an accident while I was listening to it.

Since that day, I have reflected on the impact of song and image whenever I have listened to an oldies station. These songs almost immediately elicit strong and powerful emotions connected with certain events from that period of time in my life.

Amazingly, just by listening to a certain song, we can remember many things from the past. Here is another example from my life of this principle. Any time I hear the Byrds rendition of Bob Dylan's song *Turn, Turn, Turn (To Everything There is a Season)*, I am back in my old university fraternity house, AEΠ. Surrounded by my former fraternity brothers, I can see their faces vividly, as the Byrds sing Dylan's song. Just play that song, and I am back there.

Some researchers believe that we record experiences in our minds in much the same way that records were organized in the old jukeboxes. The work of the brilliant researcher Penfield, at McGill University, strongly corroborates this conclusion. In his research and the ensuing treatment for temporal lobe epilepsy, Penfield selectively froze areas of his patients' temporal lobes. In the process, he discovered that as these areas of the brain were stimulated, distinct memories, even those from the earliest times of life, were recalled by his patients. These memories had not been collected in a large pool of memories, but were neatly compartmentalized in specific areas of the brain.

This insight can help us Take-Charge of our lives today. Just as we can change the radio station, CDs, or songs on our iPods, we can Take-Charge of our inner states and change the tunes from something painful and miserable to something positive and helpful. All we have to do is change what we listen to in life.

Let's say we love a person who recently died in a car accident. We can focus on her painful, tragic death, or we can focus on the beauty of her character and the wonderful times we spent together. The former focus inevitably creates additional pain. The latter focus inevitably creates joy in the midst of grief.

I was visiting with the family of a friend of mine who had died. The family members and friends who were gathered together were experiencing terrible sadness and grieving. Suddenly, someone remembered something funny that our friend had done. All at once, we all were howling with laughter. Were we being disrespectful, or were we choosing to experience joy and laughter in the face of our loss?

Instead of remaining focused on the tragedies and pains of life, we can choose a life of rejoicing.[1] We can change our negative perspective and our negative thoughts. From early on in history, this is how God desired us to live. The first example of this is when He appeals to Cain, who is immersing himself in bitterness and self-pity. Does He give Cain years of psychotherapy? No! God gives him just one sentence, because that sentence is all that is necessary to change Cain's life if he follows it: "Do what is right and you will be happy again."[2]

PLAY GOD'S SONGS

The songs of the Bible are given their own place in the Bible. They are called the *Songs of David*. These are the most powerful, moving songs ever written. Amazingly, we can play them at any time, day or night. They give us a vast array of help on which we can focus our minds during times of difficulty. These songs, as they fill our hearts and our minds, will help us to Take-Charge of our lives.

These songs will bring us to a new place. They will, as they say of themselves, "set our feet on a rock and give us a solid place on which to stand."[3] When we are in despair, and feel as if we are falling into a deep pit, or are submerging in rushing water—whatever the case may be—we can call out to God. He will place us on a solid rock and give us a firm place on which to stand.

This Bible song book, the *Song's of David*, is also known as the *Book of Psalms*. It is God's gift of one hundred and fifty life giving, life renewing, and life restoring songs from God to us. We are meant to play them day by day in order to experience the mercies of God, which are "new every morning."[4] When we play them, these songs will enable us to Take-Charge of our hearts and minds, and bring positive change into our lives. Yet, we have to reach out and play them, instead of grasping for temporary things that may bring momentary pleasure, but will, in the long run, only bring pain. If we do not reach for them, they sit unplayed and can not help us.

When we learn how to play these songs, we can quickly, dramatically, and effectively exercise mastery over our thoughts and feelings. These songs from heaven can remind us that even during our darkest moments God will see us through, as He enables us to Take-Charge of our life. We can use them when we feel discouraged or when we want to focus on God. These songs teach us that God deeply loves us and is with us throughout all the circumstances we face. One way I know how extremely helpful these songs are, is based on my personal experience with them. I have been reading and singing the Psalms all my life.

A Sample Song

Nearly every psalm contains helpful encouragement for troubled or despairing believers. Consider Psalm 20, which deals with depression.

David opens saying, "May the Lord answer you when you are in distress."[5] Another way to word this is, "May the Lord answer you when you are in *tsuris*." The Hebrew word *tsuris* conveys "anguish," "affliction," or "deep depression."

David then continues: "May the name of the God of Jacob protect you."[6] What does "the name of the God of Jacob" mean? This phrase immediately reminds us of Exodus 3 when God reveals Himself to Moses from within the burning bush. After telling Moses to take off his sandals, God says, "I am the God of your father, the God of Abraham, Isaac, and Jacob."[7] Then He says that He has come down to rescue the Israelites from bondage, and has chosen Moses to be their leader.

Moses feels insecure and inadequate when given this job promotion. In fact, he is downright afraid. "Who am I," he asks, "that I should go to Pharaoh and bring the Israelites out of Egypt?"[8] God replies, "I will be with you."

Moses anticipates the difficult challenges he will face. "Suppose I go to the Israelites and say to them, 'the God of your fathers has sent me to you,' and they ask me, 'What is His name?' Then what shall I tell them?"[9]

God answers from the midst of the burning bush, "I AM WHO I AM. . . . Say to the Israelites, 'The Lord, the God of your fathers—the God of Abraham, the God of Isaac and the God of Jacob—has sent me to you.' This is My name forever."[10]

The name for God that David uses in Psalm 20 means the Eternal God. What David is saying to us is that the Eternal God who delivered Israel miraculously, mightily, and powerfully from unbearable, unendurable slavery will hear us, answer us, be with us, and protect us. What a wondrous truth!

We may be facing great distress. Our friends or family may have hurt us or deserted us. All the people around us may have failed us. Nevertheless, we can always know that the Lord will care for us. He will hear us. He will answer us. He will protect us.

David continues, saying, "May God send you help from the sanctuary and grant you support from Zion."[11] Truly, when we are in trouble, we can expect the help and support of God to bless us and protect us. He will send us help from the most sacred, holy place—from His heart.

Isn't this exciting! We receive life-giving truth that fills us with the hope we need in the midst of great trouble and distress. We have a portrait of a person being rushed into an emergency room, profusely bleeding from a terrible injury. As soon as he receives a blood transfusion, his life is restored.

When David writes that God will grant us support from Zion, he reminds us that God sees everything that we do. Interestingly, the literal sense of this phrase is that God *records* all that we do. He is aware of all that we have done that has seemed to go unnoticed. God records them on His heart.

David continues by reminding us of the source of real joy. Real joy does not come from people or circumstances. Real joy comes from God. As the song continues, "We will sing for joy . . . and in the name of our God we will set up our banners."[12] Later, this same truth is mentioned in the New Testament: "Finally, rejoice in the Lord! . . . Rejoice in the Lord always . . . I will say it again: Rejoice!"[13]

We need to see just how relevant this song is in living a Take-Charge life. The focus of our joy is to be God—not ourselves, not our emotional state, not even our experience of happiness, satisfaction, or well-being. We are to rejoice in the Lord because He is the basis of our joy. In spite of ourselves, in spite of our thoughts, in spite of our feelings, in spite of our experiences, we possess a God in whom we can rejoice.

If we rejoice in how we *feel*, we are in trouble. We may feel great today, and terrible tomorrow. Satan uses that "up and down" roller coaster to condemn, judge, accuse, and destroy us. God's way is so much greater. We can rejoice regardless of how we feel at any given moment because of who God is and what He has done for us.

The joy David describes is unrelated to circumstances. Let's say we are in despair and our life does not seem worth living. Then we remember that we really do have something worth rejoicing over: We can rejoice in God and in His mercy to us. Suddenly, we are raising banners in the name of God. As we sing such songs as these, our focus turns more and more to God. This inevitably leads to prayer. As we sing the Psalms, we are reminded that God hears our voice and considers all our requests. What could be more encouraging than to know that God delights in blessing us and helping us not only to rise out of despair, but to do so with His power?

Where does that power come from? David answers as he continues in the song: "Now I know that the Lord saves His chosen one; He answers him from His holy heaven with the saving power of His right hand."[14] God answers us from heaven with real saving power. He does not just "get us through" the day. He does not even just "get us through" our lives. His purpose for us involves our full and perfect deliverance, regardless of what we face or experience in this life.

It is important for us to see just how powerful this song is as it breaks into our lives. It is a positive, personal, power-filled God who engages with the deepest concerns of our hearts. This song prepares us to face even adversity with joy.

When God opens our hearts to see the great work He is doing in our hearts, be thankful. Of all the many things for which we can be thankful, the work that God does in our hearts is the greatest work of all. As we recognize and take hold of God's great salvation and power, He will renew us deep within our minds. "We will be able to test and approve of God's good, pleasing and perfect will."[15]

Sometimes in my seminars I ask, "How many of you want to be depressed? If you do, please raise your hand." Nobody ever does. Yet many of us regularly make choices that lead to depression.

For example, we make that choice in the music we listen to. The hugely popular country western music is filled with lyrics of adultery and desertion. Rap is all about violence and degradation to women. The movies we watch have the same themes, except with a visual depiction added to it. Our computers are just a click away from some of the most horrific pornography anyone could ever imagine. What are we doing? We are focusing our minds on ugliness, on lewdness, and on violence. Even if we are not engaged in the music, movies, or internet activities, all we need are our minds, with which we focus on bad memories and even worse experiences.

Our lives are filled with degradation, depravity, corruption, despair, and deceit. Even Hollywood's most successful actors and actresses living with the world's acclaim—people who we think have everything—are desperate to escape from the indwelling despair that consumes their souls. How do they do this? They use their enormous wealth to purchase enormous amounts of drugs. Many have died in their flight. Compare this to the new songs of life God gives us in the Bible.

A NEW FOCUS

I began my career doing psychoanalytic psychotherapy. I was trained to help people free-associate, to say anything that came into their minds. I then had to interpret these associations in connection with my patients' psychosexual stage of development, their relationships with their parents, and most especially their relationship with me, their therapist. This interpretive process often goes on for years, numerous times per week at great expense (and even greater expense for those who live long enough to endure the full treatment).

Although most therapies are not as extensive or intensive as psychoanalytic treatment, they *are* committed to some extended probing into the patient's deep, buried past. The assumption is that the patient cannot really be helped until he has relived past traumas, pains, and hurts. Based on the assumption that one's past experiences can build up to an explosive level if they are not reduced in some way, these therapies endeavor to facilitate a reliving and relieving of the pain. They aim to open up repressed negative memories, hoping that such reliving, along with some measure of interpretation, will relieve the patient's pain. Such a therapy does not acknowledge that some behavior is objectively better than other behaviour. Thus, there is no direction, no standard, and no goal toward which to guide one's patients.

Let's look at this from a common sense perspective. Are things best for us when we have just delved into the absolutely most horrible and terrible experiences of our lives? Does this approach really help us to live, behave, and perform better? The answer is *no!* Standard psychotherapies often produce more pain than they alleviate. Sad, hopeless people move from therapist to therapist, from cure to cure, from one hopeful approach to the next hopeful drug.

The character portrayed by Woody Allen in one of his early movies, *Sleeper*, reflected on the 200 years his body had been frozen. He said, "If only I'd been in psychoanalysis all this time, I'd almost be cured by now." This cynicism is well deserved as it relates to the hope for personality change through the standard therapeutic approaches.

Please do not think that I am suggesting that change is easy for anyone, even believers. The process of becoming more like Jesus is a complex, life-consuming process. It demands an honest appraisal of our thoughts and actions that have bogged us down in misery and despair. At the same time, the more we dwell on what is bad, ugly, and hurtful, the worse we will feel. That is why the Bible calls us to focus on what is good and true and beautiful.[16] The easiest way to focus on the right things is to "first forget about the miseries that are behind us, and then push forward to what is ahead."[17]

At the same time, we need to remember that our lives are made up of a variety of experiences. Some of our experiences are good; some of them are bad. How we experience life today is determined to a great extent by how we have *responded* to all of these experiences, not just what the experiences have been. One of the failures of psychotherapy has been the idea that the difficulties we experience in life are because of difficult experiences. This is not true! Our difficult lives are an outworking of how we have responded over time to the difficulties we have experienced.

The Bible provides us with the necessary tools so that we not only cope with our difficulties, but thrive in spite of them. As we are seeing in Psalm 20, every verse of this song is relevant to our lives. We need to focus and concentrate on what it says and let this song of God empower us.

Our focus deepens when David urges us to realize that many individuals "trust in chariots and in horses." David's concern is neither chariots nor horses. We are his concern. Our trust is not to be in man's strength. Instead, "we trust in the name of the Lord our God."[18]

Notice how personal these words are. We are trusting in God. In an age of darkness, superstition, and idolatry, we are not looking to the chariots or idols of this age. We are looking to God. We are not boasting in being consumers of the things of this age. In fact, we are not boasting in anything earthly on which people rely. Our lasting defense against the despair of the world is never found in placing our trust in the things of the world. Beautiful cars rust. Beautiful women grow old. Beautiful money becomes worthless with inflation. Our lasting defense is God; the eternal, ever-loving God.

David goes on to explain in his song that when we trust in the things of man, we will ultimately be "brought to our knees and fall."

David gives us hope when he says, ". . . but we rise up and stand firm."[19] David understands that none of us can be raised upright and at the same time be in despair.

In a "Peanuts" cartoon, Charlie Brown is standing hunched over, saying, "This is my depressed stance." Then he says, "When you're depressed, it makes a lot of difference how you stand." Finally, he concludes, "If you're going to get any joy out of being depressed, you've got to stand like this."

In a psychiatric hospital in which I worked, one of my patients, Marvin, spent his life laying in a fetal position on the floor. I urged him to speak with me, but he would not respond. He just lay there, sucking his thumb. I said, "Marvin, I know that you have had every kind of psychotherapy there is, and nothing has helped. I am convinced I can help you." He just lay there and continued to suck on his thumb. Finally, I shouted, "Marvin, in the name of Jesus Christ, stand up!"

Do you know what Marvin did? He jumped up immediately and was no longer depressed. Why? Because he was enraged. "How dare you speak to me about Jesus?" he shouted. "I am a Jew!" Both the intern and the nurse that were with me were positively bewildered at this unusual interaction!

When Marvin stood up, it demonstrably changed his inner state. It was the beginning of an external change as well. He was coming to understand one of God's incredible songs: "Jehovah's perfect law restores the soul again."[20]

No More Excuses!

Sometimes people say to me, "When I'm depressed, I don't want to read the Psalms. I don't have the energy. I don't want to open my Bible. The last thing I want to do is start singing the Psalms or even reading them aloud."

"Okay," I may respond, "but why do you want to go deeper into depression? Why aren't you willing to do whatever is necessary to Take-Charge of your life and get out of your depression? You say you don't want to go into depression, but you don't take me seriously when I tell you what to do that will move you out of it. You act as if you can't get out of it. What makes you think that way?"

The Psalms were written to help us get through our difficulties. Just getting up to get your Bible will start to bring about a Take-Charge change in your life. Opening it will make another Take-Charge change. Opening it to Psalm 20 will make another Take-Charge change. Opening to Psalm 37 will make another Take-Charge change. Doing things consistent with what the Psalms are saying, through the power of the Holy Spirit, will make all the Take-Charge change in the world.

Let's say that we are anxious, depressed, and angry and are looking for help. We could run to a counselor or a psychologist. We could do something really revolutionary. We could run to Psalm 37, which reads, "Be still before the Lord and wait patiently for Him; do not fret when men succeed in their ways, when they carry out their wicked schemes. Refrain from anger and turn away from rage; do not be anxious, because it leads only to you doing what is wrong."[21] David understands the connection between depression, worry, and anger, and gives us incredible insight into our emotional states.

Using the Bible can change our lives faster than any antidepressant known to man. When we use the Psalms, we understand that we have all the songs that we need. The thing is, we need to listen to them, even when we do not feel like it.

I wish that I could talk with you in person so that I could motivate you to use the Psalms. The more we use the Psalms, the more adept we become at discerning which psalm is right for which occasion. When we are depressed we go to Psalm 20. When we are anxious we go to Psalm 37. When we want to see the contrast between those who follow God and those who do not, we go to Psalm 1. When we want to see the significance of enemies in our lives, we can go almost anywhere in the Psalms. This is about living the abundant life God wants for us. This is about living a Take-Charge life. Moses said it best: "I have set before you life and death, blessings and curses. Now choose life, so that you and your children may live."[22]

What about us? Will we choose life, or will we choose death? Will we choose blessing, or will we choose cursing? Will we choose depression, anger, anxiety, and fear, or will we reflect the love, joy, and peace of Jesus? Will we luxuriate in self-pity? Will we keep playing the old songs of darkness and despair? Or will we be sons and daughters of Light, living out of the glory of God? Will we consistently open our Bibles to Psalm 20, Psalm 19, Psalm 37, or any other psalm, and apply to our lives all that God is revealing to us in these songs of life?

Many of us feel that our voice is not good enough to actually sing the Psalms, or we do not have music to go with the Psalms. We can at least read them aloud. When we do that, it will make a tremendous difference in our lives and in the lives of others around us. It is time for us to turn off the old songs and begin playing the new ones. As the Bibles teaches, "God's power gives us everything we need for a godly Take-Charge life."[23] Let's go and live it.

Let us use what God has for us! We must "*make every effort* to add to our faith, goodness; and to our goodness, knowledge; and to our knowledge, self-control; and to our self-control, endurance; and to our endurance, uprightness; and to our uprightness, kindness; and to our kindness, love."[24] We need to make that choice to get out from under feelings and thoughts that wound and crush us. We need to make every effort to use and appreciate the gifts that God has given us. We are sons and daughters of Light. It is time to Take-Charge of our lives by living in that light!

TAKE-CHARGE ACTION INITIATIVES

1. *What kinds of "songs" have you been listening to recently?*

   _____

   _____

   _____

2. *Do you find it easier to rejoice in the Lord or to immerse yourself in the pain and difficulty of your life? Why?*

   _____

   _____

   _____

   _____

3. *Have you ever sung any psalms or at least read them out loud? If so, what was your experience? Did you find it helpful? If so, how? If you have not done this, are you willing to give it a try? If not, why not?*

   _____

   _____

   _____

4. *What does God promise to do when you call out to Him for help?*

   _____

   _____

   _____

5. *What excuses do you use for not reading the Bible and praying?*

   _____

   _____

   _____

6. *In what ways do you rejoice in what God has done in your life?*

    _____

    _____

    _____

PART FIVE

The
Mentality
of a Take-Charge Life

18

The Power Of Thinking In A Take-Charge Life

A spiritual battle is taking place for your mind. Your thoughts (the words and ideas in your mind) have incredible power to either disable you or empower you. As you live a Take-Charge life, you can choose even how to think!

The Bible teaches that "those of us who belong to Jesus have decisively killed everything connected with living selfishly and self-servingly, which includes even our most cherished lusts and desires."[1] As we take this idea seriously, our lives are changed. We are being taught that we are capable NOW of successfully exercising self-mastery in order to Take-Charge of our lives.

It is a well-known fact that there is tremendous power in thinking. The Bible tells us that "as a man thinks in his heart, that is what he is."[2] We need to consider that statement! When we think something, that is what we are. We have the amazing power to determine what we are, but that power depends upon what we think. We can choose to think accurately or inaccurately. We can choose to think in ways that empower us or in ways that disable us.

What would happen to an Olympic athlete who gets into the swimming pool to compete and thinks, *I can't win today?* We know the answer. He probably won't!

Think about a time when you heard someone say something about you that you did not like, and you allowed yourself to become unsettled about it until you were affected in negative ways. Think also about a time when you compared yourself to another person, thought you came up short, and gave up trying to improve. Think again, now about the time when you tried something new, failed at it, and said to yourself, *I'll never be able to do that. There is no point in even trying anymore.*

We have all thought negative thoughts about ourselves and other people. Some of us spend years thinking negative thoughts about ourselves, other people, and life in general. Here is a new thought: *We do not have to think negative thoughts.* We can Take-Charge even over the thoughts we have!

What kinds of thoughts should we allow ourselves to think? The answer is clear. We need to think accurately. Amazingly, the Bible tells us what such thinking looks like. It tells us, "Whatever is true, whatever is noble, whatever is right, whatever is pure, whatever is lovely, whatever is admirable, the most excellent and the most beautiful, these are the things you are to think about."[3]

We need to be clear about the fact that this verse does not say, "Whatever is false, whatever is demeaning, whatever is wrong, whatever is impure, whatever is ugly, whatever is despicable—if anything is imperfect or destructive—think about these things." The Bible makes it clear that we must not think in this manner.

When we are around people who have a very positive outlook on life, what happens? How do we feel? We know that we are influenced in a positive way. Their happiness and joy is infectious. We enjoy being with them. In contrast, people who have negative thoughts about everything and who are miserable and complaining all the time, also influence us. Our culture has coined a term for these people. We call them "downers." They are depressing to be around.

We have all heard the expression, "Misery loves company." This is not accurate. It should be: "Misery loves miserable company." A miserable person wants company that is as deeply negative, complaining, or despairing as he is.

When we think accurately according to these truths we have just seen in the Bible, our whole manner of life is changed. It leads to positive, proactive, powerful living. The more we think this way, the more capable we become at thinking and acting well, even in difficult situations. For example, a woman came to me for help about an adulterous relationship in which she was involved. As we talked, I asked her, "How do you feel about ending this relationship?"

"I feel terrible!" she said. "I know it's wrong. I feel miserable, but part of me still wants to be with him."

Later, after she broke off this relationship, I asked her, "Are you glad that you broke it off?"

"Oh yes," she replied. "I was miserable. The process was terribly difficult. But I'm so glad I ended it." She thought accurately, and she acted on that. She did not let her feelings or other pressures be her final determination. This was difficult for her, but she was able to do what she needed to do.

Accurate, Bible-based thinking is always positive, even though it is not always easy. As powerful as it is, such positive Bible-based thinking is not all there is. It is not the end result that we are after. Notice how the passage we just referred to continues: "Whatever we have learned or received or heard or seen—*put it into practice*."[4] God calls us to put the good, positive things we are to think about into action! When we do this, the Bible promises us something wonderful. It goes on to say, "the God of peace will be with you."[5]

Our Bible-based thinking and action leads to God's peace-filled presence both guiding and guarding our lives. This is what He does for us as we Take-Charge of our thought lives.

DISEMPOWERING POWER

Sadly, many of us turn away from accurate biblical thinking. We actually choose to disable ourselves by allowing debilitating thoughts to take up residence in our minds. Let's Take-Charge, even of our minds and our thoughts!

How sad and foolish it is for us to disable ourselves. We do it every day. The results are devastating. Notice just a few things that result from disempowered thinking:

- Teenage sex, drunkenness, and drug use.

- Parents who think about everything but the tragedies they can help to avert. These are the tragedies that are happening right in front of their eyes with their own children.

- Marriage partners whose commitment lasts only until a seductive escape is possible.

- Kids dropping out of school.

- Suicide becoming the leading cause of death in teenagers.

- Families thinking they can buy now and pay later, thus becoming part of the huge debt crisis.

- More and more kids getting involved in witchcraft, occult, and Satanism.

- Loss of the extended family. The elderly becoming viewed as a burden and shoved into nursing homes so that the idea of convenience living can be continued.

‣ The debasement of love through degrading and misogynistic pornographic sex.

The list could go on and on.

We allow what I call "disablers" to enter into our lives every day. These disablers are our debilitating thoughts. They zero in and destroy our days, our lives, and the lives of others as well. They are often the difference between life and death, between doing well in the race of life and dropping out completely. They put us into mental hospitals and at times even destroy us.

We see disablers at work in a disgruntled employee who complains, "Here I am spending my life in this rotten job," instead of Taking-Charge and taking steps to change the job or at least appreciate the fact that he has a job. We see disablers at work in the young person who says, "I'll never get a good job, I might as well just get high with my friends." We see disablers at work in the young girl who says to herself, "Maybe if I sleep with him he'll love me." We see disablers at work in the wife who asks, "Is my marriage really worth saving? What's the use anyway?"

I read a book several years ago written by a prominent coach. He described his work with champion athletes. He described how the play of the top ten internationally ranked tennis stars is close to indistinguishable.

He wondered, "What makes the winning difference between them?" As he researched their habits and their performance, he made a discovery. The difference is not how they actually play on the court—their serves, volleys, speed, footwork, and so on. He figured out that the time they actually spend playing tennis is approximately 10 percent of the time they spend on the court. He realized that the difference between these ten players is not what they do *during* the actual playing time, but what they *think about* on the court between volleys.

This coach has become able to predict with a good degree of accuracy which players will lose their matches and which will win, simply by how they walk back to the line. Some of them walk with their shoulders stooped and their heads down, muttering to themselves. He can visibly see the results of the thoughts that say, *This is no good. Things are really going against me. I'm having a lousy day. I'll never win this match.*

This principle is at work in our lives as well. We feel better, and our attitude improves, when we think accurate positive thoughts instead of negative and disabling thoughts. I have seen this in my life over and over again. I have seen positive or negative thoughts influence the outcomes in my life. I have seen that as I think in my heart, so am I.

For example, I have run a marathon and other long distance races. During these races, it is easy to wrestle with disabling thoughts. Instead of fighting my way to the finish line, I fight my way through disempowering thinking. Instead of my energy being used to run my race, my energy is used to clear my thinking from distracting disabling thoughts. I will find myself thinking, *Why am I doing this? Why am I killing myself? Why don't I just do something else?*

Clearly, such disabling thoughts have never helped me to win a race. These are *my* thoughts. No one else in the entire world is responsible for them. Saying, "I thought that way because so many people were ahead of me in the race," is not a valid excuse. I still could have chosen to think, *I only have so many people to pass before I am in the lead.* I then could have done everything I could to win the race, instead of giving up any hopes of success. If we think we are going to succeed, or if we think we are going to fail, we are right.

A mesmerizing event happened at the 1988 summer Olympics in Seoul, South Korea. A Canadian Olympic diver froze on the high board. Standing up there, she was unable to even move. Suddenly, a diver from the United States climbed up and spoke with her. Only then was she able to dive.

What stopped her from diving in the first place? We know the answer. It was a debilitating thought. Maybe she remembered that she had missed that dive during a practice three weeks earlier. Maybe she was thinking that she might make a fool of herself in front of one billion television viewers around the world. Maybe, as she mentally prepared to do her complex routine, she kept thinking about one particular twist that she had missed two days earlier. Maybe she worried about creating too much of a splash when she entered the water.

What is so amazing is that a *thought*, just a little, tiny thought, came within seconds of ruining everything she had worked so hard to achieve. It is astounding! Just a simple disabling thought, not her ability, nor an Olympic official, stopped her, and would have ruined her had not another thought, spoken to her by another diver, got her moving again.

Maybe we are thinking that thoughts are not really that important or powerful. Think about it! That Olympic diver had done that particular routine over and over, thousands of times. She was not just a six-year-old kid approaching a diving board. She was a world-class diver who could perform her dive perfectly. Her failure was not due to a lack of talent, skill, or ability. Her failure was due to her allowing a disabling, debilitating thought to Take-Charge of her life.

Only one thing makes this diver's situation unique: It happened on international television. It happens all the time in our daily lives, but we often do not realize it. In fact, we are encouraged to disable ourselves. There is a battle for our minds.

THE BATTLE FOR OUR MINDS

For over thirty years, my ministry has focused on people and their problems. Wherever I go, I meet people whose lives have Taken-Charge of them. I have found time and again that their difficulties are caused by inaccurate thinking.

Warren and Jane came to me for counseling after she discovered that he had been having an affair. Warren indicated that he hoped to save his marriage. He then agreed to end the affair. Jane was very pleased with what was taking place in Warren. After several sessions, she mentioned that he was more affectionate and loving than he had been in years.

One day Warren telephoned me. "I know I'm doing what's right, but I am still miserable. I can't control my thoughts about the other woman." His actions had changed; his thoughts had not. He had decided to end his affair, but had never addressed his thinking. His thoughts continued to focus on someone besides his wife. Was it any wonder that he was not living a Take-Charge life?

Mark, a man in his twenties, came to me for a completely different reason than Warren. He desperately wanted to get off of heroin. Before long it became clear that, in spite of his best intentions, his life continued to run roughshod over, and to Take-Charge of, him. He stopped coming for counseling. Before he stopped though, he said, "As much as I want to stop using drugs, part of me is desperate to continue."

Like many of us, Warren and Mark illustrate how thoughts keep us from becoming the Take-Charge men and women God calls us to be. Warren's thoughts and behavior were in conflict. Mark's thinking was contradictory. The Bible addresses this seeming contradiction: "What I do is not the good I want to do; instead, I keep on doing the evil I do not want to do."[6] This thought is continued a few verses later: "I see another law at work in me. It wages war against my mind.

It makes me a prisoner to a law that has me doing what I am not supposed to do."[7]

These statements are not in the Bible to discourage us. Rather, they describe the outer manifestation of our deepest inner struggles—laws that wage war against our minds and seem to be imprisoning us. Notice what is said: "laws . . . waging war against the laws of my mind." The undertone of this battle describes a sense of imprisonment. People everywhere are imprisoned. They are trapped by their thoughts and kept from breaking free in Take-Charge victory. This is a dilemma that is "common to man."[8]

James, the brother of Jesus, writes that our deepest wrongs start in our inner life. Here, in our inner thought life, we are "tempted when, by our own selfish desires, we are dragged away and enticed. Then, the desire gives birth to sin; and sin, when fully acted upon, kills."[9] The Bible indicates that our wrong actions follow our wrong thoughts.

The focus in this passage is on the wrong action. This wrong action is the direct result of wrong thinking. Notice: The lust (inner thought) gives rise to the wrong action (behavior); this behavior leads to death. Death comes when a corrupt thought life is put into action and then wholeheartedly embraced without regards to the consequences. There is an utter refusal to turn from such wrong behavior. At this point, if there is no restoration, death triumphs. To Take-Charge of our lives, we must be ready to fight a deadly enemy. We need the full armor of God.[10] We need as well to be on the alert.[11]

It does not take a great deal of knowledge to realize that if we want to stop the pattern that leads to death, we had better start as soon as possible; we had better start in our minds. We need to stop destructive, unwholesome thinking from the outset.

Unwholesome thoughts compel and propel us in a certain direction. If we allow them to run their course, we will be in terrible danger.

If we do not acknowledge debilitating thoughts for what they are and get rid of them immediately, we will wind up being disempowered and disabled by them.

DEADLY THOUGHTS

When we are honest, we admit that negative, debilitating thoughts lead to improper actions. These thoughts can even lead to death. They seem to hit us with the intensity and speed of an enemy missile. It is not as if we stand in our living room, see a disabling thought coming, and say to ourselves, *Oh, here comes a disabling thought. If I let it in, it is going to make me feel unhappy. I had better avoid it. I had better Take-Charge of it.* This is just not how we think.

In a sense, thoughts can be compared to emotions. Both hit us with power and can easily dominate our lives. Regardless of whether we believe that we have generated our disabling thoughts or that they have come to us from other people, situations, satanic forces, or something we have seen or done, it does not matter. We still experience these thoughts.

Every day we are inundated by thoughts. They come at us from images and words that flash across the television screen. They come at us from workplace conversations, song lyrics, billboards, books, friends, family, and many other sources. Often these words and images revolve around consumerism, greed, lust, violence, power, and improper living. Most of us never stop long enough to evaluate our incoming thoughts. It is so easy to think, *It is just a few words. I can handle it.* We do not realize that over time these images and words become the images and words that dominate how we live.

Have you ever watched a video, and replayed a certain portion of it again and again? Instant replays are quite popular during sporting events. People want to see a certain angle of a play replayed again and again. Likewise, the images and words that enter our minds are replayed over and over.

We often try to resolve the hurts, pains, injustices, and disappointments of our lives. We replay these situations over and over again in our minds, hoping by that process to somehow change them. We cannot change them, because they have already happened. The painful experiences from the past will never be any different. We can only learn from them and move on. Replaying these debilitating thoughts only facilitates these thoughts Taking-Charge of us.

Once we learn how to click off the replay button, we have taken a giant step towards a positive Take-Charge life.

THE POWER OF CHOICE

When I was about ten years old, I chose to watch science-fiction thrillers that played at our neighborhood movie theater on Saturday afternoons. Without fail, I experienced weeks and sometimes even months of terror and nightmares after watching each of those terror-packed films. I still remember a movie about outer space seed pods that took over a town. I even remember the name of the main character in that movie—Kevin McCarthy!

Why did I experience so much fear? Because of the choices I made. These choices are the working out of our thoughts. When we consider our thoughts, it is easy to think that our thoughts, almost as if they are independent of us, possess their own, autonomous power. At times we feel as if we are innocent bystanders watching our thoughts take on a life of their own.

Scientists send giant telescopes into outer space that can film the universe's outer reaches and send back pictures from thousands of light-years away. Researchers discover genetic secrets that enable us to heal diseases that were considered incurable just a few years ago.

Yet very, very few people (scientists included) seem able to exercise mastery over their thoughts.

The quality of the life we live is based upon what we choose to do with our thoughts, day by day, moment by moment. If we choose to think about things that will bring grief, anxiety, fear, or despair into our lives, we know what our experience of life will be. Without question, it will be grievous, anxious, fearful, or despairing.

Very few families today choose to pray and read the Bible each day. Instead of such family-oriented and God-directed patterns, families today sit before their televisions and DVD players watching disturbing shows filled with violence and sex, fear and anger, loneliness and confusion. Would our lives improve if our minds were filled instead with truth from the Bible? It does not take much thought to answer this question. Our lives would be enormously improved if our minds were filled with what is beautiful, true, and good.

We can choose whether or not we will give credibility to our thoughts as they pass through our minds, urging us into certain types of action, while, at the same time, leaving us images in our minds that further represent the thoughts we are thinking. For example, if a man thinks an impure thought, it is dangerous for him. If he continues by portraying the object of his thought in his mind, he is adding to the danger. If he portrays this in terms of impure sexual activity, he has gone even further still. These are the realities of the thought life that have to be watched over.

We can choose whether or not we will listen to these dangerous and negative thoughts, and allow them to damage and disable us, or whether we will empower ourselves and Take-Charge of these negative thoughts. It is all the more difficult to Take-Charge of them when we enjoy them. Nonetheless, it can be done. It is what a Take-Charge life is all about. We have the power to choose upon which thoughts we will focus our attention. We have the power to choose which strong influences of thought and image will influence our actions.

We see this ability to choose operating from the very beginning of our race. We see such an operation of choice demonstrated in the lives of Cain and Abel in the opening chapters of the Bible.[12] Abel was a shepherd who brought portions of meat to sacrifice to God. Cain, Abel's brother and a farmer, brought vegetables instead. When God accepted Abel's offering but not Cain's, Cain became angry and depressed.

God said to Cain, "Why are you angry? Why are you depressed? If you do what is right, you will be accepted. If you do not do what is right, evil is crouching at your door. It desires to take control of you, but you must take control of it instead."[13]

God did not wait for Cain to answer after asking these two questions. He did not give Cain an opportunity to whine and complain, "You didn't accept my sacrifice, God. You like my brother better than me." Instead, God got right to the heart of the issue. He said in effect, "Take-Charge of your life. Do what is right, and you will be happy!"

Cain did not listen to God. He wallowed in self-pity and filled himself with bitterness. It was not long before Cain killed his brother Abel. His murderous behavior did not just materialize from thin air. It began with Cain's thoughts, in which he saw himself as a victim. He considered himself to have received unfair treatment from God. He became jealous of his brother. Cain's thoughts led him to choose terribly evil actions.

Cain refused to exercise mastery over the situation and to Take-Charge of his anger and his self-pity. He let his thoughts and emotions Take-Charge of him. The result is murder.

The fact that we can Take-Charge of our thoughts is very exciting. This power to Take-Charge of our minds is the ultimate practice of self-mastery. As we obey God, as we think and act according to His guidelines, we can exercise joy no matter how difficult our circumstances may be.

Moses, the leader of Israel, fully understood how vitally important it is to choose godly thought patterns. He said to the people:

> Now what I am commanding you today is not too difficult for you or beyond your reach. It is not up in heaven, so that you have to ask, "Who will ascend into heaven to get it and proclaim it to us so we may obey it?" Nor is it beyond the sea. . . . No, the word is very near you; it is in your mouth and in your heart so you may be able to obey it. See, I set before you today life and prosperity, death and destruction. I command you today to love the Lord your God, to walk in His ways, and to keep His commandments, decrees and laws. . . . This day I call heaven and earth as witnesses against you that I have set before you life and death, blessings and curses. *Now choose life, so that you and your children may live* and that you may love the Lord your God, listen to His voice, and hold fast to Him. For the Lord is your life, and He will give you many years in the land he swore to give to your fathers, Abraham, Isaac and Jacob.[14]

There is no question that, in the ultimate sense, to "choose life" is to commit ourselves wholeheartedly to God. Many who think they have chosen life lack joy and peace. They have not understood that choosing life has meaning for TODAY as well as for eternity.

Right thinking brings the peace of God.[15] Right action brings the God of peace.[16] From Genesis through to Revelation, the Bible calls us to a life of joy. We need to learn how to Take-Charge of the wrongs, the fears, the doubts, and the failures in our lives. As we Take-Charge of our minds, we will see changes in us that we never thought or dreamed were possible.

We often fail to appreciate that the decisions we make TODAY with our thoughts will affect our lives, both today and for years afterward. We need to choose what will bring us freedom and life. We need to learn never to choose what will bring us slavery and death. The mental chaos that rules this world is not meant to rule our minds and our lives. We possess the mind of Christ.[17] "The mind of those given over to evil is death. The mind set on the Spirit is life and peace."[18]

We can Take-Charge of our disabling thoughts and choose life. The pattern of godly living involves Take-Charge determination. Each of us can Take-Charge of our minds (thoughts), and in so doing, win the battle for our lives!

TAKE-CHARGE ACTION INITIATIVES

1. *What disabling thoughts have you allowed to keep you from a Take-Charge life?*

   _____

   _____

   _____

2. *What impact have these disabling thoughts had on your life? On the lives of others?*

   _____

   _____

   _____

   _____

   _____

3. *Describe a time when a positive thought turned a difficult experience into a better one.*

   _____

   _____

   _____

   _____

4. *What choices are you making to put accurate, Bible-based thoughts into your mind?*

_____

_____

_____

5. *What choices are you making that allow bad and corrupt thoughts to take root in your mind? What are you doing to Take-Charge and move from bad thoughts and actions to good thoughts and actions?*

_____

_____

_____

19

HOW TO CHANGE YOUR THINKING IN A TAKE-CHARGE LIFE

Take-Charge of your thoughts! This is your responsibility! Only you can confront your disabling thoughts, take them captive, and replace them with Take-Charge thoughts that honor and exalt God.

When disabling thoughts hit us hard, we reel from the impact. Instead of acknowledging them for what they are and getting rid of them immediately, we allow ourselves to be disabled by them. Do we have to go through life unable to Take-Charge of our disabling thoughts? No!

In the previous chapter, I wrote about how the science-fiction thrillers I watched as a child terrified me and gave me nightmares. Those experiences of terror taught me a very valuable lesson: If I did not watch that kind of movie, I did not experience that kind of terror. In a childlike way, I was learning what the Bible teaches: "As a man thinks in his heart, so he is."[1]

How do we do this? How do we Take-Charge of our disabling thoughts?

PRINCIPLE 1: TAKE-CHARGE

How we think is pivotal in a Take-Charge life, because we never act independently of our thoughts. The amazing reality is that we have the ability to Take-Charge of our thoughts. Even though most of us do not realize it, we possess a kind of control button that allows us to Take-Charge of our thoughts.

Remember how God told Cain to Take-Charge of his thoughts and focus on the right things? Cain chose to think about the wrong things. It has been said that an adult has 50,000 thoughts every day, and that 80 percent of them are negative. Think about what our life is like if 80 percent of our time is spent in negativity! In spite of this dire assessment, we have the ability to Take-Charge of our thoughts. Cain chose to focus on his anger and jealousy. "As a man thinks in his heart, so is he." What is Cain? Cain is a murderer. Anger and jealousy lead to murder.

We need to ask ourselves a vital question: *Right now, at this very moment, am I willing to admit that I can, with God's help, Take-Charge of my thoughts and think enabling thoughts that are good, true, and beautiful, instead of disabling thoughts that are bad, false, and ugly?*[2] We must Take-Charge of the inner dimension of our life—our thoughts.

PRINCIPLE 2: TAKE-CHARGE FOR LASTING CHANGE

In the Bible, the word "heart" describes the deepest part our being. It is the core of our identity. In order for us to experience a Take-Charge life, our heart must change. In order for our heart to change, it must be changed by God. From out of a changed heart, changed thoughts, attitudes, and behaviors will emerge.

With changed hearts we will live changed lives. Out of our love for Jesus, we will "do what He commands."[3] We do what He commands because living with a new heart makes us want to honor and please

God. Changing our behavior is very important. I want us to understand that. At the same time, however, learning to Take-Charge of our mind involves even more than behavior change. It involves lasting change.

This lasting change enables us to live lives that are like the life of Jesus. It involves our minds, our thoughts, and our hearts as well. Lasting Take-Charge change involves the transformation of our lives. This transformation comes about by the "renewing of our minds."[4]

PRINCIPLE 3: TAKE-CHARGE OF YOUR PROBLEMS

Successful people rarely stumble upon success. Biographies about them reveal that they fail time and again. These biographies also reveal that each time these successful people fail they learn some new, valuable, lesson they can use in the future. The honest examination of our failures is foundational to a deeper and more vibrant Take-Charge life.

We have a choice today. When we experience difficult challenges, we can react to them and think ourselves into the heart of despair every time. We can think, *I am a complete failure. I will never do anything right.* Or we can choose to look forward to the next opportunity, thinking, *I learn from each past mistake and use it for good.*

What, though, are the consequences of saying, "I will never do anything right"? Such a manner of thinking will inevitably move to "I am just no good as a person." This will become "It is not my fault that I am a failure. I have no power over this," which will lead to "Why bother trying? My life will never be anything but failure. Nothing will ever change."

We have all experienced such thoughts. We are all familiar with this train of thinking. We all at times react to situations in this manner. On the other hand, none of us have to get trapped by our disabling thoughts. They do not have to Take-Charge of our minds.

We are capable of banishing thoughts of shame, despair, hopeless-ness, anger, and so on. This is known as Taking-Charge of our thoughts.

Consider Susan. She came for help for a very serious problem. She was deeply troubled by blasphemous, terrifying thoughts that caused her to experience deep self-accusation, paralyzing fear, and despair. "I have these evil thoughts about God," Susan sobbed tear-fully, "and because of them I know I can't be a Christian. I have been thinking that God is waiting to hurl me into hell because of them." As we thought through her situation, we could find no area of known sin that might have led to these thoughts.

Susan longed to be at peace and to have good thoughts. She took action to confront these thoughts and not allow herself to be victim-ized by them. She learned that her thoughts did not have to rule her life. She had given them power. She could now remove that power. That proved to be the end this particular problem in Susan's life. She learned how to put away thoughts which were crippling her and replace them with thoughts which were edifying and uplifting.

PRINCIPLE 4: TAKE-CHARGE
THROUGH EMPOWERED CONFESSION

Susan needed to see that her thoughts were not sovereign. She needed to realize that they did not have to dominate her life. She needed to remember that only God is sovereign. The Bible teaches us how to handle invading and satanic thoughts, when it says, "The weapons we fight with are not worldly weapons. On the contrary, they have God's power connected to them for the purpose of tearing down strongholds. We are tearing down arguments and every element of pride that sets itself up against the knowledge of God. We are taking every thought captive, and making it obedient to Christ,"[5] We are "overcoming evil with good."[6]

It is not enough for Susan to confess her negative thoughts to God and then simply try to think about the right kinds of things. She needs to strive to live a God-pleasing, Take-Charge life. She has to Take-Charge of her thoughts every time they pop into her mind. She has to live by faith, trusting that she can continue to live as a child of God in spite of her disabling thoughts. She has to remember that she has been saved by grace through faith in Jesus. She has to actively repudiate her disabling thoughts and re-evaluate them. She has to regularly confess as sin these thoughts whenever they erupt in her consciousness. She needs to remind herself of her love for God, and God's love for her. She has to overpower and replace any evil thoughts with good and upright ones.

Susan experienced many rotten ideas and thoughts about God. Realizing that fact is quite different from maintaining a belief that she is rotten. It is one thing to say, "Everything I believe about myself as a child of God must be a lie because I think these thoughts." It is quite another thing to say, "I know that I love God. These thoughts can't be trusted because they are alien to what I know myself to be."

We need to ask God to help us when we are troubled by disabling thoughts. We need His help to Take-Charge of our thoughts and guide us in a direction in which our thoughts will honor Him. In His power, we can Take-Charge of disabling thoughts and actually take them captive! While I have already mentioned that confession of sin is not the only thing, it may indeed be both the starting point and the most necessary thing for a Take-Charge life and victory over our thoughts and problems.

PRINCIPLE 5: A TAKE-CHARGE MIND

When dealing with pride and excessive self-concern, the Bible says, "You can have the same mind inside of you which is also in Christ Jesus."[7]

The word translated "mind" means "thoughts" or "attitude." The remedy for the kind of thinking that gets us into terrible trouble is to think like Jesus Christ. In order for us to learn how to deal with attitudes and thought patterns that are deadly, we need to be able to think like Jesus.

Everything in our life revolves around those things upon which we focus our thoughts! The Bible confirms this: "Those who live according to the old ways, are always thinking and planning to do the old things, but those whose thoughts are in accordance with the Spirit, do what the Spirit desires."[8] Each day, we need to ask God to give us the mind and attitude of Jesus. With His mindset, we will be helped to Take-Charge of our life as we think godly thoughts.

Principle 6: A Take-Charge Focus

The Jews involved in the holocaust lost everything. They lost their families. They lost their fortunes. They lost their lives. In spite of the demonic plan to destroy every Jew, some survived. The survivors have testified time and again that in the midst of the cesspool of evil in which they found themselves, they saw, heard, or experienced a thought, word, or image that changed their lives. They said that this thought, word, or image spoke to their souls, turned them around, and even went so far as to produce within them a will to live. One survivor said, "Thoughts make a person free. The Nazis couldn't take away our thoughts."

This is true! We do best when we fill our minds with and think about things that are "true, noble, right, pure, lovely, admirable; the best things, not the worst; the beautiful things, not the ugly; the things that bless, not the things that curse."[9] As we do this, "the God of peace will be with us."[10]

What a contrast there is between words that are *true, noble, right, pure, lovely, admirable, excellent, and beautiful*, and the cruel and ugly thoughts and words that capture the mindset of people today. It is sad to see how many people are more interested in evil than they are in good and beauty. This can only mean that people desire ugliness and pain, because this is the focus of their time and energy.

Will such a focus on the wrong things accomplish any good in our life? Does the Bible encourage misery? No! We have the power to focus on what is good and beautiful, or on what is bleak and ugly. It is our choice. We need to choose well. We need to Take-Charge!

Most of us want our lives to be characterized by what is true, good, and beautiful. The problem is that we want a movie, television show, or how-to formula to accomplish this for us, rather than committing ourselves to training our minds. What the Bible calls a secret,[11] is the teaching that we possess the capability to live a life directed by Bible truths under the power of the Spirit. Only then can we be permanently joy filled and Spirit led. Only then will we hunger to think the right thoughts and flee from dishonorable thoughts.

We need to Take-Charge of our thoughts, developing thought patterns that are true, noble, right, pure, lovely, admirable, excellent, and beautiful. A Take-Charge life is not an easy life. It is not easy to respond in new ways. It is not easy to direct our minds toward new, Bible-based truths. Take heart! God delights in empowering us to Take-Charge and focus our minds on the right things. With time and practice, it will become easier. Take-Charge!

Our Take-Charge experience of life will expand into newly developing frames of reference in our lives. A frame is a boundary for what is placed within it. Our frame of reference is a portrait that is true, lovely, excellent, and beautiful. This is *our* frame of reference. We decide what goes inside the frame! Disabling thoughts might hit us like missiles, but they do not have to stay in our minds! We need never allow them to be part of our *frame* of reference.

God delights in empowering us as we Take-Charge of our thoughts. He loves us so much that He sent His Son to die for us. He promises to be with us no matter what our situation may be. He wants us to be released from a disabled life, which is a consequence of disabled thoughts. He wants us to be transformed by the renewing of our minds.[12]

TAKE-CHARGE ACTION INITIATIVES

1. *What types of situations, relationships, music, videos, and so on trigger disabling thoughts within you?*

   _____

   _____

   _____

   _____

2. *What steps can you take right now to accept responsibility to Take-Charge of your thoughts?*

   _____

   _____

   _____

   _____

3. *The Bible teaches us that when we prayerfully, earnestly, and thankfully present our concerns to God, His peace will guard our hearts and minds. What difference does this truth make in your life?*

   _____

   _____

   _____

   _____

4. *Describe five things you have learned recently from difficult situations.*

_____

_____

_____

_____

_____

5. *Which negative thoughts are disabling you? In what ways are they damaging your life? What do you need to do about them?*

_____

_____

_____

6. *What are the benefits of having your mind focused on what is good, true, etc., instead of focusing on the old, ugly, disabling ways that used to dominate your thoughts and your life?*

_____

_____

_____

7. *As you read Philippians 4:8, how do these words compare to the thoughts you have in your mind at this time?*

_____

_____

_____

20

TAKE-CHARGE
OF ANXIETY

Do not let anxiety tear you to pieces. Do not let your life Take-Charge of you. When you live one day at a time, not only will you triumph over anxiety, but also you will realize that TODAY IS YOUR LIFE.[1] Take-Charge of anxiety and make today count!

For many people, anxiety is a great disabler. It is a pervasive problem that affects people of all ages, socioeconomic groups, and nationalities. The word *anxiety* means "to rip," "to divide," "to tear apart." Anxious people feel as if they are being ripped to pieces.

Anxiety causes us to give up control in the battle for our minds. When we are anxious, we are sick, depressed, tired, joyless, and, in many ways, lifeless. It is impossible to Take-Charge of our life and focus properly if anxiety is tearing us apart and robbing us of joy.

A recent self-help book encourages us to get rid of our anxiety by getting rid of whatever triggers our anxiety. To this end, it even recommends getting rid of our spouse! Is this the way we want to solve our problems? In fact, I could put it this way: *Does* this solve our problems? Should we ever attempt to solve our problems by running away, by destroying relationships, by doing things that are irresponsible?

There is a better way! Knowing how prone we are to worry, Jesus teaches us how to face anxiety. He teaches us the key causes of anxiety and how to deal with them.

CAUSE #1: CONCERNS IN DAILY LIVING

These are difficult times. Some of us do not have even enough food and clothing. It becomes very easy to put all of our energy into obtaining these basic necessities. A life such as this can be filled with anxiety. Imagine what it is like to never know if you are going to have a meal on the table.

Jesus understands that we need all these things. He also recognizes that our greater necessity is to learn how to deal with our needs properly. After saying that God takes care of His people, Jesus asks, "Who of you by worrying can add a single hour to his life? . . . So do not worry, asking, 'What shall we eat?' or 'What shall we drink?' or 'What shall we wear?'"[2] He challenges us to look to Him for what we need rather than being preoccupied with obtaining earthly things that will not last. "I give food and shelter to the birds, and I splendidly clothe the lilies of the fields in beauty. What are they compared to you? Surely I will take care of you. I know you and I love you."[3]

CAUSE #2: CONCERNS FOR THINGS

We see how wonderfully God takes care of our lives. If we truly appreciate His care for our lives, why do we get so anxiety-ridden about the little things in life?

Jesus deals with our concern, as He continues and says, "Unbelievers are frightened that they will not have what they need, so they spend all their energy getting these things, even though your heavenly Father knows that you need them."[4] It is easy for us to always want more and more material things. It is easy for us to be anxious when we do not have everything we think we need. In these days of easy consumer credit, we know what happens to people who overextend themselves financially. We know what happens to families when they put more emphasis on obtaining things than on building relationships within the family. We all know people who are anxiety-filled wrecks. Their lives are thoroughly unpleasant. Instead of pursuing "these things," we are to pursue the greater things, the things of the faith.

Cause #3: Concerns about Living Faith

In addition to dealing with our unnecessary concern for things, the passage we quoted above also reveals that we become anxious when we do not really believe in God's unchanging character.[5] In our last point, the concern is the more obvious one. People everywhere are concerned that they will always have enough of the things they think are necessary. The passage deals with a deeper concern as well: The problem of little faith. Even though our heavenly Father knows that we need certain things and is concerned that we have those things, we live as if we must provide everything for ourselves. Let us not forget what the Bible teaches: "If God is for us, who can be against us? He who did not spare His own Son, but gave Him up for us all, will He not also graciously give us all things?"[6] Since this is so, we ought to banish anxiety and live in confidence.

We are to display our trust and our confidence in God. We are to do this at home, at work, and in all of the relationships of our lives. When we do this, anxiety is banished because we cannot live trusting and anxious at the same time. Let's keep anxiety far from us. Our lips should be vessels of praise, not worry.

Cause #4: Concerns Regarding Uncertainties

Another reason we experience anxiety is that we allow our minds to dwell on the future, over which we have little control. We easily become plagued by common worries such as: "Will I have a job next year?" "What if my child becomes terminally ill?" "What if I am involved in an accident?" "What if I get sick and can't work?" "What if my spouse leaves me for someone else?"

The Bible's teaching remains clear. Jesus says, "Seek first God's kingdom and His righteousness, and all these things will be given to you as well."[7] Jesus then continues, "Therefore do not worry about tomorrow, for tomorrow will worry about itself. Each day has enough trouble of its own."[8]

Life is much more than food, clothing, shelter, or any material thing. We are to have a distinctly different focus. We are to remember that we live "not by bread alone, but by every word that comes out of the mouth of God."[9]

Regardless of its source, anxiety results in physical and spiritual destruction. It tears us up and consumes us. It robs our time, our attention, our thoughts, and our life. It removes us from the present, in which we can really Take-Charge and experience joy. It moves us into an uncertain future over which we have no control. Anxiety directs us away from the unchanging character of God and toward our frailties. As we behold the beauty and glory of God, we are enabled to Take-Charge of our lives, and live empowered and trust-filled lives.

TAKE-CHARGE OF YOUR ANXIETY

Since no individuals in the world except Adam and Eve before the Fall have known what it is like to have no anxiety, how can we be free from it? Four times Jesus told His disciples to have no anxiety: "Do not be anxious about your life,"[10] "Who of you by being anxious can add a single hour to his life?"[11] "Do not be anxious,"[12] "Do not be anxious about tomorrow."[13] There is no other subject in the Bible that is dealt with four times in such a short passage.

Anxiety is a serious problem. Jesus has a very simple point: STOP IT! He is saying that anxiety is wrong. It will not help us. It displays a lack of true faith and confidence in God. Anxiety robs us of living a Take-Charge life.

As we saw earlier, anxiety means to be "distracted," "divided," or "torn apart." It makes sense then, that living without anxiety means being single-focused, single-purposed. Once we have done everything we can to accomplish that which God has set before us, we must not be weighed down and burdened by a problem we cannot solve at a given time. Instead, we must focus on God. He made us, and in our creation endowed us with meaning and significance. He desires to care for us and meet our needs.

We do not have to become anxious about whether or not we can keep all the details of our lives running smoothly. Life is filled with difficulties. God provides during the good times as well as the bad.

Jesus makes it clear that nothing we do will add a single moment to the time allotted for our lives. This means that neither our best thoughts nor our best attitudes—certainly not our anxieties—will add a moment to our lives. Our option is simple: Face TODAY with courage and confidence in the freedom and joy of the Lord. Instead of being anxiously consumed with things, trust in God while pursuing a Take-Charge life.

We need to remember that life is more, much more, than anxiously seeking "all these things." This does not mean that we have no interest at all in "these things." It simply means that we are not to live as if this life is all there is. God calls us to pursue a greater faith, a faith rooted in His character.

When we come to faith in God, we know that God knows us personally and loves us. Knowing His love should break the hold that anxiety has on us. Situations that used to be anxiety provoking come to lose their hold on us.

The Bible is not a secret. It is a revelation. It is a manifestation of the presence and person of God. It teaches us about joy and contentment. It says that we can "learn to be content in whatever circumstance we are in. We can know what it is like to be in need. We can know what it is like to have abundance. We can learn the secret of being content in any and every situation; whether we have just had a wonderful meal, or happen to be hungry; whether we live in a land of abundance [such as the U.S. or Canada], or in a land of poverty and famine [such as Ethiopia or Sierra Leone]."[14] What is this secret? "I can do everything through Jesus, because He gives me Take-Charge strength."[15] We are empowered to triumph over anxiety through Jesus.

THE ALTERNATIVE TO ANXIETY

The alternative to anxiety is very simple. We are to live one day at a time. We need to remember that TODAY is our life. We need to remember to make it count. We need to remember that each day has all the trouble we will ever need.

Existentialists distort this concept and say, "Live for today and for the moment, because that is all there is. Nothing has meaning. Neither the future nor the past have any meaning."

The famous sixties folk singer, Joan Baez, came closer to the truth. She sang, "I live one day at a time. I dream one dream at a time. Yesterday is dead and tomorrow is blind, so I live one day at a time."

For us it is to be the same, and yet different. We are to live one day at a time, for God. Living this way keeps us from being anxious during our short, earthly existence. The past is real, and has consequences. The future will one day be real as well. We live between the past and the future. We live TODAY. We are meant to live it in freedom and joy, knowing that God is with us.

Regardless of how we have lived the past, or how we will even live the future, we can be sure of one thing. God has given us *this* moment! God has given us TODAY. If we live for more than this, we are making a mistake, and, in the process, losing today.

There is a story in the Bible about a man who completely fills up his barns with crops, and then makes plans to build bigger barns. He does this because he thinks incorrectly about the future. He says to himself, "I have plenty of good things stored up for many years. I am just going to take life easy. I am going to eat, drink and be merry." This man, who thinks he finds security in larger barns filled with food, is told that he is a fool. God says to him, "This very night your life will be taken from you."[16]

We can never be ready for God today, if we are consumed with the worries of tomorrow. Jonathan Edwards, possibly the greatest theologian from the United States, said, "I will never, ever, do anything now, which I would never do if it was the last hour of my life." He gives us a pattern for living: *Live now as if it were the last moment of your life.*

Antidotes to Anxiety

Let's look at five easy ways to focus our mind on God and not on our anxieties:

- ► *Focus on Today*— "This is the day the Lord has made; let us rejoice and be glad in it."[17] Let us focus on the positive things that are happening in our lives TODAY.

- ► *Focus on Thanksgiving*— "Do not be anxious about anything, but in everything, by prayer, and request, and thanksgiving, present your concerns to God."[18] Let us not forget that it is impossible to be both anxious and thankful at the same time.

- ► *Focus on Truth*— "Whatever is true, whatever is noble, whatever is right, whatever is pure, whatever is lovely, whatever is admirable—if anything is excellent or beautiful—think about such things."[19] Every instant of our thinking is to be like this.

▸ *Focus on Action*— "Whatever you have learned or received or heard from me, or seen in me—put it into practice."[20] Paul wrote this so that we would not just think properly, but so that we would do the right thing as well. God wants us to act responsibly in dealing with every area of our life in which there is anxiety.

▸ *Focus on God*—When our focus is right, "the God of peace" will be with us.[21] We can trust Him when He says that we are to "cast all of our anxieties on Him because He cares for us."[22]

We have a choice today. Will we live the rest of today thankfully? Will we focus our mind on the right things and be upright in our actions? Will we keep God and His promises clearly in mind? Will we Take-Charge of our anxieties and give them over to God? He says that He is glad to carry them for us.

TAKE-CHARGE ACTION INITIATIVES

1. *Which situations tend to make you anxious?*

   _____

   _____

   _____

   Take a few moments right now to talk with God about them.

2. *What actions can you take to help reduce your anxiety?*

   _____

   _____

   _____

   _____

3. *List a few of the things that God has done for you that reveal His loving care for you.*

_____

_____

_____

_____

4. *What Take-Charge changes will you begin to make so that you can focus on the challenges of today instead of worrying about tomorrow?*

_____

_____

_____

5. *If you knew that Jesus was going to return tomorrow, how would you change your life spiritually, physically, emotionally, and materially, TODAY?*

_____

_____

_____

_____

_____

6. *In what ways can you demonstrate a living, Take-Charge, non-anxiety-filled faith, and trust in God on a daily basis?*

_____

_____

_____

2 1

TAKE-CHARGE
WORD POWER

*The words you think and speak are powerful. You can
Take-Charge of every word you speak. Choose today to
stop using words that are harmful to anyone. Only speak
words that will encourage, uplift, and be gracious.*

We have all heard the statement, "Sticks and stones can break my
bones, but words can never hurt me." The reason that we remember
these words is because we know they are a pack of lies! We know that
some of the worst pain we have ever experienced has come through
people who aimed mean, cruel words at us.

On some level, we all know the power of words. They may not kill,
but they can crush our spirit and destroy us in other ways. The words
we hear and say have a profound impact on the thoughts we think!
Thus, if we are going to Take-Charge of our thoughts, we also need to
Take-Charge of our words.

THE RIGHT WORDS

The right words can motivate a team or an army to reach heights
of performance they never thought were possible. For example, in
the Revolutionary War, a badly outnumbered colonial militia had
no bullets to waste. Their commanding officer, Colonel William
Prescott, mobilized, motivated, and directed his men with these

simple, yet enduring words: "Don't fire until you can see the whites of their eyes."

Patrick Henry was one of the colonies' greatest patriots. He was also their greatest orator. He gave one speech that is remembered to this day because of one line in that speech: "*Give me liberty or give me death.*" His speech leaves us with a call to action that has not been surpassed in over 200 years of U.S. history.

In a battle in which General Douglas MacArthur's troops were seriously outnumbered by enemy troops, he ordered a retreat. At the same time as he ordered the retreat, he said these now famous words: "We are not retreating. We are advancing in the opposite direction."

A final military quote comes from the Battle of Pusan in the Korean War, in which U.S. troops were surrounded by an over-whelming number of the North Korean People's Army. The now famous words that led to the holding of the Pusan Perimeter were these: "They've got us on the left, they've got us on the right; they've got us in front, and they've got us behind. They'll never get away this time."

Moving from military to sports produces numerous additional memorable quotations that demonstrate the power and mobilizing quality of words. One will suffice for our purposes. It is from the legendary Vince Lombardi, head coach of the Green Bay Packers. In a sport that conducts itself almost like a war, his words went far to demonstrating the intensity and battle in pro football. He said, "Winning isn't everything. It's the only thing." Imagine being one of his players. You know what you have to do. You are not out there to have a good time. You are out there to win.

Let me end these examples on a more humorous note. The words here are not meant for motivation or mobilization. They simply show us how words can make us glad. There is no better person for this than Yankee Hall of Famer, Yogi Berra. He brought humour to his fans throughout his storied career. After a particularly upsetting loss, he told the press, "This is like déjà-vu all over again!" It seems only fair to let him have the last word about his numerous hysterical quotes. When asked about a lifetime of such hilarious statements, his response was, "I didn't really say everything I said."

THE POWER OF WORDS

Words can soothe a hurt, make someone laugh, and convey deep passion and love. On the other hand, words can completely discourage, defeat, and even disgrace. They can keep reminding us of our seeming failures, weaknesses, and shortcomings.

The Bible recognizes that although it is difficult for us to Take-Charge of our words, it is absolutely possible. Notice: "With our tongue we praise our Lord and Father, and with our tongue we curse men, who have been made in God's likeness. Out of the same mouth come praise and cursing. Dear friends, this should not be. Can both fresh water and salt water flow from the same spring? Can a fig tree bear olives, or a grapevine bear figs? No! Neither can a salt spring produce fresh water."[1] What a clear and honest perspective about the power of our words!

Notice for a moment the power of the *perspective* of our words. When NASA heard that the Apollo 13 space team would probably die from carbon monoxide poisoning, one leader said, "This is going to be NASA's greatest defeat." Another leader said, "This is going to be NASA's finest hour." They were both looking at the same situation, but from entirely different perspectives. The words of one man displayed his despair. The words of the other man displayed his confidence. This man's confidence motivated the entire ground team into a Take-Charge mentality that enabled them to discover the solution to each of the space team's numerous problems.

Our perspective is vital. Our perspective is intimately involved with what we think. What we think will lead to what we say. We must remember that we have the capability to choose our perspective in every situation we face. The words we use demonstrate our thoughts and perspective. They demonstrate whether we have chosen despair or hope, hatred or love, sadness or joy, fear or courage.

Our words though, do more than reflect our perspective, our inner commitments, and our feelings. Our words also help to form the perspective, beliefs, commitments, and lives of everyone who hears them.

Our words have tremendous effects, both on ourselves and others. During World War II, Winston Churchill said, "We have nothing to fear, but fear itself." This of course is not really true. The British people had the powerful Nazi army to fear. However, Churchill's words gave them resolve in the face of fear. Later, Churchill would speak about the possibility of the Nazis taking over Great Britain. His response left no uncertainty. The nation was mobilized when he said, "Never, never, never."

After Pearl Harbor was bombed, Franklin Delanor Roosevelt mobilized the people of the United States with these words: "Today is the day that shall live in infamy." John F. Kennedy, in his inaugural address, said these memorable words: "Ask not what your country can do for you. Ask what you can do for your country."

On September 11, 2001 Todd Beamer was a passenger on Flight 93, when hijackers took over the plane. When he learned the details of what was going on, and realized that the plane was being used as a missile to crash into the Pentagon, he knew exactly what he had to do. After calling his wife to say goodbye, he marshalled the men around him to take over the plane with these few simple words: "Let's roll."

There is no question that these statements are all powerful. Jesus as well uses words to teach, mobilize, and save His people, but He adds a little addendum to His words. Whereas other leaders' words may just motivate, Jesus says that God's word is truth.[2] Therefore, when He says, "Come to Me all you who are weary and burdened down, and I will give you rest,"[3] He means it. He has a real, lasting, and satisfying rest for His people. When He cries out from the cross, "Father, forgive them,"[4] it is full and everlasting forgiveness that He has in mind. When His disciple Stephen is being stoned to death by a mob, and cries out as he lies dying, "Lord, do not hold this sin against them,"[5] he is continuing the very ministry of Jesus.

Our words are significant. That is why the Bible says, "Be careful about what you say. Let nothing bad or dirty come out of your mouth. Say only what is helpful for building up and encouraging people. Make sure that what you say helps them and is a benefit to them."[6]

Words spoken carelessly can be very dangerous. This is why the Bible tells us to think about and use words that are "true, honorable, right, pure, lovely, admirable, excellent and beautiful."[7] In order for us to think and speak in such an encouraging and edifying manner, we need to begin by thinking and speaking these words to ourselves.

Take-Charge of Your Words

We all know that when we sincerely tell someone something beautiful, most often those words lead to an experience that is uplifting and beautiful. Conversely, when we speak words in anger and contempt, we create bitter situations. In both of these situations, the outcome originates from our words.

Just as our thoughts are expressed in our words, our words are expressions of our thoughts. Words help to form thoughts, which have certain actions attached to them. If we entertain happy thoughts, we will likely exhibit numerous actions connected with happiness. Perhaps we will smile, be peaceful, or be generous. If, on the other hand, we entertain angry thoughts, we might gnash our teeth, speak loudly, and use harsh words while clenching our fists.

We have the ability to Take-Charge of our mental and spoken thoughts. If we think and speak rotten words, it is because we have chosen to do so. We must not blame our wrong use of words on other people, or on what they may have done to us. What they have done is their responsibility. We need to recognize that we are responsible for how we think and how we respond.

A Take-Charge Response

We need to ask ourselves why we respond in one way rather than another. As we answer ourselves, we decide, on some level, that a certain response is more beneficial or necessary than another response. This is supported by our beliefs, which affect what we think, and determine what we say. We do not speak just for the sake of producing words. Even people who so monopolize a conversation that the people to whom they speak never get a word in edgewise, also have a purpose. Their purpose may be to silence or intimidate their hearers.

Consider this: If a man believes that a certain woman should be his wife, he will think about her. At a certain point, he will tell her how beautiful she is, how much he loves her, and how he hopes she will marry him. His hope is that she will say yes. Thus, his words are carefully designed to facilitate a desired end, which is that she would say yes. On the other hand, if he comes to her and says, "I think you are ugly and have a horrible personality. Will you marry me?" unless there is something very wrong with her, she will walk away from this man, greatly unimpressed and unsympathetic to his proposal. His statements are bizarre in that they are counter to everything that he says he wants.

We develop certain beliefs that support what we want in a given situation by saying things that will facilitate us getting what we want. What we say, is said so that a certain response will ensue. The presidential candidate who gives a powerful speech, does so with the hope of receiving several moments of thunderous applause. The mother who appeals to her difficult child to change his behavior, hopes that the appeal will be met with, "I'm sorry Mom. I'll do whatever you want." It is amazing how incredibly powerful our words can be in making other people's behavior bend to become what we want it to be.

Countless young girls have had their lives and futures ruined. Young men, with no concern for these girls, convince them with their cold, calculated use of a few words, that sexual intimacy is a direct declaration of their mutual love. We may look at these girls and say, "How could they ever believe a line such as that?" We could also say that they are just being stupid. Their belief though, that they are loved, is met by words, which, on their face value, support such a belief. They are responding to those words regardless of their truth.

Words are powerful. How often we say things we wish we had never said. I can remember something I said to someone thirty years ago, and I still regret that I said it. I wish I could take it back, but I cannot. We so easily believe words that are nothing more than empty, hollow lies, because they are consistent with what we are so desperate to believe. We cannot take back our words and actions that we regret. We cannot take back any action, even if our action was based upon a hope that the words said to us were the answer to our dreams. Not only do we have to be careful with what we say, but we also have to be careful with what we do based upon what we hear. Done carelessly, both lead to disaster and regret.

I am writing this during the Presidential Election year of 2008. I am especially interested in Barak Obama's campaign. My interest lies in his incredibly creative use of words. He speaks about this "generation of change," this "time of hope," and this "age of change." He speaks of the "break with past traditions." Although I have followed him carefully, I do not know what the change he speaks of is all about. His words reflect to me an ability to use words, but with little or no content connected to them. Since he has not spoken of what his changes would look like, I assume that he desires change simply for the sake of change.

This is a masterful stroke on the part of Obama. He is speaking to a nation of people who are not articulate in expressing their desire for change. The only question to be asked of the citizens of the United States is this: Do they really want such a vapid, insubstantial individual whose expertise is with words but not with substantive policy? I could put it in these words: Be careful about what you wish for, because you may get it. Even more importantly, as we listen to the rhetoric of our political leaders we must remember one thing: Words are enormously powerful. The future of the United States may be drastically influenced because of a man's rhetorical and linguistic prowess.

TAKE-CHARGE OF WHAT YOU THINK AND SAY

Habitually wrong ways of responding are not impossible to change. We may object, *I have learned how to think and say things that hurt other people and myself. They leap out of my mind and my mouth before I can do anything about them.*

As difficult as it may seem, our patterns of speaking can be changed. We can do this as we become more and more aware of our thoughts and our words. We can begin to monitor ourselves and even change language that we may have used all our lives. Perhaps a certain situation leaves us wanting to explode with anger. This may take place when a family member is late getting into the car for church, a loud family pulls into the public campground at two in the morning and wakes us up by yelling, or a cab-driver cuts us off in traffic. Instead of letting the anger surge, we need to Take-Charge of our thinking, by saying to ourselves, *This is not worth getting mad about. Which edifying words can I focus on that will help me to be gracious in this difficult situation?*

We need to remember that *situations and circumstances do not make us furious.* A situation or a circumstance is just that, and no more—a situation or a circumstance. We can choose how we will think, speak, and respond to them. A challenging situation does not have to provoke our wrath or our despair. Instead, such circumstances can be stimuli for us to go deeper in developing a positive, Take-Charge attitude and overcoming all the negative circumstances that come our way.

We can change our negative thought and speech patterns. To accomplish this, it is necessary for us to stop making excuses for such negative thoughts and actions in our lives. Making this adjustment can radically alter our lives.

For example, Robert is a fifty-year-old former boxer. Following his boxing career, he became an alcoholic and even came to live on the streets. He began to change his life when he had a very simple thought. He said to himself, "This is killing me." He then poured out his lunch—half a gallon of vodka—on the ground. He further communicated with himself. He said to himself, "I need to help others to make changes in their lives as well." He developed a thirteen-step program that restores one in every three drug abusers or alcoholics as a functioning member of society. It costs only $3,000 per person, per year to operate.

The sign that greets anyone entering Robert's program is, "The day you stop making excuses, that's the day you start a new life." This principle applies to an alcoholic, or to a drug addict. It applies to each of us as well. I am sure we have all wondered why people continue in thinking, saying, and doing things that inevitably destroy them. They draw on a basketful of excuses that allow them to perpetuate all the wrong thoughts, words, and deeds that they are unwilling to change.

Not long ago, I was a guest on a live call-in radio show. A caller asked why he continued to use crack even though he had been through every treatment imaginable and was desperate to stop. "You do not really want to get off crack," I answered, "You like the *idea* of wanting to get off crack. But you like doing crack more than you like never using crack again."

Sad to say, the caller agreed. He was saddened because he had been telling himself that he really wanted to stop using crack. He was frightened to acknowledge to himself just how much he loved the experience of getting high. He was an expert at using words to both excuse and condone his behavior. All I did was press him to see how he had been using these thoughts and words to deceive himself, and others as well.

We need to change our thoughts and words. To accomplish this, we need, first of all, to Take-Charge of what we say to ourselves.

TAKE-CHARGE OF SELF-TALK

Once we commit ourselves to stop using words in our minds and speech that allow us to continue thinking, saying, and doing things that harm us and others, we have made a commendable start. Now let us go further. Let us change what we tell ourselves about our circumstance or situation before we have even entered into it.

For example, Robert remained a drunk as long as he told himself such things as: *I can never win; by drinking I can avoid all the rat-race hassles; I'm not hurting anyone*, and so on. Finally, he used the power of his words in a brand new way that was destined to change his life and the lives of others as well. He asked, *What am I doing with my life?* Then he honestly answered his question. He admitted that he was destroying his life. As he spoke truthfully to himself, Robert was finally able to move away from giving the worst possible meaning to his life's circumstances. He continues to this day to positively impact other people.

Sadly, Robert is a rare example of a person who has learned to Take-Charge of a life that was wildly out of control. He learned what we all need to learn how to do. He learned how to speak to himself truthfully, and act wisely and in the best possible interest for his life. He had broken free of a self-destructive, self-deceptive, lifestyle. Robert also enacted one other thing, to which we will now turn.

TAKE-CHARGE THROUGH REDIRECTION

As we Take-Charge of our thoughts, we change what we tell ourselves. We begin to say encouraging and edifying things to ourselves. Redirecting our words involves using our speech in a new and powerful way that enables us to handle difficult circumstances with power, grace, love, and kindness. Such a redirection invariably helps us to deal with the actuality of a circumstance rather than the subjectivity of it; that is, we deal honestly with the circumstance rather than simply focusing on how we feel in it.

Our feelings are just one part of the total picture of our lives. They are not the total picture. When we learn how to accurately redirect our words, such redirection will always keep us from speaking to ourselves disabling words of pain, rage, bitterness, powerlessness, and defeat. We can instead speak to our own hearts and the hearts of others, bringing the joys of grace and edification.

This is so far removed from our former lives of self-defeat and self-destruction. It is time NOW to embrace the path of grace and edification. There is a way to live that is consistent with a truly gracious and edifying life. It is different than what we often think of how life is meant to be.

Sadly, we rarely live our life to the fullest. Instead, we live as though our main purpose in life is to be true to ourself. One of the most quoted expressions is, "To your own self be true." This expression is not true. I have seen people destroy their lives and their families living out this idea. Even today as I write this, I am faced with a family in just such a crisis. I received a telephone call from a man whose wife of thirty years sat him down and said, "I'm leaving you." Her justification, amongst many things, is a desire to be "true to herself." For this woman, this means getting involved with an attractive musician, while telling herself that her behavior is okay because she deserves this.

Our purpose is never to be true to self. Our purpose is to *die* to self.[8] This involves putting to death any negative, destructive, disabling, or disempowering thoughts and words that come to our consciousness. When we redirect our words during the times we are caught up in swirls of powerful emotion, our words can become a language of love and edification. Our new language meets all the needs of our circumstances, and will actually be gracious and helpful to those who hear us. We can create new experiences for ourselves if we let ourselves experience things in new ways. When we do this, we will find that we are building others and ourselves up, and providing grace as it is needed, moment by moment.

TAKE-CHARGE IMITATION

Several years ago, I was in Europe doing counseling seminars. The driver of the car I was riding in unintentionally blocked the view of a woman in another car who intended to make a turn. Although we spoke a different language, we did not need an interpreter. She was cursing at my driver a mile a minute. The veins on her neck bulged, and she glared with hatred as the words tumbled out of her mouth. What happened next was very interesting. As the driver of my car looked at her, he smiled and graciously shrugged his shoulders. In an instant, her demeanor changed. She returned his smile as she drove off.

This illustrates what redirecting our words can accomplish. The woman in the other car was disarmed by my driver's smile, and could not help but return it. Earlier, she had probably imitated drivers who had been rude and nasty to her. Now she was courteous, even though at first she had responded both angrily and rudely. It is even possible that this new pattern of response manifested itself in the next difficult situation she faced while driving. Perhaps it even spread to situations where she was not driving, such as at work or at home. At the most basic level, though, we know two things about this interaction. First of all, a gracious response changed the direction of her response. Secondly, she replaced her rage by imitating the behavior of my driver.

Imitation gets bad publicity. People like to think that they have no need to imitate anyone else. This is ridiculous. Great athletes, great actors, and great preachers model themselves continually after greatness. How often as parents we are either excited or depressed at how our children imitate both our good and bad behaviors.

Jesus calls us to imitate Him. Notice the pattern of imitation. It is not His style of dress. It is not the way He walks. It is not His diet. We read, "Be imitators of God. Therefore, since we are dearly loved as children, live a life of love *just as Christ loved us* and gave everything of Himself for us. Let us love like that."[9] This is the type of Take-Charge action-oriented initiative that is meant to be the standard of our imitation. It is the love of Jesus. Just imagine how glorious our life will be as we live with a Take-Charge Christ-like love.

TAKE-CHARGE WORDS

Let us consider some words Jesus left for us as models to imitate.

- ▸ "*Blessed* are the merciful, for they will be shown mercy."[10]

- ▸ "Seek first His *kingdom* and His *righteousness*."[11]

- ▸ "*Follow Me.*"[12]

- ▸ "I tell you the *truth.*"[13]

- ▸ "I have come to bring you life in *abundance.*"[14]

- ▸ "I am the way and the truth and the *life.*"[15]

- ▸ "Father, *forgive* them."[16]

When we compare the words of Jesus to our own words, we are compelled to ask a few questions: What is the focus of our thoughts and our words? What kinds of thoughts, emotions, and attitudes do our words create in us? What kinds of thoughts, emotions, and attitudes do our words create in others to whom we speak? Have we, by our words, encouraged and demonstrated a Take-Charge life, both in us and in others?

TAKE-CHARGE OF YOUR EXPERIENCE

We have all heard the expression, "I want that word out of your vocabulary." Why? People understand the powerful impact that words have in our lives. We need to redirect our words both in our minds and in our speech. Such redirection of our words helps us to attain the encouraging and edifying speech we long to be part of our lives. We come to see, for example, how a kind word from us can go a long way in changing someone else's experience as well as our own. As we redirect our words, we will be redirecting our interpretation of our experiences.

We want to Take-Charge of our lives and see others Take-Charge of their lives. To do this, let us remember to never stop short of Taking-Charge of our words. It is great to Take-Charge of our thoughts. Let us put this into action as we Take-Charge of our words as well. As we work on our words, we may begin to realize just how many of our words are negative and corrupt. These words that we think and say, influence every aspect of our lives—our feelings, our thoughts, our behavior, and how we experience our circumstances.

I love the opportunity to teach my seminars. Almost always I experience a wave of nausea before I speak. I interpret this as part of the excitement that accompanies the work I do. Other people who experience this same nausea call it dread and terror, and choose not to speak publicly. What is the difference between our responses? It does not seem to be our experience, because we both have the same experience. The difference is our interpretation *of* the experience. There is a big difference between "I can't wait to ..." and "I can't stand to. ..."

In the movie *The Sound of Music*, one of the songs centers around Maria's fears. Julie Andrews, as Maria, sings about her "favorite things," and the song ends with this line: "Then I don't feel so bad." Not many of us are public speakers, but we all experience many things that make us "feel so bad." Some of these things may even make us feel the deep-gut nausea I just mentioned. When we experience that feeling, what do we do? Do our words reflect how badly we feel, thus reinforcing our worst feelings? Or do we just redirect our words so that we experience greater empowerment in our lives?

The Greek word *peirazo* means "trial," "temptation," or "test." The precise meaning of the word depends on the context in which it is used. For example, the same situation can be a temptation, leading us into sin; or it can be a test that we pass with flying colors. Most of us see our circumstances in terms of the worst possible scenario. We focus our thoughts on troubles and worries, rarely thinking about our blessings.

Words can make or break our lives. When we use words with wisdom, even a single word can have a radical impact. A single word can change the course of history.

Notice this in an example from the Bible. Moses introduced the Old Covenant with these words: "This is the blood of the covenant."[17] When Jesus ate the Last Supper, He introduced the New Covenant saying, "This is *My* blood of the New Covenant."[18] Two little changes, and "all the old things have passed away; everything has become new."[19] Such a small change, yet nothing has been the same since!

I am sure we all agree that our words have tremendous power. We need to consciously and deliberately have a Take-Charge attitude about our words. We need to employ words that edify, encourage, and empower.

TAKE-CHARGE ACTION INITIATIVES

1. *Describe a time when you used words to make someone laugh or be encouraged.*

   _____

   _____

   _____

   How did you feel about that time later?

   _____

   _____

2. *List several people whose words have had great influence on you. For each person, list at least one word from them, and describe the impact it had on you.*

   _____

   _____

   _____

3. *Which situations tend to particularly irritate you?*

_____

_____

_____

What can you do to redirect your thoughts and words when these situations occur?

_____

_____

_____

4. *Take a few moments and write down what you are thinking and saying about yourself (and others) that is false, evil, ugly, and will ultimately tear you down or hurt other people. List three kinds of situations where you have used such language. What specific changes could you have made in each one of those circumstances?*

_____

_____

_____

_____

_____

_____

5. *In what ways should you be "an imitator of God"? For each one, list how you can put this into practice.*

_____

_____

_____

_____

22

A COMMITTED
TAKE-CHARGE LIFE

As you Take-Charge of your life, determine how your commitments toward God, other people, and yourself are meant to be lived out. Deal uprightly with all thoughts, actions, and conflicts that need to be corrected. Follow the leadership of those who already live Take-Charge lives and who are willing to help you Take-Charge of your life.

Living a Take-Charge life is never easy. Distractions come. We are tempted to listen to "old songs." People let us down. We feel we are not progressing fast enough. We are still hit with negative thoughts. We are still discouraged at times. Even so, we are still living a Take-Charge life as we discover new, godly ways to live.

As we live a Take-Charge life, we can expect obstacles to be in our path. We must determine that we will not let them stop us. God continues to empower us to do the right thing in our lives. He helps us attain the new goals He gives us. He loves, comforts, and aids us in all our circumstances.

The following three guidelines help us to persist in a long-term Take-Charge approach to life.

1. Take-Charge of Your Commitments

Effective business leaders know the importance of clarifying their core commitments—excellence, integrity, service, and so on. This awareness of core commitments is sadly lacking, and is desperately needed, in our homes, families, and nation. Many people have little idea of what their core commitments really are, and do not understand the significance of those commitments.

As believers, we are committed to Jesus Christ. What does that commitment mean? How does it influence our personal commitments to ourselves and others?

For example, if we are married, our commitment is to our spouse. What does that mean when the relationship becomes strained? Recently, I counseled a married couple considering separation. The wife felt that her husband did not love her, did not care for her, and was not committed to her. I asked the husband to write out a statement of his commitment to his wife in concrete terms. He wrote out specific commitments that he could fulfill each day. Statement after statement flowed onto the page. His list was an example of how marriages can be reignited.

We need to understand our commitments. Are we willing to pursue our commitments in an honorable way? Are we willing to strive to meet these commitments consistently in God's power and wisdom? These commitments not only strengthen businesses, marriages, and nations, they radically affect our life as well.

Our commitments are absolutely unique. No one else will ever be committed in the same way to the people, purposes, and priorities to which we are committed.

Our commitment as believers means that we bring the truth, love, and mercy of Jesus into every area of our life. It means that we are prepared to do the right things in the right ways, on a personal level, and in every relationship in our life. It means that not only do we have the Bible, but that we are prepared as well to use the Bible as our standard for a Take-Charge life. As part of a God honoring Take-Charge life, we will endeavor to faithfully carry out every good and noble commitment to which we have set our hearts and minds. Sometimes, these commitments are tested to the limit. How do we handle this difficulty?

2. Take-Charge and Restore Your Commitments

We need to evaluate our core commitments. We need to then determine to be the kind of person God wants us to be. Our path is beginning to unfold. We must both own and Take-Charge of our commitments. As we will see, we also need something to help us when we do not meet these commitments. We will not always hit the mark we are aiming at, but we can keep trying for it.

Notice how this works. Bill is a master at making commitments that he hopes to keep, but he finds himself failing in spite of his best efforts. He wants to speak kindly to his wife, yet he responds with harshness. Should Bill give up on his commitment because of his failures? Absolutely not! He made the right commitment, even though he continues to fail at it. What can he do?

Admit the Wrong

Bill needs to admit and own up to his wrong behavior and his continuing failure to correct it. This is an incredibly important starting place.

Confess the Wrong

The next step is never easy. Not only should Bill own up to what he has done, he should deal with it. Bill needs to confess both to God and to his wife that he continues to speak improperly to her. He needs to then ask forgiveness, both from God and his wife. He has wronged them. He should not justify his failure and rationalize it away, or deny it. When people notice his wrong behavior and address it, he should not be angry with them. He should realize that they care enough about him to want to help him change his behavior for the better.

We need to ask forgiveness whether we feel like it or not. When we do the wrong thing, we need to make it right. The Bible says, "If we confess our sins, God is faithful and just. He will forgive us and cleanse us from all the wrong things we do."[1]

CORRECT THE WRONG

As important as confession and forgiveness is, it is not the final step. Bill needs to correct what is wrong. It is not enough for Bill to be sorrowful for his treatment of his wife. He needs to turn from his improper and inappropriate thoughts, words, and actions and reverse his direction by pursuing what is good, right, and true.

Such correction, called repentance, involves a change of heart and mind. A Take-Charge life turns away from what is wrong and heads off in the opposite direction towards what is good.

Sadly, many people have the wrong idea of what this correction is all about. Harold came to me after he had already left politics. While he was in politics, Harold had gone to a resort area and solicited a man at the resort for homosexual purposes. The man he chose, however, was an undercover police officer involved in a sting operation. The resulting publicity destroyed Harold's political career, and threatened to destroy his personal life as well.

I asked Harold if he recognized his homosexual behavior as sin. He answered, "Yes," so I asked him if he repented of this sin. "Absolutely," he stated. "There's no question that I have repented of it." However, as we continued speaking, I realized that he was not going to stop his homosexual behavior. I realized that when Harold said

"I repent," what he really meant was, "I am so, so, sorry that I got caught, and I will never let myself get caught again."

What Harold meant by "repentance" was that he would be more careful about not getting caught, not that he would change his thinking and his behavior. He remained committed to his homosexual lifestyle. Rather than learning how to relate in a godly way to men and women, and replace his sinful patterns of thinking and behavior with what is good and right, he wanted to continue these encounters without getting caught.

As I write this, the state of New York is reeling from the results of a recent politically motivated sex sting operation. Unlike the example I just mentioned above, this one has had national significance in the United States. The object of the sting operation was Eliot Switzer, the governor of New York. Until this sting occurred, Switzer was being touted as a possible democratic candidate for the vice presidency. A banking institution had been concerned about large sums of money being funnelled into a high-priced escort service.

It turned out that over the last ten years Switzer has spent close to eighty thousand dollars on high-priced prostitutes. I watched him at a press conference, as he stood with his wife at his side. What most affected me was what he said: "I want to apologize to my wife and three daughters for my behavior." I waited for something else to follow. Nothing did. There was no sorrow, there were no tears. He was apologizing as if he had done nothing more than accidently spill some coffee on his wife's dress. He had betrayed the trust of his family and the state he served in its most powerful political position, and was content to simply say, "I apologize."

It is also remarkable to me that in the numerous television and newspaper stories about this event, not one that I saw or read mentioned anything about this thoroughly inadequate apology. This shows us something. Even at the highest levels of political power, most people have almost no understanding of how to either honor our commitments or restore them when they are broken.

Barbara Walters, host of the popular daytime talk show "The View," weighed in on the situation. She said, in effect, "If there was a choice between my husband being emotionally involved with a woman or going to a prostitute, I would choose him going to the prostitute." While I do not have the exact quote, this is what I remember to be the essence of her comment. It shows the plight of our nation. We have nothing to gauge right and wrong. We have no way to determine how to live. It is difficult to engage in the process of correcting our thoughts, words, and actions. We often do not even realize how wrong they may be. We need to return to absolutes if we have *any* desire to correct what is wrong in our lives and in our culture.

Let me give you one final example. Yesterday, I was asked to counsel a couple that is in the process of getting a divorce. As we talked, it came to light that another pastor had learned of their situation second or third hand. He began telling people in his congregation all kinds of things about their divorce. The husband involved told me that what this pastor was saying was incorrect, so he called him to speak to him about this. He said to me that what amazed him was that the pastor said six times to him, "I apologize." Never once though, did he ask his forgiveness for saying things that could have hindered the possibilities of reconciliation. He also never, by his actions or his words, indicated that his interest was to correct or restore this broken relationship.

Talk is cheap. If our words are not meant to build up, restore, or be gracious, they probably should not be spoken. Whether it is in our government, or our church, or our families, or our marriages, it seems as if we have very little understanding about how to make things right.

Thankfully, there is an answer for the terrible failures in which we often find ourselves engaged. True Take-Charge repentance involves more than making an apology. It is also more than being sorry. True Take-Charge repentance involves an active turning away from what we should not be doing, and instead choosing the right path. It involves actively turning away from the habitual patterns that have been destroying our life and harming others as well. It involves the deliberate replacement of what is wrong with what is right.

True Take-Charge repentance is most clearly seen when there is a need for restitution. In these cases, it is not enough to say, "I'm sorry," or even, "Forgive me." If a person has stolen from you and says he is repentant, then he is willing to pay back to you all that is necessary to right the wrong that he has committed. In the Bible, there is a man whose life is touched by Jesus. After Jesus frees this man from his enslavement to money, the first thing the man says is, "I will pay back fourfold to anyone I have wronged."[2] Restitution shows that we are serious about our commitments.

Take-Charge repentance leaves us transparent. We are no longer hiding or rationalizing. We have set the tone for a new way of living. We are telling ourselves that the wrong behaviors that have dominated our lives "will not be our master."[3] We are not saying that we will never again do wrong. Rather, we are saying that our lives are no longer going to be dominated by such behavior. We have found the Light at the end of a dark tunnel, and we are persistently heading in that direction. We do not give up when we reach an impasse. Instead, we keep bringing our wrong behavior to God, and repenting of it.

We do not have to remain in our sins. "Sin is no longer our master."[4] Our sins no longer have control over us. Our life no longer has to be dominated by sin. We now have the Take-Charge power, given to us by God, to resist the pull of evil. With God ruling our lives, we are enabled and empowered to Take-Charge of all the wrong things we think, say, and do.

Of course, we still do things that are wrong. The Bible tells us that we are liars if we deny this truth. Through forgiveness and repentance, we become more like Jesus. We keep "putting off the old ways of living and putting on new ways of living, which are true and right and holy."[5]

As we seek to live godly Take-Charge lives, we will have to deal with old patterns of thinking and behaving. As we continually choose to acknowledge our sin, ask forgiveness, and repent, we are establishing new response patterns that become easier to live out in time.

Teaching ourselves to employ godly words and actions in order to break habitual sinful patterns of thought and action is a bit like breaking a new trail in the snow on our farm in Canada. This past week, we had snowstorms that left us with four feet of new snow. Added to the snow already on the ground, in some places the snow was over my head. Even to walk out of our house meant breaking through that snow. The first walk through the snow was exhausting, but a slight trail was being made. As I walked over it again and again, the snow packed down and the contours of a little, tiny path became clear. Soon, we had a walkable path. It took many efforts to get the path packed down. So too it is with our habitual sinful patterns. Breaking into them is not easy. They need to be addressed again and again. As we do so, the path becomes easier to travel.

3. Find a Take-Charge Mentor

Many of us were brought up in families where certain negative behaviors were common. We naturally perpetuate these same behaviors because we have never known anyone who did things differently, or anyone who was willing to teach us the right ways of living. We need mentors who can help us learn better ways of living.

As we use the ideas we are learning in this book, remember that very few of us work best alone. It is an immeasurable benefit when we find a gifted, godly person who can help guide us through the difficulties that we encounter and the choices that we make.

For example, not many of us really know the Bible well. We can benefit immensely if we have a good Bible teacher. One of the first needs I recognized in my life as a believer was that I needed to know the Bible better. One of my earliest prayer requests to God was for a good Bible teacher to help me to learn properly.

We all know people who are battling depression and finding it difficult to handle everyday life. These people almost always benefit when they have someone to help them sort out the important issues they are facing.

Through the years, I have realized more and more the importance of having at least one wise, godly person standing beside me. This is a person who believes in me, seeks to know God better, lives a Take-Charge life, and holds me accountable to meet my core commitments. We need to be mentored. We need to be held accountable. We need a coach.

Here is an example of what it is like without a knowledgeable coach. The first time I decided to jog, I laced up a pair of tennis shoes and stepped out into 95 degree heat and what felt like 200 percent humidity. Off I ran at top speed. Even a non-runner can anticipate what happened next. I collapsed within three hundred yards. I had symptoms of heatstroke, as I fell exhausted into a bush filled with poison ivy! My desire was strong, but my knowledge of jogging was weak.

Jogging is not just about taking off down the street. It requires the proper clothing and shoes; warm-up exercises beforehand and cool-down exercises afterwards. Today, three decades after my plunge into the poison ivy, I run six days a week, often doing intervals at a pace of better than six minute miles. Who would have dreamed it possible that I would be a runner at all, let alone a competent runner, after my first running experience left me with heatstroke and covered in poison ivy? As I look back on that pitiable start, I am well aware that my terrible initial experience could easily have been my last running experience. What could have made a difference that first day? I needed someone to guide me and teach me how to run.

Many people never jog again after an initial experience like mine. Similarly, many of us jump into a commitment with an initial burst of enthusiasm. We then stop, discouraged, because of a lack of proper planning and execution. We drop out of these commitments, even though we have read motivational books or attended seminars. How can we guard against this result?

What might I have done differently when I started to jog? I should have thought, *If running is what I want to accomplish, and some people do this well, I need to find a good runner who is able to teach me what running is all about.* I should have learned the principles first before facing unnecessary failure.

Some of us have watched winning athletic teams in a practice session. During each practice, excellent coaches train the team members, showing them exactly what they have to do, and motivating them to excel in doing those things correctly. Every incorrect movement of a player is scrutinized so that team members can correct mistakes, focus on the right actions, and do those actions smoothly and properly, both individually and as a team. Likewise, the church needs its mature members to coach those who are less mature. We all need models who can help hone our skills and help us to live a more successful, God-honoring life.

The Apostle Paul faced many challenges throughout his life. He recognized the value of imitating the right people and pursuing after the right goals. He challenges us to imitate his behavior. He challenges us to "be imitators of God."[6] He further urges us to imitate what is good, lovely, and right.[7]

Was Paul being conceited when he wrote that the only way to obtain the peace of God that passes all understanding is by living a life exactly like his? No. A godly life is not an accident. Paul was trained and taught how to be godly. Sad to say, most people in the church do not learn godliness through the teaching of other believers, but through trial and error. This is wasteful, costly, and dangerous.

A consistent and godly Take-Charge life should be a high priority for us. We need men and women who live this way to help us see what is involved in living such a life of self-mastery. If we are looking right now for someone after whom we can model ourselves in our quest for a godly life, there is no question about the type of person we are seeking. We are not impressed with someone who has great material wealth but whose life is in disarray. We are looking for someone who is successful in handling life's struggles and difficulties with a God-given confidence and a hope. We are looking for someone whose life is filled with the fruit of the Spirit—love, joy, peace, patience, kindness, goodness, faithfulness, gentleness, and self-mastery.[8] These qualities are the inner reality of committed believers. They are available to each of us who trust Jesus.

LIVE A TAKE-CHARGE LIFE

Character transformation is available to all of us. God has given us the power to Take-Charge of our life. We must not sit around waiting to be changed. Love is not what others give us. It is what we give to others. Without loving others, we are always going to feel loveless. If we want a changed life, we must begin by Taking-Charge of our life. We must think and do the things that are joy-filled, love-filled, and so on. We must think of how we can love and serve others rather than how others can love and serve us.

It is possible for us to be filled with joy at all times. As we read, "I have learned to be content in every circumstance I am in."[9] In that same passage, we learn that the *secret* of a Take-Charge life is allowing ourselves to constantly receive strength from God.[10] We are able to Take-Charge of every situation we face in life, and represent it to ourselves in a way that will lead to either joy or despair. The choice is ours. We need never become mired in the muck. Just as we have the power to focus on what is bad, ugly and false, we have the power to focus on what is good, beautiful, and true. This is *our* choice!

If we want to live a Take-Charge life, we need to move in that direction, starting TODAY. We do not have to run away from problems, hoping to find a meaningful life in some haven far removed from reality and trouble. We owe it to ourselves to experience the joy and the blessing of living a Take-Charge life in the face of life's most powerful difficulties.

TAKE-CHARGE ACTION INITIATIVES

1. *List six of your core commitments, one per line:*

   _____

   _____

   _____

   _____

   _____

   _____

2. *Next, write out what you are doing in practical ways to help you live out each core commitment.*

   _____

   _____

   _____

   _____

   _____

   _____

Having done this, are there changes you need to make to your core commitments? If so, what?

_____

_____

_____

3. *Think about your life right now. From whom do you need to ask forgiveness for sinful words or actions?*

_____

_____

_____

_____

4. *Determine the best way to contact each of these people and ask for forgiveness. Please be specific.*

_____

_____

_____

What do you need to do to correct those wrongs?

_____

_____

_____

5. *Why is it important for you to confess your sins to God and man (1 John 1:9), and to ask God to help you to repent as well?*

_____

_____

_____

6. *List three godly character traits you most admire and desire for a Take-Charge life:*

_____

_____

_____

_____

7. *List at least one Take-Charge person who exemplifies each of these traits:*

_____

_____

_____

_____

Go to these people one at a time and speak to them about the trait(s) you would like to develop. Ask them if they are willing to guide you in becoming a Take-Charge person, and becoming more like Jesus. Learn from them. Imitate them. As you apply what you learn from God, the Bible, and these godly people, your life will change!

PART SIX

The
Extent
of a Take-Charge Life

23

A TAKE-CHARGE
LIFE EXAMPLE

You have been given everything necessary to live a Take-Charge life. When you open your eyes, you can see just who you are meant to be, what you are meant to be, and what you are meant to do. You need to open your eyes, get going, and live.

Most of us make New Year's resolutions. How long do our resolutions usually last? I had an experience at the gym the other day that helped me to answer that question. I noticed that although the year is less than a month old, a number of people who had recently joined the gym had already given up and quit. They had joined, wanting to get into shape, or wanting to lose weight, or wanting to get a black belt, or wanting to learn how to fight, but they left anyway.

Later that day, I thought back to when I had joined the gym over five years ago, also right after New Year's. Shortly after I had joined, an instructor at the gym told me that only a few of us who had joined in the New Year would still be attending by the end of the year. In fact, by the end of that year, this particular instructor was no longer working at the gym.

Today, five years later, as I think about the instructor's comments, I have just heard a fascinating interview on the radio. This interview was conducted by the well-known sports show host Jim Rome. He was interviewing Jim MacLaren, who had been a top student at Yale

University and a star on the university football team. Jim seemed destined for a wonderful life. Then, while he was on a training run through the streets of New Haven, he was hit by a bus. His injuries were so severe that his leg had to be amputated.

Jim did not give up. He recovered from his injury and returned to sports, becoming a successful marathon and Ironman competitor. He beat most of the "able-bodied" athletes, and began setting records. Then, while riding a bicycle during his training for an Ironman Triathlon competition, he was hit by a truck and left a quadriplegic.

During the ensuing two years of rehab in the hospital, Jim determined that he would somehow survive this catastrophe. Instead, after he left the hospital he wound up becoming a cocaine addict. It did not seem that he would survive. At this point, Jim decided that he had no reason to live. He was rushed to the hospital in a coma.

When Jim came out of the coma, he knew that he had a huge decision facing him. It was *the decision of whether to live or to die.* He decided that as ruined as his life seemed to be, *life* was still better than non-life. When Jim Rome asked him what happened that made him change his outlook, he replied, "*I chose to live.*"

Jim MacLaren went on to say that every day of his life starts with him receiving four hours of specialized care, just to go to the washroom and have himself prepared for the day. Nevertheless, he realizes that his life is a gift.

Jim has come to see that TODAY is truly a gift, no matter how terrible his afflictions may be. No matter how he feels, no matter how painful the day is (Jim says that his body feels like a truck filled with wet cement), no matter how horrible the pain or the torment may be, he is going to Take-Charge of his life TODAY. Whatever else might come to pass, he will live TODAY fully. Through this mindset, Jim has come to realize that his enjoyment of life is not dependent upon him having the use of his body. What he realizes instead, is that *the enjoyment of his life is dependent upon him having that life to enjoy!* He has come to see that as long as he is alive, he has reason to rejoice and enjoy his life NOW!

In the interview, Jim Rome asked, "If you could receive a pill that could make you like you were *before* the accidents, would you take it?" Jim MacLaren responded, "NEVER." He went on to describe how the blessings he has received as a quadriplegic mean more to him than being able-bodied. He explained that there is more to life than walking. When Jim asked him to describe some of those blessings, he replied, "People talk to me. They tell me their stories. They know that when I ask them, 'How are you doing?' that I really want to know. People tell me about themselves, and I get to know people because of this." What an attitude of gratitude!

GETTING ON IN LIFE

Think about this from our perspective. People like us have every advantage. We have everything necessary to do just about anything we want to do. Yet so often we wind up like the people from the gym I mentioned earlier. We sign up for life, and then, after a month, we quit. Why? How is it that we can see just who we are meant to be, what we are meant to be, and what we are meant to do, and then still just pretend? What is it that we pretend? We pretend anything. We pretend anything we want to pretend, anything we can pretend, anything at all, as long as we do not have to ever try to be what we are meant to be.

Let me put this another way: Why is it that our life shows so little progress? Notice that I am not saying it is our "work" life, or our "spiritual" life, manifesting meager results. It is our *life*, in its totality, which is either meager or magnificent. It is our life which is meant to be a manifestation of God's work in our heart. It is our life which is meant to be magnificent. What then about the progress we desire to see in our life?

When we learn how to Take-Charge of our life, progress will show itself in *every* way. Attempting to Take-Charge of our life should not be done by seeking to change one area alone. We need to appreciate that every area of our life is intimately related to every other area of our life. We will never have the blessing God desires for us if we break ourselves up into tiny little pieces, each piece to be worked on separately.

Think again about Jim MacLaren. What if he had let the meaning of his life be determined by his ability to use his arms or his legs? The answer is obvious. His life would have been rendered meaningless. There was no unbroken part of him except his head. In fact, coming out of the hospital and seeing himself as a collection of broken, useless parts, left him thinking that suicide was his only option.

Then Jim came to see the bigger picture. He came to see that life is more than arms or legs, walking or running, playing football or winning triathlons. He came to see that life is about living TODAY. From that point on, he understood that his life is more than any single aspect of his life. His life is more than the mastery, or victory, that even the highly successful use of the parts of his body can ever bring to his life.

CHANGE AND PROGRESS

We should not expect to see just a part of our lives grow. We will grow or we will shrink. Growth and progress reveals growth and progress in every area of our lives.

At the same time, this progress is never all or nothing. Jim went through despair. Jim considered suicide. It was through immense, blinding darkness, that Jim began to see what life is all about. We will never see all that we hope to see all at once. Why not? Because often, only after darkness is there light. This is the kind of principle Jesus calls us to live by, when He says, "I am the Light of the world.

If you follow Me, you will not be stumbling through the darkness, because you will have the light that leads to life."[1] Jesus is speaking about movement from darkness to the light. This should be the movement of our lives.

Please use the acronym that we looked at earlier. The simple idea of GISI-DICI helps us to have a Take-Charge life. We need to remember it.

Gradual Improvement, Steady Improvement!
Daily Improvement, Constant Improvement!

The problem we have is that we want instead: Immediate Improvement, Total Improvement; Instant Change, Rapid Change. When we do not get what we want, we quit. We become like Jim MacLaren when he thought life was hopeless. The only difference for us is that we have more ability to move around and run away from the pain. Instead of accepting a formula for success, we adopt a guaranteed formula for failure.

This is why so few people make any real progress in almost any area of their life. A Take-Charge life demands consistent and progressive effort in order to bring about consistent and progressive growth. GISI-DICI is a tool to help us remember not to despair when the improvements in our lives are more gradual than we would like. That is the way of life. We become expert at something by taking small steps, and consistently practicing over time.

As we increasingly Take-Charge of our life, we will experience the growth and joy we so passionately long for. The "quick fix" has never been, nor ever will be, the answer. It has not worked for us in the past. It will not work for us now. I am suggesting something so much better. I am suggesting a Take-Charge life. If we walk away from Taking-Charge of our life, our life will invariably Take-Charge of us.

TAKE-CHARGE ACTION INITIATIVES

1. *If your resolutions do not last long, what accounts for such a failure to accomplish what you resolved?*

   _____

   _____

   _____

2. *What was most important in helping Jim MacLaren determine to not give up and die when he had already determined that he no longer had anything worth living for?*

   _____

   _____

   _____

3. *How do you think that you would respond to such tragedy in your own life? What resources might you have to get you through such a disaster?*

   _____

   _____

   _____

4. *How can you begin TODAY to look at your life as a whole, instead of breaking it up into tiny little pieces?*

   _____

   _____

   _____

5. *How can TODAY be a Take-Charge day for YOU?*

   _____

   _____

   _____

24

A Principled Take-Charge Life

When you choose life in Jesus Christ, you are choosing full and abundant life TODAY. You are choosing your best life, NOW and FOREVER!

We need to ask ourselves if we really believe it when Jesus says, "It is through the most terrible difficulties that you will enter the Kingdom of God."[1] There is no mistaking it. All of us, at one time or another, face the "terrible difficulties" that Jesus is talking about. We are not alone in life's struggles. Jesus told us that He "will never leave us or abandon us."[2]

When we speak of life's terrible difficulties, it is helpful to reflect again upon the life of Jim MacLaren. It is reasonable for us to wonder, "How does a man who is a quadriplegic and not a believer in Jesus, live a life that is closer to biblical truth than most of us ever live?" One thing stood out for me in Jim Rome's interview. It was when Jim MacLaren said that he "made a choice." He made a commitment and "chose life"! Life is what it is all about. It is certainly what it is all about to those of us who follow Jesus Christ. To choose life is the heart of our commitment to Jesus, who said, "I have come so that you would all have life in all its fullness."[3]

From our heart commitment to choose life in Jesus, other commitments flow. We must consider what we need to help us make the commitments for our life to be what they are meant to be. The answer is surprising in its simplicity, as we are once again reminded to *choose life*. Choose life TODAY. Choose the abundant life Jesus died to give us. Choose this life, by choosing Jesus Christ. Real life, the full and abundant life in Jesus, begins with a choice, a commitment to Jesus, a trust in Jesus and in all that Jesus has done for us.

Once our commitment to Jesus is settled, our choice does not end. Day by day, we actually have the opportunity to choose to live the abundant Take-Charge life He offers us. It is a tragic choice that so many of us make day by day to neglect the abundance that is ours in Jesus. Jesus promises us our best life NOW, and our best life EVER, *now*. As Jesus keeps this promise, it is something that can help us experience the best in life, and the best life, if we take His promise to heart.

In Jim Rome's interview, Jim MacLaren said something very interesting. He said, "We are all in wheelchairs." He may not have understood the full implications of what he said, but he is right. Sin has crippled all of us. None of us live as we should. None of us measure up to what we are meant to be. None of us in our own strength can ever hope to regain the use of our faculties that have been devastated by the explosion of sin that has broken us in pieces. We *do not* live as we should. We *do not* love as we should.

This though, is not where we end. We are not to conclude on a note of sin-broken uselessness and helplessness. Not at all! Our hope is not simply to be taken up with God when we leave these broken-down bodies and lives. We have a present hope that "cannot possibly disappoint us now."[4]

This present hope will strengthen and refresh us, especially as we work through and implement the Take-Charge life giving principles in this book. As we get ready to conclude our journey together, let me leave you with a goodbye gift: SEVEN TAKE-CHARGE PRINCI-PLES that will never fail you in the trials and struggles of your life.

As we come to these principles, let us not forget that we live at a time when people realize the enormous benefits of coaching. We have coaches for sports, coaches for acting, coaches for business, etc. I have heard that the NFL Washington Redskins have 53 paid coaches on their team! I am hoping this book has been a coaching manual for you. In fact, it is my desire for you to see this book as a new type of coaching venue: *Coaching for life*. This is the most important coaching you may ever receive, because *this is your life. These are your principles*. Keep them in mind, and you will be well on your way to an honorable, well-lived, Take-Charge life.

These principles will not keep you *from* trouble. They will though, help get you *out* of trouble. They will though, help get you *through* the trouble. All you have to do is to be willing to use them *in* the trouble.

1. KEEP YOUR FOCUS

Our attention is always given over to that upon which we focus. We must not forget that *we can only focus on one thing at a time*. If we want God to be real and significant in our lives, we must make Him our focus. We must learn to look to God and be interested in Him. Jesus says, "The food and drink that nourishes Me day after day, is to do My Father's will. After all, He sent Me here, and I agreed to come. How can I possibly just go My own way?"[5] Then He says, as He faces the cross, "It is not what I want to do that is uppermost in My heart, but what You, My Father, desire for Me to do."[6]

This is what it means to focus on God. This is how a Take-Charge life should be lived. If we want to eradicate the distress we experience as we face the difficulties and troubles that assault us, we should be looking to God and be focused on God. We will always have troubles and trials. Difficulties will consume us if we let them. We need to determine to make God the focus of our life.

A.W. Tozer says, "As we begin to focus upon God, the things of the Spirit will take shape before our inner eyes." Just as the sailor locates his position on the sea by focusing on the sun or the North star, we get our moral bearings by focusing on God.

Once we have made the determination that our focus is on God, we, like Jesus, have decided to do God's will. How do we do this?

2. DELIGHT YOURSELF IN THE WORD

It is not sufficient to know *about* the Bible. We have to *know* the Bible. We have to *study* the Bible. We have to *read* the Bible *regularly*. We have to *meditate* on the Bible, absorbing what is being said *in the Bible*. As we do this, we ask: 1. *What does this mean for my life?* 2. *How can this lead me into a changed, Take-Charge life?* We are reading, studying, and meditating on the Bible in order to see our lives changed in this manner. We want to be changed Take-Charge people.

This is no different than anything else. We use our skills to change things. Likewise, we use the Bible to help change *us*. This happens as we apply what we are learning as we read the Bible. For example, when the Bible says, "I am giving you a new command, to love one another,"[7] we need to ask, *What does this mean for me?* We remember that the essence of biblical love involves the giving and sacrificing of ourselves. It involves opening our hearts and our lives to those around us, so that we might lovingly aide them in some way.

The Bible speaks with life-changing power. Notice: "I have hidden Your word in my heart so that I will not sin against You."[8] "I will not neglect Your word."[9] "I will obey Your word."[10] "Strengthen me according to Your word."[11] "Preserve my life according to Your word."[12] "I trust in Your word."[13] "I have put my hope in Your word."[14] "Your word, O Lord, is eternal."[15] "Your word is a lamp to my feet and a light to my path. Direct my footsteps according to Your word, so that no sin rules over me."[16] "Give me understanding according to Your word."[17]

Here, in just one chapter of the Bible, is a snapshot of the significance and the importance of the Bible as a change agent for our lives. It can change us when it is part of our lives because it is right, it is true, it is instructional, it is eternal, it is strengthening. It helps us become pure. It keeps sin from dominating us. It increases our understanding of all that we will ever face. It gives light to our paths. It helps us to distinguish between a good path and a corrupt path. It flawlessly reveals the person and character of God. It possesses all of His direction for us.

If we want the life the Bible speaks about, we need to take time to read the Bible, and to challenge ourselves while we are reading it. We need to ask ourselves if we are living according to the standards that are presented in the Bible. These standards are high, but we can reach them when our heart and life is submitted to and focused on, not just the Word of God, but also applying His Word to our life.

3. Strength Through Prayer

Prayer is tough. It is tough for strong believers. It is incredibly tough for the weaker ones. When we are strong in prayer, we are STRONG, because we are "near to God." A strong life of prayer keeps us near to God.

Many of us want a strong Take-Charge life without prayer. People often say they are too busy to pray. A vibrant life needs vibrant prayer. Homer Hodge puts it this way: "Prayer should be the breath of our breathing, the thought of our thinking, the soul of our feeling, the life of our living, the sound of our hearing, and the growth of our growing. Prayer is length without end, width without bounds, height without top, depth without bottom; limitless in its breadth, exhaustless in height, fathomless in depth, infinite in extension." E.M. Bounds writes that prayer "is the secret of the saints' power. By prayer, the ability is secured to feel the law of love, to speak according to the law of love, to do everything in harmony with the law of love."

If we desire to live a Take-Charge life, it needs to be a consistent life. We need to choose the right things again and again in our lives. We need to acknowledge our need for God's help, and that we even need His help to make the right choice. We need to pray. The Bible says, "Pray regularly. Be devoted to prayer. Wrestle in prayer. Keep praying."[18]

A.W. Tozer says that "those who want to know God must give time to Him." Why? Tozer goes on to say, "We are called to an everlasting preoccupation with Him." To be strong, powerful, and victorious, we need to keep on praying. After decades of missionary frustration, William Carey said, "Prayer, secret, fervent, believing prayer, lies at the root of all personal godliness."

4. Deal Quickly With Sin

The more that we honestly come before God in prayer, the more it reveals our weaknesses, our shortcomings, our pride, our arrogance, our flaws, and our blindness. Prayer is a starting point in experiencing dynamic change in our life. When we see what we need to change, we need to make these changes immediately. We need to resist taking even a moment to defend, justify, or rationalize what is wrong in our lives.

If we want to avoid dealing with the unsatisfying, unsettling, and sinful areas of our lives, we always will. If we would rather have a life filled with personal conquest over what is wrong, what is unsatisfying, what is mediocre, and what is revolting, then we need to live boldly and Take-Charge of every area in our life that needs change. We need to acknowledge and deal with every area of deficiency speedily.

Every second that we permit sin to have power in our lives (and that means ANY sin) enables those areas to grow stronger and more difficult to eradicate. It is all too easy to let ourselves think that our weak and passionless faith is not our fault. It is always convenient and easy to blame our spouse, our pastor, our colleagues, our children, or our friends for our difficulties.

We must not blame our lethargic lives on anyone or anything other than ourselves. We really need to look at, and Take-Charge of, ourselves. We need to look at our own life, not someone else's. As Jesus says, "Why are you worrying about a speck in your friend's eye, when you have a log in your own eye? How can you think of saying, 'Let me help you get rid of that speck in your eye,' when you can't see past the log in your own eye?"[19]

If we are concerned about wrongdoing, we need to look first at ourselves before we jump on and correct others. We need to take heed to ourselves. We need to deal with ourselves. There is no one else on the face of the earth that can do this for us. We need to Take-Charge of ourselves.

The following is an example of one man who went from living in the depths of despair to the heights of worldly success. While worldly success is not our goal, the way in which he accomplished his success is both revealing and helpful. Listen to Robert Ringer's account.

I have often said that the difference between success and failure is much smaller than most people might suspect. For example, a right or wrong turn in the road can sometimes be the deciding factor in a person's life. But there are many other things that can be responsible for that small difference as well.

Experience has taught me that one factor, in particular, plays a major role in how one's life turns out. The factor I am referring to is *synchronicity*—achieving long-term success by getting all areas of your life in synch.

When I was in my late twenties, I found myself at the bottom of a very deep financial ravine. No income ... no friends ... no connections ... no prospects ... and living on a Ryder truck! Those were pretty grim times.

I haven't been asked about those dark days for many years, but early in my career as a bestselling author, a number of television talk-show hosts inquired about my climb from the financial abyss to fame and fortune.

I vividly recall one of my appearances on *The Merv Griffin Show*, when *Merv* (who, by the way, was a great guy and a fabulous interviewer) asked me, "How in the world did you go from living on a Ryder truck to a sprawling beach-front home in Malibu?"

It was the first time I had ever publicly discussed the gory details of my miraculous turnaround, and my answer was direct. I explained to Merv that by selling off some of my furniture and other belongings that were on the truck, I was able to raise enough money to move into a seedy little apartment.

Surprisingly, I have fond memories of that wretched little abode, because it's where I bottomed out. I not only was broke, I was grossly overweight, I was out of shape, and I had no real plan for changing things.

Then, one night, I fell asleep on the floor in front of my black-and-white television set. When I awoke, I did something that puzzles me to this day: I tried to do a pushup ... just one little pushup. It was an impulsive act, but an act that turned out to be a major turning point in my life.

Notwithstanding my youth, I could not push myself up off the floor... not even once! I cannot tell you what an impact that had on my psyche. The next step, I thought to myself, was a heart attack ... followed by a trip to the poor folks' cemetery.

With great effort, I managed to get up off the floor and onto my feet. Then, as though I were on autopilot, I walked to the bathroom, turned on the light, and looked in the mirror. To put it mildly, I did not like what I saw staring back at me. Truly, it was an epiphany moment in my life.

I was immediately conscious of the fact that the guy in the mirror was responsible for my predicament. There was not a question in my mind that he was the one who had destroyed my life.

Sure, there were a lot of unscrupulous characters along the way who had added to my misery, but they were nothing more than enablers. The sorry soul in the mirror was the one who had always been at the controls.

I then did something that forever changed my life: I ran my right index finger over a bar of soap that was on the sink, then made an X with it on the mirror—*right through my face*. It was a symbolic act, meant to signify that I was striking the Robert Ringer in the mirror from my life.

That single act opened the door for the *new* Robert Ringer to emerge. While staring at that X on the mirror, I made a vow. It wasn't a vow to get rich. It was a vow that I was going to change *everything* about my life.

It was an instinctive thought. I suddenly realized that the only way I could hope to change *anything* was to change *everything*. And it was the only way I could ever hope to *have* everything — including purpose, prosperity, and peace of mind.

From that point on, through the power of free will, the most important decision I made was to employ relentless self-discipline in everything I did. Self-discipline translates into habits, habits translate into consistency, consistency translates into speed, and speed translates into results.

Everyone experiences a certain degree of success for some length of time. In extreme cases, it may be only for a few days. But when we use the term *successful person*, we are usually referring to someone who has experienced a *high level* of success over a *long period of time*.

Such a person doesn't just do the right thing now and then. Rather, he develops habits that consistently and quickly move him in the right direction.[20]

It took Robert Ringer a lifetime to become fat, unhealthy, impoverished, and hopeless. It took him an instant to begin his turnaround. It would then take a lifetime for him to live out that turnaround. Why? Because changes that are worth making are permanent changes.

For example, the word "diet" for most of us means "a temporary change to eat more properly to lose some weight." Let's face it, that is how people think. We know that because people on diets inevitably fail. This is because diets inevitably fail. People always return to their pre-diet eating habits. They wind up gaining more weight than they lost. What would it be like if we took our diet changes seriously? Let us remember that the word "diet" means "way of life," not, as it does for most people, "die"!

We should never wait until we are hopelessly and helplessly out of shape physically, spiritually, emotionally, and economically. It is much easier to get into shape if you are twenty pounds overweight, than if you are two hundred pounds overweight. Not that it cannot be done, but the principle is obvious: *The sooner you start, the easier it is.* This applies for every area of our life.

Deal quickly with every area that needs to be changed. Remember: God calls us to Take-Charge of ourselves right NOW!

5. Sing Your Way Through Life... (on key, if possible!)

Dealing with areas of personal failure is both difficult and challenging. When we are facing these life challenges, one of the best things we can do is what we rarely do. We can sing. Listen to this song: "When I spoke openly of all my wrongs and did not cover them up, when I said, 'I will confess all these things to the Lord,' an amazing thing happened. You forgave not only all of my sin, but also all of the guilt that had been connected with it."[21]

When we are praying and desiring to live a Take-Charge life near to God, His songs will cover us, protect us, and bring us joy. Listen to this song: "Let us praise God with all our hearts. Let us be happy and rejoice in Him, especially while we are singing praises to His name. Let us not forget, His name is high above the heavens."[22]

These songs are written in the face of trouble and enemies. What do they teach us? They teach us that we can praise God with all our heart, even in the face of overwhelming difficulty.

Such singing inevitably brings rejoicing. This how we should live, instead of letting ourselves get beaten down by every trial that comes our way.

How can we help but be glad when we are singing to God? After all, He is *El Elyon*, the Most High God. He is the God of whom there is none higher. He is the God of ultimate power. That is why we can sing with confidence that "the Lord will take care of us forever."[23] Let us sing and be glad forever. In our "gladness, we can sing joyfully forever,"[24] shouting out all the wonderful things He has done. We can sing "because He has been good to us."[25] We can keep on singing for joy because even though "we were weeping in sorrow-filled darkness, He did not leave us there. Instead, He has taken us and brought us into the morning's light and given us great joy and gladness."[26]

With confidence in our forgiveness in Jesus, we sing and "we rejoice in the Lord and are glad. We are now upright, even in our hearts."[27] This is because, our song goes on, "You are the God who saves me."[28] It comes down to this: We "sing joyfully to the Lord, because this is the right thing for us to do, to praise Him."[29] This is the way we live. Our life is filled with songs from day to day, from dawn to dusk. Let them be beautiful songs such as this: "Awake O my soul, for my soul awakens the dawn."[30]

These songs, which bring rejoicing to our lives, also help us through enormous troubles. We can sing of deliverance even when we are "in the midst of lions, of ravenous beasts, of men whose teeth are as sharp as spears, and whose tongues are as sharp as swords."[31] This is our song, as God helps us through the worst troubles that we could possibly imagine. Even in the adversity, His greatness reminds us that "great is Your love. It reaches as high as heaven, and Your faithfulness to us reaches into the skies."[32]

These songs encourage us as we step out and begin a Take-Charge walk through a dark and hostile world. These songs move our focus from the troubles in our life to the greatness of our God. As we leave a crippling life of sin behind us, we do so with songs of praise to God.

We need to focus on the songs of God, not the songs of this world. The songs of this world are the songs of lostness, of lust, of alienation, of anger, and of greed. God's songs are songs of salvation. They are NEW songs. He tells us to "sing a new song to the Lord."[33] These new songs glory in the abundant life that God gives us. These are songs of salvation. These songs enable us to be more than we are in and of ourselves. These new songs bring us to "God's mercies, which are new every morning."[34] In our new life, we "sing and make music in our hearts to God."[35]

Israel's greatest king, David, sang when he was depressed. It got him through depression. Let us sing when we are depressed. David sang when he was rejoicing. It got him through the high times of life. Let us sing when we are rejoicing.

Singing makes our hearts joyful. It enables us to move beyond ourselves. It enables us to get out of a rut. It enables us to break free from bondage to ourselves. It enables us to move to a better, a higher place, a place where we can behold God. It enables us to Take-Charge of our life, and in so doing, to appreciate that a Take-Charge life of victory does not necessarily change our circumstances. The victory comes as our hearts and our minds remain secure in the face of life's greatest battles.

6. FOCUS ON OTHERS

God calls us to be *other person oriented*, because a Take-Charge life is a life in which we shift our focus from *ourselves to others*. What does this mean? It means that we are not concerned about whether or not people love us. We are concerned that *we* are loving other people. Our focus is not on whether or not people are concerned for *us*, but whether we are concerned for *others*.

Over and over, the Bible says, "Love one another." Of course, this is a blessing for the people we are loving. It is also a blessing for us. Our souls are strengthened as we love others. Our lives are encouraged as we give to others. Our walk with God is deepened as we are concerned to benefit others.

People all around us are hurting, and we can help them. God says, "Love one another."[36] God says, "Pray for one another."[37] God says, "Be devoted to one another."[38] God says, "Accept one another."[39] God says, "Encourage one another."[40] God says, "Serve one another."[41] God says, "Counsel one another."[42] God says, "Always greet one another."[43]

As we can see, a Take-Charge life means that we focus not on ourselves, but on one another.

7. A TAKE-CHARGE FOCUS

The focus of a Take-Charge life is never what God will do for us, because He has *already* done it ALL for us. We need to live out of the perfect and finished life-giving, death-defying work of Jesus. If we really want to Take-Charge of our life, our focus must be, our focus has to be, *How will I let myself be used in the lives of others?* As we think this way, doors of service, windows of opportunity, will, seemingly miraculously, open to us. As we Take-Charge of our life, we will find ourselves not hiding from opportunity, but taking advantage of all the opportunities that come our way.

TAKE-CHARGE ACTION INITIATIVES

1. *How can you start to live a meaningful life, if your life seems to be completely wrecked?*

    _____

    _____

    _____

2. *What is involved in keeping the right focus on God?*

    _____

    _____

    _____

3. *What is involved in a practical study of the Bible? Give some concrete examples from your own study of the Bible.*

    _____

    _____

    _____

    _____

4. *What is the purpose of prayer, and how does prayer help us?*

    _____

    _____

    _____

5. *How does speedy action against the sins in our life benefit us?*
   What are the consequences of letting sin go unchecked?

   _____

   _____

   _____

6. *List every way you can think of in which you have lived the one-*
   another life spoken of in this chapter, this past week.

   _____

   _____

   _____

7. *How do you demonstrate that yours is a Take-Charge life?*

   _____

   _____

   _____

8. *In what specific ways can you be used in the lives of others?*

   _____

   _____

   _____

25

TAKE-CHARGE AND LIVE WITH PASSION

Let your purpose be Jesus. Let your focus be Jesus. Let your starting and ending point be Jesus. Do not compare yourself with your family, friends, or colleagues. Let your only reference point be Jesus.

A Take-Charge life is an active life. We are not sitting around waiting for God to change us. He already has. We jump into life. We TAKE-CHARGE. We act on what we know is true. We want more and more of God. We pursue God vigorously.

Jacob is an example of such a Take-Charge pursuit of God. He wrestled with God and would not let go of God until God blessed him.[1] God's blessing came to Jacob with tremendous pain in Jacob's body. The pain would be a constant reminder of his encounter with God. God touched Jacob's hip, and Jacob walked with a limp for the rest of his life. His encounter with God was costly. Pain followed him every step of his life, for the rest of his life. There is not though, in the ensuing account of Jacob's life, even a hint of regret because of his pursuit of God.

Jacob's passion for God saw him being plucked from a life of grasping what was not his (the name Jacob means "the Grasper"), and bringing him into the gates of splendor. He was now living in the deepest possible fellowship with God.

A.W. Tozer reflects on this when he says that a true follower of Jesus will not ask, "What will it cost me if I embrace this truth?" Rather, he will say, "This is truth. God help me walk in it, let come what may."

Such passion for God, such pursuit of God, is everything. The Bible puts it this way: "As the deer pants for water, so my soul pants for You, O God. My soul thirsts for God, for the living God. When can I go and meet with God?"[2] There is even more: "O God, You are my God. I am passionately seeking for You. My soul is thirsty for You. My body longs for You. Without You, I am in a dry and weary land where there is no water."[3]

Let us consider as well the prophet Elijah. After Elijah performs one of the greatest miracles ever, God provides an extraordinary commentary about him. He says, "Elijah was a man just like you and me."[4] One of the greatest, most powerfully used men in the Bible, is no different than any of us. He just *lives* his life out differently.

One of the things that marks out people such as Elijah is that they deal quickly with the wrongs in their lives. They spend their lives learning more and more about God, and praying faithfully. God is always in the forefront of their lives. They are driven by God-honoring purpose. Billy Sunday, the great evangelist of the nineteenth century, said that "more individuals fail through lack of purpose, than through lack of talent."

The Bible has this to say about purpose: "Whatever purpose my life used to have, whatever profit I used to be able to gain, I consider all of this a loss simply for the sake of Jesus. In fact, I consider everything in my life a loss when I compare it to how incredible it is to know Christ Jesus as my Lord."[5] This knowledge of Jesus gives us a great purpose in life. What is this purpose? The Bible is clear: "*That I may, day by day, gain Jesus.*"[6] Self-interest and self-serving are to be gone from our life.

MAKING OUR FOCUS CLEAR

How do we get to this point in our life? One thing is clear. Our purpose is Jesus. Our focus is Jesus. Our starting and ending point is Jesus. We do not compare ourselves with our families, friends, or colleagues. Our only point of reference is Jesus. We say, "There is only one thing I need to do. I must forget all that is behind me, and strain forward to what is ahead of me. I must Take-Charge of my life with all my strength as I move toward the goal to win the prize for which God has called me heavenward in Christ Jesus."[7]

It is this passion, purpose, and pursuit which grips our heart and empowers us both to serve and to know Jesus. Our desire is to gain Jesus. We do not simply want to be better believers. We want Jesus. We eliminate all that stands in the way of a Take-Charge life. We pray ceaselessly. We study fervently. We minister diligently. We do this because Jesus is the beginning and the end. He is the beginning and the end of all things, our life included.

Perhaps you are wondering: *How can I ever get to that point in my life?* As followers of Jesus, we are all, in principle, at that place of prayer, diligence, and life. The Bible says, "We already have everything we need for an abundant and God centered life."[8] Followers of Jesus have had this life for the past two thousand years. The wonderful surprise is that we can have it NOW. Our life really does not have to Take-Charge of us. We really *can* Take-Charge of our life.

Let us be Take-Charge men and Take-Charge women, and live our lives fully for God. The Bible says that "all of us who are mature should see that we are meant to live Take-Charge lives; that we should live up to the standard that we already know to be true."[9] The Bible is teaching us to *do what we know to be the right thing.*

GET UP AND GET GOING

It is time for us to get up and get out of whatever self-imposed wheelchair we have placed ourselves in. If a man can live abundantly without the use of his hands and feet, arms and legs, how much more should we be grateful for all that we have. Some of us may be worrying about whether we are capable of such an adversity-conquering life. Perhaps we are afraid that it will hurt us. Perhaps we are afraid that it will be too difficult. Dear reader, we need to get up and get out of the wheelchair that we have sat in perhaps our whole life. As believers in Jesus, we can do it. We have everything that is necessary to move ourselves from where we are (mentally, physically, emotionally, spiritually) to where we need to be.

There is a world out there dying without Jesus. Most of this dying world will never, ever possess the personal strength to move when they are feeling that they are nothing more than a truckload of wet cement. They are sitting helplessly mired in the weight of their own despair. They need us! They are waiting for us to demonstrate to them how to move a truckload of wet cement. They are waiting for us to give them real, honest answers for the hell they are living in.

Over thirty years ago, I spoke to a man who came as close to successfully killing himself as it is possible for a man to come. God used me to bring words of life into this man's dead heart. This man came to life. I did not see him again for almost twenty-five years.

One night, while I was praying, God put this man on my heart, and led me to find him and call him. The place where I finally spoke to him was once again in a hospital. This time, it was in a hospital in which he worked. He was not working at the time we spoke, but was being prepared for stomach cancer surgery. The doctors considered his case terminal. He was speechless that I had come to him at a point when he was facing death once again. We prayed together just before he was wheeled into surgery. When we spoke after the surgery, he said he felt as if God's hand was on him, guiding him through the darkness.

One day, several years after that, I received a letter from him. He wrote: "I tell people that I am the poster child for the grace of God. To have gotten that call from you just before my surgery makes me feel like an Old Testament character who has felt the hand of the Lord" (as of this writing, this man is still alive and well).

We have been working together on what a Take-Charge life is all about. The story I just shared with you reflects what is involved in moving from inertia to Take-Charge action. God brings people into our thoughts, into our hearts, into our prayers, into our lives. In some ways, living a Take-Charge life begins with acting on these opportunities that God presents to us, and doing so consistently. These are opportunities that abound for all of us. We just need to open our eyes and be available when God gives us these opportunities. Some of these opportunities may be before us right now.

We do not have to be perfect. We cannot be sinless. We just need to be available. In spite of our sin, our weakness, and our problems, God will use us "beyond all we can ask or even imagine."[10]

TAKE-CHARGE ACTION INITIATIVES

1. *What does God want you to Take-Charge of right NOW?*

_____

_____

_____

_____

_____

2. *Have you ever faced something you believed God wanted you to do, that you felt unable to do? If you did not do it, what did you tell yourself that kept you from doing it? If you did do it, what principles enabled you to accomplish it?*

   _____

   _____

   _____

3. *How do you understand passion for God?*

   _____

   _____

   _____

4. *What are the implications for us if, as the Bible teaches, "Elijah really is a man just like you and me" (James 5:17)?*

   _____

   _____

   _____

5. *What does the Bible say about the purpose of your life?*

   _____

   _____

   _____

6. *In what ways can you Take-Charge of your life for the sake of Jesus Christ (Philippians 4:12)? In what ways can you Take-Charge of your life TODAY ?*

   _____

   _____

   _____

26

A FINAL TAKE-CHARGE CALL

*Stand up and be strong. Break free from any bondage
that enslaves you and leaves you weak and powerless.
Remember that you possess a new life filled with power
and blessing. Take-Charge of that life, and live it in the
freedom of the sons and daughters of God.*

Wake up! This is the last word. I hope that you have enjoyed this
journey with me into a Take-Charge life. This is your call to "wake up
and put on your strength."[1]

Living out of strength rather than weakness and powerlessness
often seems impossible to most of us. We cannot imagine that we
have the power to "advance from strength to strength."[2] God tells us
to put on our strength. He wants us to be strong. He wants us to wake
up from a sleep that keeps us from seeing things as they are. He wants
us to wake up from lives that are being destroyed because of how we
are living. Instead of tottering around, God wants us to "rise up from
the dust"[3] and Take-Charge of our life.

We are to stand up and be strong, but that is not all. God tells us to
do more than just stand up. He says, "Get up out of the dust, shake it
off, and remove the slave chains from around your necks."[4] He wants
us to rouse ourselves, and break free from the bondage that has left
us weak and powerless.

BREAK THE CHAINS

God wants us to Take-Charge of our life and remove the chains that keep us in slavery. God asks us why, since we have new lives in Him, do we live like drunken, foolish slaves who are bound and chained.

It is sin that leads to slavery. This slavery is doing the very things that are most horrible and destructive for us. Amazingly, the Bible tells us that "we are no longer slaves to sin."[5] The question is: If we are no longer slaves to sin, why are we still living like slaves? Why do we stay bound?

We live powerlessly because we strongly believe that we have no power over the habits that have controlled us for years. This is not true. God calls us to *get up!* This *getting up* does not take a lifetime to accomplish. It takes only as long as it takes to shake off the stupor and to break the chains. A Take-Charge life can be accomplished in an instant, and further accomplished in every instant after that.

We can live Take-Charge lives, even as we deal with things that have strangleholds on us. These destructive patterns of living do not have to be seen as if they are some malady that afflicts us and leaves us hopelessly out of control. It is not that way at all.

Everything we do that is wrong can be changed in an instant. God expects us to change these things in order to accomplish an upright Take-Charge life.

STAND UP WITH STRENGTH

How are we able to stand up, and break the power of the destructive thought, word, and deed habit patterns in our life? The Bible presents a rather ominous sounding idea, when it says that "we should consider ourselves dead to sin and alive to God."[6] If this is the case, if it is really possible to consider ourselves *dead* to everything that has us chained, what are the implications for us? We cannot let ourselves stay self-pityingly wallowing in destructive-strewn and damage-filled lives. We have to Take-Charge by shaking the sleep out of our eyes and standing up.

We can do this. The Bible is clear that we do not have to let "corrupt behavior control the way we live, nor do we have to give in to our old way of life."[7]

We are not meant to be naïve. There are always going to be powerful desires hitting us, trying to knock us off our feet. We do not have to give in to those desires. We do not have to believe the lie we tell ourselves: "Oh, I can't do anything about it. I might as well give in now." This is just not true. The Bible makes it clear that we are "not to let a single part of our body be used for anything at all that is wrong."[8]

We want God to live an upright life through us. We want God to live our new life for us. We often think, *God, work it all out for us. You gave this new life to us, now work it out for us.*[9] He says instead, "Work it out *yourself*, and be careful as you do it. Remember that I am working in you all the time for you to both desire and to do these things, and to accomplish them for Me."[10]

We are radically new men and women. We can now live uprightly. We have the power to say *no* to what is wrong and *yes* to what is right.

What is this radically new life? The Bible says that it is "giving ourselves over completely to God, because we have been given a completely new life."[11] God does not want to hold us back from anything that He has for us. He does not want to keep anything back from us. We have a new life that is given by Him. He has given us a new power in that life. He wants us to use the power of our new life for Him. He wants us to live a Take-Charge life.

We become complacent in living out of our new life, because we know that God has done everything for us. This attitude becomes dangerous when we come to live a genie-in-the-bottle kind of life. We say, "God, do this for me. God, change me. God, don't let me do this anymore." God not only expects us to *know* what is right, He expects us to *do* what is right.

The Bible goes on to say that "sin is no longer our master."[12] Do we realize that? Do we understand that we are not controlled by a lust or a frenzy to do the wrong kinds of things? Even though we still do the wrongs things at times, we are not in slavery to the rotten and corrupt things of life. In our old life, before we believed in Jesus, we could not help but do the things that God hated. It is hard for us to comprehend that our lives were so much less than we ever realized.

The Power to Please God

Now our lives are different. Now we have the power to do all that pleases God. We have "everything necessary for living the right kind of life."[13] All we have to do is remember who we are and what we have been given, and use it all to the glory of God.

We can break the chains that are choking us. "God's grace has made us free."[14] We are free, not simply from an oppressor like Russia or China, but from a far greater oppressor. We are free from the oppressive power of evil.

This freedom that we have been given by God means that we have the power to not sin. Perhaps that is a new thought for us. *We have the power to not sin*. That is incredible! Every time we are confronted with a temptation or a sinful possibility, we have the power to say *no* to sin and *yes* to God. *We* have that power. We must not make excuses for ourselves. We must not justify ourselves. We must not rationalize away the rotten things we do. We must change them. We can do this because we have the power to do what is right. This is who we are. Let's live this way. Let's live Take-Charge lives.

Many of us, at one time or another, ask ourselves, "How can I go on living such a miserable life? God has given me a new life."[15] The Bible answers this question by saying that "whatever we *choose* to obey, this is what becomes our master."[16] The Bible says that we have a choice when it comes to masters. We can choose life or we can choose death. If we choose a life that is destructive and corrupt, we are going to die. There is no way around it. We can delude ourselves as long as we want, but such delusional power will not change things one bit. It does not matter how good our rationalizations, justifications, and denials are. We are dead. If we choose the momentary *pleasures* of such a life, we are dead.

God says we do not have to choose a corrupt and destructive way of life. He says that because we "know Him and have been redeemed by Him,"[17] "*we can choose to obey Him.*"[18] This is what is so incredible about knowing God. We no longer have to live in defiant opposition to Him. We now have a choice. We can *choose* to obey Him.

LET YOUR ATTITUDE BE GRATITUDE

What should our response be to His gift of such a God-favoring choice to us? "We can be thankful."[19] We can be grateful. We need not be angry with God because He keeps us from the things that are going to kill us. I do not know how many times we all have said how angry we are with God because He has taken something from us to which we are really attached. In fact, what He has taken is often so deadly that it will kill us. Even though we know just how deadly these things are, often we do not care, because we like them so much.

Let me illustrate this. Our oldest grandson is not yet two years old. Two young men were working at our home today with chainsaws. While my wife and I were walking with our grandson, he stopped to look at one of the chainsaws. He went over to touch it. We immediately moved his hand, and gave him his play saw, which he did not want and refused to take. Instead, I watched him get angry with us for not letting him play with a deadly chainsaw. He could not imagine that this appealing "toy" was deadly. It looked so inviting.

We often do not see things as they really are. This is what I am talking about. We play with things that look so appealing, and yet are deadly. God keeps us from being destroyed, while we get angry at what is nothing other than His mercy.

What should our response be when we loosen our grip on the things that hold us and are destructive to us? Let us thank God for that. Let us not be angry at God because He has kept us from things that are deadly. He reminds us that "once we were slaves of all these deadly things. Since we were in such slavery, we were living in filth,"[20] but not any longer. Now we are living Take-Charge lives.

Recently, in a counseling session, the man I was counseling paused to reflect on his now long past adulteries. What made this situation so unusual is that I had counseled him at that time as well. He and his family were being getting torn to pieces. At *that* time, he hoped that somehow I would be sympathetic to him and say, "Dear boy, it's okay. It's okay."

By God's grace, this man got out of that terrible, deadly life. As he reflected back on this period of his life, he said, "I never had a guilt-free moment during the entire time. Every moment was misery, but I wanted her anyway." This is a good definition of sin. *It was horrible. It was guilt-full, but I wanted it anyway.*

This above definition is in agreement with the Bible's teaching, when it says: "In those days you were slaves of sin. You were not concerned with doing what is right. What was the result? It was not good. Now you are ashamed of the things you used to do, things that end in eternal doom for you."[21] When we see the wrongs that we have done, what are we to do? We thank God for our ability to see what is wrong, and we do the right thing.

God has a Take-Charge word for us from heaven. His message is: *GET UP!*[22] *Be what you are supposed to be*. We are to be what we are supposed to be.

WHAT WE ARE SUPPOSED TO BE

What are we supposed to be? We are supposed to be living a Take-Charge life that is united to Jesus. His life is our life. In this Take-Charge life, we are wide awake. We are sober and vigilant. We are living in purity.

Living a Take-Charge life does not mean that bad things will not happen to us. It also does not mean that difficult things will not happen to us. It just means that we are clear-minded and able to hear the call of God. Being clear-minded and wide awake, we are ready to deal with all that is in our life and all that harms our life. We are ready to deal with all that we do that harms the lives of others. We are vigilant in our battles against all that is corrupt in our life. We are committed to living well.

The man I mentioned earlier was living in the dust. Now that he is clear-minded and awake, now that he has risen from the ash heap,[23] he can see with his new eyes. He looks back and what he sees is no longer, "Oh I want her sooo much!" What he sees is that he was a slave. He sees that when he "gave into such evil temptations, it led to evil actions, and the actions were killing him."[24] He was enslaved. He was a slave of all manner of corruption. He was chained like a slave.

A TAKE-CHARGE BREAK

Try telling a slave, "Take those chains off from around your neck." He can not do it, because he is enslaved. God though, tells us to take the chains off from around our necks.[25] He tells us this because we *can* do it. We can do it because we are not slaves of sin. We have been delivered by Jesus, and we dare not live as slaves any longer. We do not have to wait for God to deliver us yet again. He has already done it definitively once. We do not have to sit moaning, "God there's a chain around my neck, can you please take it off?" He says to us, "Take it off."

We live as if what God has told us to do is impossible for us. We live in fear of taking responsibility. We plead: "I need that chain, God. I am so used to it. I have been wearing it all my life. Don't make me get rid of it."

Imagine living with a chain around our neck. Imagine getting to the point where we feel comfortable with this chain. Imagine saying, "I am used to this chain. I like the choking sensation of this chain." All of this, while God is saying to us, "Get rid of it!"

To many of us, getting rid of our slave chains seems impossible. It's not. We can do it, because God empowers us to do it. He enables us to do it. Nothing disempowering ever has to be a part of our lives.

God IS speaking to us. He is speaking to those of us whose life already belongs to Him. He says, "Listen to Me, My people."[26] When He continues to speak, He does not say, "*I* will break your chains." It is not that He *can* not, nor is it that He *could* not. He can do whatever He wants. The reality is that He *will* not. He says, "YOU remove the slave chains from YOUR neck."[27] As little as we may like it, there is divine glory in that declaration.

Countless times I have heard people pray, "God, deliver me from this. God, deliver me from that." There is real glory when, in the crippling and crushing power of tempting evils, you realize that God is not keeping that cigarette from your mouth. There is real glory when you realize that God is not keeping that woman's lips from your lips.

We come to realize that God is not doing these things for us, because God wants US to Take-Charge of our lives and do it. We have to be ready and knowledgeable to say NO to evil and YES to God!

God is saying to us, "You are going to do it. I am not picking you up, because you are going to use your own two feet to stand up in the face of every struggle that is being hurled at you. Stand up, because only when you get up will you see the power I have given you. I have not used My power to pick you up. I did not stand you up. You have used My power to stand up on your own."

TAKE-CHARGE ENCOURAGEMENT

There is tremendous encouragement in this. We know that we have the power to face all that we have to face. We are not being asked to do anything that we cannot do. God has shown us how, and He has empowered us to do it. He will not baby us all our life.

Think about it this way. When our children are very young, we do all kinds of things for them that we will never do for them when they are older. As they get older, they start doing more and more of these things for themselves. They also start to make decisions for themselves. It is a serious hinderance for them when we get involved in their life and both do things for them and make decisions for them which they are capable of doing and making for themselves. They need to learn *how* to do these things, then they need to *do* them. What an encouragement when they see they have the power to stand up against evil and terrible things.

Let me give you an example of how early on this decision-making principle can take hold in a child's life, and in our life as well. My wife and I started home schooling our oldest daughter, Shoshannah, when she was four years old. She had spent a semester in four year old kindergarten just prior to that. We were called into the school by her kindergarten teacher, because our daughter was "disruptive." Shoshannah had not said anything to us. We only found out about the problem when we were called into the school by her teacher. For the week prior to that meeting, Shoshannah had been seated alone at the back of the room.

It turned out that the public schools had been celebrating a native praise day. The children were ordered to bow down and worship a totem pole. Shoshannah refused. She said she would never bow down to an idol. The teacher was furious at Shoshannah's refusal to participate, and punished her for it. Shoshannah was just a little child, but she stood up.

COMING DOWN THE HOME STRETCH

God delights in us standing up against the evils in us, as well as the evils that are hurled at us. He wants us to stand up and say *no* to what is bad, evil, and wrong, and *yes* to Him, for as long as we are alive. He will not baby us. He calls us to wake up. He calls us to stand up. He calls us to strengthen up. He calls us to be what we already are.

This is what a Take-Charge life is all about—standing up against, and smashing, the idols in our lives. These idols want our devotion, our emotion, and our passion. God wants us to *stay* free. He says, "If you know the Son, you shall stay free indeed."[28] It is in just such freedom as this that He calls us to live a Take-Charge life for Him. We live this when we are four. We live this when we are eighty-four. We live this in university. We live this in four year old kindergarten.

Jesus calls us to become like little children. If His little ones will stand up in the face of man's fury, so will we. When we stand, we live.

This book is about life—full and abundant life. This is not a dreary life. This is not a boring life. This is not a hopeless life. This is an abundant Take-Charge life.

Dear reader, I hope that your life will become an adventure. As you live out what you have learned in this book, soon you too will be saying of yourself: "I have learned in all things the secret of Taking-Charge of my life for the sake of Jesus Christ."[29]

TAKE-CHARGE ACTION INITIATIVES

1. *Why does God give you an action call to WAKE UP (Isaiah 52:1)?*

_____

_____

_____

_____

2. *What does it mean to "Get up out of the dust, shake it off, and remove the slave chains from around your necks" (Isaiah 52:2)?*

_____

_____

_____

_____

3. *Why do most believers in Jesus still live like slaves?*

_____

_____

_____

_____

4. *How are you meant to consider yourself dead to all the patterns and actions of living that keep you chained?*

_____

_____

_____

_____

5. *Is your working out the life that God has given you inconsistent with the reality that "God is working in you, both to desire and to accomplish this life for you" (Philippians 2:12-13)? If it is inconsistent, how so? If it is not inconsistent, how so?*

_____

_____

_____

_____

6. *What does it mean for you to be a radically new Take-Charge man or woman?*

_____

_____

_____

What is involved in this for you?

_____

_____

_____

7. *What is God's Take-Charge word for you from heaven?*

_____

_____

_____

_____

NOTES

Chapter 2:
Breaking Into a Take-Charge Life
1. Philippians 2:9-10
2. Luke 2:34

Chapter 3:
What in the World is a Take-Charge Life?
1. Philippians 2:12
2. Philippians 2:13

Chapter 5:
The Grace of a Take-Charge Life
1. Ephesians 3:18-19
2. Romans 6:23, NIV
3. 1 John 4:10
4. 1 John 4:10-11

Chapter 6:
Living a Take-Charge Life
1. 2 Corinthians 11:23-25
2. See Matthew 17:20.
3. 1 Kings 18:21
4. 1 Kings 18:24
5. 1 Kings 18:27
6. James 5:17
7. Proverbs 29:18

Chapter 7:
Take-Charge Today
1. Seligman, Martin E. P., *Learned Optimism* (New York: Pocket Books, 1990), 55.
2. 2 Corinthians 5:17
3. For a more complete explanation of biblical freedom, see the author's book *Free Indeed* (Wapwallopen, P.A.: Shepherd Press, 2002).
4. See the author's book *Secret of Self-Control* (Wheaton, Illinois: Crossway Books, 1998).
5. John 16:33
6. Romans 5:3-4

Chapter 8:
A Take-Charge Way of Life
1. 1 Peter 5:7
2. Psalm 18:30

3. Jeremiah 33:3
4. Philippians 4:6
5. 2 Corinthians 10:3-4
6. Joshua 6
7. Judges 6-7
8. 1 Samuel 17
9. Proverbs 16:25
10. Deuteronomy 30:19, NIV
11. Deuteronomy 30:20
12. Psalm 111:10, NIV
13. Proverbs 1:7, NIV
14. Proverbs 2:12
15. Proverbs 2:16
16. Proverbs 2:20
17. Proverbs 3:2
18. Proverbs 3:8
19. Proverbs 3:17
20. Proverbs 3:24
21. Proverbs 3:26
22. Proverbs 4:7

23. 2 Corinthians 4:7
24. 2 Corinthians 12:9
25. 2 Corinthians 1:8
26. Acts 1:8
27. Acts 3
28. Acts 4:7
29. Acts 4:10
30. Acts 4:33
31. Acts 6:8
32. Acts 7
33. Romans 15:13
34. Psalm 121:1
35. Hebrews 12:2
36. Hebrews 11
37. Hebrews 12:28
38. 2 Timothy 1:7
39. Romans 5:3-4
40. See the author's book *Secret of Self-Control* (Wheaton, Illinois: Crossway Books, 1998).

Chapter 9:
Take-Charge Action

1. Proverbs 29:18
2. Philippians 4:9
3. Philippians 4:9
4. Philippians 3:14
5. Galatians 5:1
6. Philippians 4:11-13

Chapter 10:
The Benefits of a Take-Charge Life

1. Judges 21:25; see also Proverbs 3:7 & 26:12
2. 2 Peter 1:3
3. Proverbs 25:28
4. 1 Corinthians 9:24-27
5. Galatians 5:22-23, NIV
6. Galatians 5:24-25

Chapter 11:
Self-Mastery of a Take-Charge Life

1. 1 Timothy 4:7, NASB
2. Hebrews 12:14, NIV
3. 1 Corinthians 9:26, NIV
4. Tracy, Brian, *Eat That Frog* (Berrett-Koehler, 2006), Chapter 3.
5. 1 Corinthians 9:25
6. 1 Corinthians 9:25
7. Hebrews 12:11
8. Hebrews 12:11
9. Hebrews 12:1
10. Hebrews 12:7
11. Hebrews 12:5-6
12. Hebrews 12:10

13. Proverbs 5:12
14. Proverbs 5:14
15. Proverbs 5:14
16. Proverbs 10:17
17. Proverbs 10:17
18. Proverbs 10:17
19. Ephesians 4:22, Colossians 3:9-10. *Note: The two passages, Ephesians 4:22-32 and Colossians 3:5-10, describe this process in detail.*
20. See Galatians 5:22-23.
21. Hebrews 12:12
22. Hebrews 12:12
23. Proverbs 4:26
24. Proverbs 4:27, NIV
25. See Philippians 4:8.
26. Romans 12:1
27. Romans 12:2
28. Romans 12:2
29. Proverbs 12:1
30. 2 Timothy 1:7

Chapter 12:
Facing Challenges in a Take-Charge Life

1. Job 19:25, NIV
2. Psalm 42:3, NIV
3. Psalm 42:5
4. Philippians 4:11-13
5. Psalm 42:5
6. Matthew Henry, *A Commentary on the Whole Bible*, vol. 3 (Tarrytown, N.Y.: Fleming H. Revell, 1986), 394.
7. Psalm 42:5
8. Psalm 42:8
9. Psalm 42:11, NIV
10. *Military History*, 3, no. 6 (June 1987), 10, 56-57.

Chapter 13:
Power Beliefs of a Take-Charge Life

1. 2 Timothy 3:16-17
2. 2 Corinthians 5:17
3. John 3:7, NIV
4. John 14:16-17, NIV
5. Job 42:2
6. Romans 8:28
7. Genesis 45:5
8. Luke 9:23-25

Chapter 14:
The Anchor of a Take-Charge Life

1. 2 Timothy 3:16-17
2. 2 Peter 1:3
3. Psalm 119:96
4. Matthew 5:48
5. Philippians 3:14
6. 1 John 4:18, NIV
7. 1 John 1:9
8. See Matthew 18:15-17.
9. Romans 6:11-12
10. Romans 12:1-2
11. 1 John 4:4
12. Joshua 24:14-15
13. Matthew 28:20

Chapter 15:
Take-Charge No Matter the Circumstances

1. See Proverbs 3:5-6.
2. Psalms 18:2; 46:1; 91:2
3. Psalm 40:1-3
4. 2 Samuel 22:2; Psalm 89:26
5. Philippians 3:13
6. Psalm 77:1-2
7. Psalm 77:5,7-9
8. Psalm 77:10-12
9. 2 Corinthians 4:17, NIV
10. Romans 12:2
11. Psalm 77:10
12. Matthew 22:29
13. See John 15:12; Romans 5:8; Ephesians 2:4-5.
14. Hebrews 11:40
15. Psalm 77:12
16. Psalm 77:13-15, NIV
17. Psalm 77:19
18. Psalm 77:20, NIV
19. 1 Peter 1:8-9, NIV

Chapter 16:
An Obedient Take-Charge Life

1. 1 Corinthians 9:27
2. 1 Corinthians 4:6
3. Ephesians 3:17-19
4. Ephesians 4:22-23
5. Ephesians 4:25
6. Ephesians 4:26
7. Ephesians 4:28
8. Ephesians 4:29
9. Ephesians 4:31
10. Ephesians 4:32
11. See Philippians 4:22.
12. Philippians 4:4, NIV
13. Psalm 119:111-112
14. 1 John 4:10

Chapter 17:
The Songs of a Take-Charge Life

1. See Philippians 3:1.
2. Genesis 4:7
3. Psalm 40:2
4. Lamentations 3:23, NIV
5. Psalm 20:1, NIV
6. Psalm 20:1, NIV
7. Exodus 3:6
8. Exodus 3:11, NIV
9. Exodus 3:13, NIV
10. Exodus 3:14-15, NIV
11. Psalm 20:2, NIV
12. Psalm 20:5, NASB
13. Philippians 3:1 & 4:4
14. Psalm 20:6
15. Romans 12:2
16. See Philippians 4:8-9.
17. Philippians 3:13
18. Psalm 20:7, NIV
19. Psalm 20:7-8
20. Psalm 19:7, *Book of Psalms for Singing* (Pittsburgh, Penn.: Crown & Covenant Publications, 1973), 19B.
21. Psalm 37:7-8
22. Deuteronomy 30:19, NIV
23. 2 Peter 1:3
24. 2 Peter 1:5-7

Chapter 18:
The Power of Thinking in a Take-Charge Life

1. Galatians 5:24
2. Proverbs 23:7

3. Philippians 4:8
4. Philippians 4:9
5. Philippians 4:9, NIV
6. Romans 7:19
7. Romans 7:23
8. 1 Corinthians 10:13
9. James 1:14-15
10. See Ephesians 6:10-17.
11. Ephesians 6:18
12. See Genesis 4.
13. Genesis 4:6-7
14. Deuteronomy 30:11-16,19-20, NIV
15. See Philippians 4:7.
16. See Philippians 4:9.
17. See 1 Corinthians 2:16.
18. Romans 8:6

Chapter 19:
Take-Charge of Your Thoughts

1. Proverbs 23:7
2. See Philippians 4:8.
3. John 14:15
4. Romans 12:2
5. 2 Corinthians 10:4-5
6. Romans 12:21
7. Philippians 2:5
8. Romans 8:5
9. Philippians 4:8
10. Philippians 4:9
11. See Philippians 4:12ff.
12. See Romans 12:2.

Chapter 20:
Take-Charge of Anxiety

1. See the author's next book *TODAY IS YOUR LIFE... Make it Count*
2. Matthew 6:27,31, NIV
3. Matthew 6:26,28-29
4. Matthew 6:32
5. See Matthew 6:32.
6. Romans 8:31-32
7. Matthew 6:33
8. Matthew 6:34
9. Deuteronomy 8:3, NIV
10. Matthew 6:25
11. Matthew 6:27
12. Matthew 6:31
13. Matthew 6:34
14. Philippians 4:11-12
15. Philippians 4:13
16. Luke 12:13-21
17. Psalm 118:24, NIV
18. Philippians 4:6
19. Philippians 4:8, NIV
20. Philippians 4:9
21. Philippians 4:9
22. 1 Peter 5:7

Chapter 21:
Take-Charge Word Power

1. James 3:9-12
2. John 17:17
3. Matthew 11:28
4. Luke 23:34
5. Acts 7:60
6. Ephesians 4:29
7. Philippians 4:8
8. Luke 9:23-25
9. Ephesians 5:1-2
10. Matthew 5:7, NIV
11. Matthew 6:33, NIV
12. Luke 5:27, NIV
13. Matthew 8:10, NIV
14. John 10:10

15. John 14:6, NIV
16. Luke 23:34, NIV
17. Exodus 24:8

18. Mark 14:24
19. 2 Corinthians 5:17

Chapter 22:
A Committed Take-Charge Life

1. 1 John 1:9
2. Luke 19:8
3. Romans 6:14
4. Romans 6:14
5. Ephesians 4:22,24

6. Ephesians 5:1
7. See Philippians 4:8-9.
8. See Galatians 5:22-23.
9. Philippians 4:11
10. See Philippians 4:13.

Chapter 23:
A Take-Charge Life Example

1. John 8:12, NLT

Chapter 24:
A Principled Take-Charge Life

1. John 16:33
2. Joshua 1:5, Matthew 28:20
3. John 10:10
4. Romans 10:11
5. John 6:38
6. Luke 22:42
7. John 13:34
8. Psalm 119:11
9. Psalm 119:16
10. Psalm 119:17
11. Psalm 119:28
12. Psalm 119:37
13. Psalm 119:42
14. Psalm 119:74
15. Psalm 119:89
16. Psalm 119:105
17. Psalm 119:169
18. Romans 12:12, Colossians 4:1, Acts 6:4
19. Matthew 7:3-4, NLT
20. Ringer, Robert, *The Pushup That Wasn't* (weekly email, November 19, 2007).

21. Psalm 32:5
22. Psalm 9:1-2
23. Psalm 9:10
24. Psalm 5:11
25. Psalm 13:6
26. Psalm 30:5
27. Psalm 32:11
28. Psalm 51:14
29. Psalm 33:1
30. Psalm 57:8
31. Psalm 57:4
32. Psalm 57:10
33. Psalm 98:1
34. Lamentations 3:20
35. Ephesians 5:19
36. 1 Peter 1:22
37. James 5:16
38. Romans 12:10
39. Romans 15:7
40. 1 Thessalonians 5:11
41. Galatians 5:15
42. Romans 15:14
43. Romans 16:16

Chapter 25:
Take-Charge and Live with Passion

1. See Genesis 32:22-32.
2. Psalm 42:1
3. Psalm 63:1
4. James 5:17
5. Philippians 3:7-8
6. Philippians 3:8
7. Philippians 3:13-14
8. 2 Peter 1:3
9. Philippians 3:15
10. Ephesians 3:21

Chapter 26:
A Final Take-Charge Call

1. Isaiah 52:1
2. Psalm 84:7
3. Isaiah 52:2
4. Isaiah 52:2
5. Romans 6:6
6. Romans 6:11
7. Romans 6:12
8. Romans 6:13
9. Philippians 2:12
10. Philippians 2:12-13
11. Romans 6:13
12. Romans 6:14
13. 1 Peter 1:3
14. Romans 6:14
15. Romans 6:16
16. Romans 6:16
17. Isaiah 21:3
18. Romans 6:16
19. Romans 6:17
20. Romans 6:17
21. Romans 6:20-21
22. Isaiah 52:12
23. Isaiah 52:3
24. James 1:15
25. Isaiah 52:2
26. Isaiah 51:4
27. Isaiah 52:2
28. John 8:36
29. Philippians 4:12

Dr. Richard Ganz

If you would like information about the ministry, speaking schedule, or other books by Dr. Ganz, please visit his website or email him. If you, your church, or organization is interested in a conference or seminar by Dr. Ganz, please contact him.

Website: www.RichardGanz.com
Email: Rich@RichardGanz.com

Take Charge of Your Life...
Before it Takes Charge of You

To order additional copies of this book, please visit the website of the publisher, Landmark Project Press. (Bulk discounts available.)

LANDMARK
PROJECT ∞
P R E S S

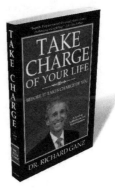

http://takecharge.landmarkproject.net